WITTGENSTEIN'S DEFINITION OF MEANING AS USE

The Orestes Brownson Series

on Contemporary Thought and Affairs

No. 6

1967

WITTGENSTEIN'S DEFINITION OF MEANING AS USE

GARTH HALLETT, S.J.

FORDHAM UNIVERSITY PRESS

NEW YORK

ACKNOWLEDGMENTS

I would like to acknowledge with gratitude the kind assistance of those who helped me most during the preparation, revision, and publication of this work: Fr. Timothy Cronin, S.J.; Fr. Frederick Copleston, S.J.; Fr. S. Youree Watson, S.J.; and Miss G. E. M. Anscombe and her husband, Mr. Peter Geach, with whom I discussed the first chapter.

I would like to express my gratitude also to Routledge and Kegan Paul, Ltd., for permission to quote from Wittgenstein's *Tractatus Logico–Philosophicus*, and to Basil Blackwell, Publisher, and Wittgenstein's literary executors for permission to quote still more amply from Wittgenstein's *Notebooks 1914–1916*, *The Blue and Brown Books*, *Remarks on the Foundations of Mathematics*, and *Philosophical Investigations*. Permission to quote from the *Tractatus* has also been obtained from the American publisher, Humanities Press Inc.

CONTENTS

ABBREVIATIONS

Books and Articles

BB   Ludwig Wittgenstein, *The Blue and Brown Books*, with a preface by R(ush) R(hees). Second edition, Oxford, 1958.

Colombo   Ludwig Wittgenstein, *Tractatus Logico–Philosophicus*, testo tedesco con versione italiana e introduzione critica di Gian Carlo Maria Colombo, s.ɪ. Milano, 1954.

FM   Ludwig Wittgenstein, *Remarks on the Foundations of Mathematics*, edited by G. H. von Wright, R. Rhees, and G. E. M. Anscombe, with an English translation by G. E. M. Anscombe facing the original German. Oxford, 1956.

LC   Ludwig Wittgenstein, *Lectures and Conversations on Aesthetics, Psychology and Religious Belief*, edited by Cyril Barrett. Oxford, 1966.

M^1, M^2, M^3 The three sections respectively of G E. Moore, "Wittgenstein's Lectures in 1930–33," *Mind* 63 (1954), 1–15, 289–316; 64 (1955), 1–27.

NB   Ludwig Wittgenstein, *Notebooks 1914–1916*, edited by G. H. von Wright and G. E. M. Anscombe, with an English translation by G. E. M. Anscombe facing the original German. Oxford, 1961.

PB   Ludwig Wittgenstein, *Philosophische Bemerkungen*, edited by Rush Rhees. Oxford, 1964.

PI   Ludwig Wittgenstein, *Philosophical Investigations*, [edited by G. E. M. Anscombe and R. Rhees] with an English translation by G. E. M. Anscombe facing the original German. Second edition, Oxford, 1958.

PM   Bertrand Russell and Alfred North Whitehead, *Principia Mathematica*, 3 vols. Second edition, Cambridge, 1925.

Proc. XIth Int. Cong.   *Proceedings of the Eleventh International Congress of Philosophy*, 14 vols. Amsterdam-Louvain, 1953.

Proc. XIIth Int. Cong.   *Proceedings of the Twelfth International Congress of Philosophy*, 12 vols. Florence, 1960–1961.

Periodicals

Arch. Filos.	*Archivio di Filosofia*. Roma.
Aust. J. Phil.	*The Australasian Journal of Philosophy*. Sydney.
Irish Theol. Quart.	*Irish Theological Quarterly*. Maynooth.
J. Philos.	*The Journal of Philosophy*. New York.
Philos. Phenom. Res.	*Philosophy and Phenomenological Research*. Philadelphia.
Philos. Quart.	*The Philosophical Quarterly*. St. Andrews.
Philos. Rev.	*The Philosophical Review*. Ithaca.
Philos. Stud.	*Philosophical Studies*. Maynooth.
Proc. Amer. Cathol. Philos. Assoc.	*Proceedings of the American Catholic Philosophical Association*. Washington.
Proc. Ar. Soc.	*Proceedings of the Aristotelian Society*. London.
Rass. Sc. filos.	*Rassegna di Scienze filosofiche*. Napoli.
Rev. Filos.	*Revista de Filosofia*. Madrid.
Rev. Int. Philos.	*Revue Internationale de Philosophie*. Bruxelles.
Rev. Meta.	*Review of Metaphysics*. New Haven.
Rev. Mét. Mor.	*Revue de Métaphysique et de Morale*. Paris.
Riv. Filos.	*Rivista di Filosofia*. Bologna, Torino.

WITTGENSTEIN'S DEFINITION OF MEANING AS USE

INTRODUCTION

"FOR A *large* CLASS OF CASES—THOUGH NOT FOR ALL—IN WHICH WE EMPLOY the word 'meaning' it can be defined thus: the meaning of a word is its use in the language."[1] This definition,[2] the subject of the present study, is the hallmark of Ludwig Wittgenstein's (1889-1951) later philosophy and consequently of much recent British philosophy.[3] It indicates both his philosophical interests and his method—his interest in individual key words, his method of merely describing their use. To understand this definition is to understand Wittgenstein's philosophy and its development, and through them some main trends in Anglo-Saxon philosophy in this century.

Yet Wittgenstein's definition, so important and so frequently mentioned, has received little detailed study. The relation of the definition to previous definitions of meaning, both Wittgenstein's and others,' has occasionally been sketched, but as part of a historical survey, not in an effort to trace precisely the development of Wittgenstein's views.[3a] For instance, nowhere have I seen a full treatment of the reasons which led Wittgenstein to abandon his earlier definition of words' meanings. And nowhere have I seen his arguments on the subject systematically contrasted with the views of any of those he clearly had in mind—Russell, for instance, and James. Nowhere have I found an attempt to go much beyond the words of the definition itself, in order to determine just what large class of cases Wittgenstein had in mind, and what sort of use. Little wonder, then, that the definition has been criticized in the most varied and often contradictory ways and that its critics have remained for the most part unanswered.

The importance of the philosopher,[4] the importance of the subject, the little detailed study done on it—these were reasons both for undertaking the inquiry into Wittgenstein's definition and for making the results available.

Before plunging *in medias res,* the reader may be helped by a few words on the general historical background of the definition, on the works in which its development can be traced, on the organization of the present inquiry, and on the central importance of this definition in Wittgenstein's later philosophy.

By routing idealism in England, Moore and Russell brought Anglo-

1

Saxon philosophy back pretty much where Hume had left it. Most Anglo-Saxon philosophers accepted once again the dichotomy stated by Hume: propositions about reality are either analytic and non-informative, or they are informative but *a posteriori,* and so provided by simple observation or scientific inquiry, without any help from philosophy. Philosophy is not informative in the way idealists had believed. But what, then, *is* the business of philosophy? Well, it may still decide which propositions are analytic and which are *a posteriori,* or it may clarify the meaning of propositions in both categories. This is, as a matter of fact, the general trend Anglo-Saxon philosophy has taken in the post-idealist era. It has become concerned primarily with meaning.[5]

Though it is doubtful whether Hume had any direct influence on him,[6] an indirect influence through Russell being more likely, Wittgenstein's philosophy obeyed the same logic. Convinced both that all necessary statements are uninformative tautologies[7] and that philosophy cannot extend the horizons of reality (6.53), he turned to the analysis of meaning. He was concerned to show how and in what sense necessary propositions are non-informative tautologies. He was still more concerned with the meaning of ordinary contingent statements—what they mean and how they mean it and what it is for words to have meaning.

Within the movement mentioned there has been a trend away from one dominant account of the meaning of individual words to another. The former tendency was to look upon proper names as the models of meaningful expressions and to correlate an entity of some sort with each word or expression. This was its meaning.[8] Such was Frege's outlook,[9] and the outlook of Bertrand Russell in his *Principles of Mathematics.*[10] Today the dominant view is that no objects are the meanings of words; words' meanings are their uses.

Once again, Wittgenstein's views reflect the general tendency, which is not at all surprising, as he was responsible more than any other person for bringing the change about.[11] In *Principia Mathematica* Russell had already taken a first step away from the extreme position of the *Principles* by introducing "incomplete symbols," in addition to complete symbols or proper names; the *uses* of the former were defined, but they were not assumed to have any meanings in the old sense, that is, any referents.[12] Wittgenstein carried this development still further; in his first book, the *Tractatus Logico-Philosophicus,* the meanings which Russell would not "assume" Wittgenstein ruled out as impossible. Only genuine proper names had referents which were their meanings. We shall see how even these referent meanings disappeared in Wittgenstein's later philosophy; not even bona fide objects referred to by names could be called the meanings of these names. The meanings of all expressions were their uses.

The two definitions of words' meanings—as their referents, then as their uses—belong to two periods in Wittgenstein's philosophical activity. There is some disagreement as to whether there were two Wittgensteins or one, and about the degree of continuity between his earlier and later views, but chronologically at least, his work falls clearly into two periods. The first period began late in 1911 or early in 1912, when Wittgenstein arrived in Cambridge to study logic and the foundations of mathematics under Russell.[13] He began almost immediately filling notebooks, some of which have survived,[14] with jottings on these and other matters. Out of these grew the *Tractatus*,[15] which he wrote while serving with the Austrian army during the First World War. Having thus given final form to his thoughts, Wittgenstein retired from philosophy for more than ten years. In the meantime the *Tractatus* became a classic of logical atomism and exercised a wide influence, especially through the Vienna Circle, whose logical positivism stemmed largely from discussions on the *Tractatus*.[16]

Wittgenstein returned to Cambridge and to philosophy in 1929. One article, repudiated by him before it was even printed, dates from that year.[17] So, perhaps, does a popular lecture on ethics, just recently published.[18] In 1930 he wrote a bulky manuscript entitled *Philosophische Bemerkungen*,[19] which he worked over during the next two years, then abandoned and replaced with an entirely new work. The former has just been published, and the latter apparently soon will be. We are informed of his thought during these same years by the notes which G. E. Moore took at Wittgenstein's lectures and published after his death.[20] In 1933-1934 and 1934-1935 respectively Wittgenstein dictated the two folios of notes which came to be known and were posthumously published as *The Blue and Brown Books*.[21] From 1937 till 1944 he put down a series of jottings from which some were later selected and posthumously published under the title *Remarks on the Foundations of Mathematics*.[22] During a similar period (1938-1946) several of Wittgenstein's students were taking notes from a number of his *Lectures and Conversations on Aesthetics, Psychology and Religious Belief*, recently made public.[22a] The only one of his later works which Wittgenstein envisaged publishing was the *Philosophical Investigations*, which he described in 1945 as "the precipitate of philosophical investigations which have occupied me for the last sixteen years" (PI ix). Part One was finished by that year; Part Two was written between 1947 and 1949 (PI vi). The works just mentioned are the only ones used in this study. Another appeared while this book was in process of publication.[23]

In the *Tractatus* the influence of Schopenhauer, whose *Die welt als Wille und Vorstellung* Wittgenstein had read when he was sixteen,[24] and especially of Gottlob Frege and Bertrand Russell is evident. No philosopher had similar influence on Wittgenstein's later philosophy, though William James's *Principles of Psychology* and Russell's *The Analysis of Mind*, both of which Wittgenstein read,[25] seem to have stimulated many of his later critical discussions. Though Wittgenstein refers with relative frequency to the views of St. Augustine and of Plato, two of the very few philosophers with whose writings and thought Wittgenstein was familiar,[26] they do not seem to be as important for an understanding of Wittgenstein's later ideas as are the writings of James or Russell or perhaps his friend G. E. Moore.[27]

However, Wittgenstein was his own principal adversary in the later writings. He said of the *Investigations* that they "could be seen in the right light only by contrast with and against the background of my old way of thinking" (PI x).[28] In my first chapter I have attempted to give enough of his early views on the use and meaning of individual words so as to render intelligible his later definition of meaning in the *Investigations*. This definition (the one already quoted) is a development from tendencies already noticeable in the *Tractatus*; and it is established in part by arguments directed against the *Tractatus* explanation of meaning, arguments which therefore can be "seen in the right light" only if the earlier treatment is known and understood.

Rather than anticipate by introducing the later definition and organizing the first chapter in terms of it, I have preferred to follow more closely the train of Wittgenstein's thought at the time he wrote the *Tractatus*, without intruding later developments. The reader will be less disconcerted by this procedure if he notices that the later definition has determined the two themes in Wittgenstein's earlier thought that are pursued throughout the chapter: meaning and use.

The next three chapters treat the immediate origin and the contents of this definition. They are drawn from three principal sources: Moore's notes, the *Blue and Brown Books*, and the *Investigations*. However, the division of the chapters does not correspond to the division of the sources. To study, chapter by chapter, the status of Wittgenstein's ideas on meaning in each of the three periods represented by these works, would result in too much repetition. In the two main sources, the *Blue and Brown Books* and the *Investigations*, Wittgenstein's views on meaning are practically identical. Instead, the division is partly temporal and partly topical. Chapters two and three give the reasoning that led to the definition, and chapter four investigates the definition thus proved, its extension and its intension.

This division, and the divisions within the chapters, do not correspond, either, to divisions within the sources, for instance to divisions within the *Investigations*. I am forced to divide where Wittgenstein did not divide and to join where he did not join. For his later writings in particular are notoriously lacking in any clear organization. In his preface to the *Investigations*, Wittgenstein himself draws attention to his inability to weld his thoughts together into an organized whole (PI ix).

These first four chapters are purely expository. All critical comment and discussion are put off till the fifth and final chapter, where the accuracy, reliability, and importance of Wittgenstein's definition are assessed.

The organization of the work would be very different were my subject Wittgenstein's whole doctrine of meaning. But it should be stressed that I am studying his *definition* of meaning, and the only definition of meaning he gave was a definition of the meaning of words. It is true that he said quite similar things about the meaning of sentences.[29] But sentences are not mentioned in the definition. Furthermore, the German word used in the definition, *Bedeutung*, is one which Wittgenstein hardly ever applied to sentences. For some reason, not even in his later period did he speak of the *Bedeutung* of sentences, unless the sentences consisted of a single word,[30] or unless he meant quite a different sort of *Bedeutung* from that mentioned in the definition, as on one occasion (§ 540).[31] So the limitation of the definition is not accidental. It is not as though Wittgenstein cited but one sort of example where he might have cited two, bringing in the *Bedeutung* of sentences as well. In his terminology, sentences did not have *Bedeutung*, but only *Sinn*.

This distinction and this limitation of subject matter allow me to avoid a number of vexing problems, such as Wittgenstein's contrast theory of sentence meaning,[32] his attitude toward the principle of verification, his criteria for meaningful sentences, his interpretation of necessary propositions.[33] But it thereby eliminates much that is of interest and importance in Wittgenstein's treatment of meaning. In fact it might seem that little of value is left once attention is restricted to the meaning of individual words. So it would seem to a large group of present-day linguistic philosophers, whose interest centers on full sentences.[34]

But not to Wittgenstein. It is no accident that his definition applies to words, not to sentences. In putting stress on individual words, the definition reflects Wittgenstein's major concern in the period of the *Investigations* and their immediate antecedents. His interest was in various important concepts, and in sentences mainly insofar as they reveal the structure of concepts. This meant interest in certain key words, for concepts are indicated by concept words. Study of the word reveals the concept.

An individual sentence is, after all, something accidental, transient, *ad hoc*, whereas Wittgenstein's main interest was always the *a priori*. In the *Tractatus*, as we shall see, he believed in a sentential *a priori*, a single way in which all sentences had to be put together, and this *a priori* dominated his thinking. Later, when this idol had fallen, Wittgenstein came to look on concepts, on individual words and their uses, as the relatively permanent tools in language and on sentences as things which are done with them (§§ 569-570). This new *a priori* held the focus of his attention.

Another reason for his concern with the meaning of individual words was the conviction he acquired, largely through his own past errors, that philosophical problems arise, not when words are at work in sentences, but when they are idling (§§ 11, 38, 132). One asks what language is, or what meaning is, or what thinking is, not what this or that sentence means in which the word "meaning" or "language" or "thinking" occurs, not what the word means on any particular occasion (BB 1). So it is necessary to consider the words one by one and show the questioner, or rather remind him (§§ 89, 127, 253), how they ordinarily work in the "language-game" which is their home (§ 116). That is, one reminds him of their meaning. Thus meaning—the meaning of words—is the central preoccupation of Wittgenstein's later philosophy.

For such therapy as this is the whole program he proposed for himself and for present-day philosophers.[35] "Philosophy," he said, "is a battle against the bewitchment of our intelligence by means of language" (§ 109).[36]

The indispensable first step in this campaign is to get clear about "meaning" (BB 1, § 1). The solution to this problem is the lead to all the rest,

indicating the form every solution should take. If the important thing
about a word, its meaning,[37] is the way it is used in the language, "this
is what we need to understand in order to resolve philosophical paradoxes"
(§ 182).[38]

Chapter I

MEANING AND USE IN THE *TRACTATUS*

I. THE SEARCH FOR MEANING

WITTGENSTEIN'S BASIC ESTIMATE OF PHILOSOPHY SEEMS NEVER TO HAVE changed: past philosophy was full of confusion and error; present philosophy must undo the mess. Its business is philosophical therapy—philosophical in the double sense that the therapy is applied to philosophy (of the traditional sort) and that it is carried out by means proper to philosophy (of the new sort).

This estimate of past philosophy is expressed clearly in the *Tractatus,* and at the same time Wittgenstein's diagnosis of the reasons for philosophical problems:

> Most of the propositions and questions to be found in philosophical works are not false but nonsensical. Consequently we cannot give any answer to questions of this kind, but can only establish that they are nonsensical. Most of the propositions and questions of philosophers arise from our failure to understand the logic of our language.
>
> (They belong to the same class as the questions whether the good is more or less identical than the beautiful.)
>
> And it is not surprising that the deepest problems are in fact *not* problems at all (4.003).

This repeats what he had said in the preface: "The book deals with the problems of philosophy, and shows, I believe, that the reason why these problems are posed is that the logic of our language is misunderstood."[1] Language is not misunderstood by those who use it, but its logic is by philosophers.[2] Wittgenstein explains why this is so:

> Everyday language is a part of the human organism and is no less complicated than it.
>
> It is not humanly possible to gather immediately from it what the logic of language is.

Language disguises thought. So much so, that from the outward form of the clothing it is impossible to infer the form of the thought beneath it, because the outward form of the clothing is not designed to reveal the form of the body, but for entirely different purposes (4.002).[3]

The remedy Wittgenstein suggested in the *Tractatus* was to construct a language for this purpose. In order to avoid the fundamental confusions (3.324) produced in philosophers by confusing grammar, "we must make use of a sign-language that excludes them," for instance "by not using the same sign for different symbols and by not using in a superficially similar way signs that have different modes of signification" (3.325); by using a notation with exactly the same logical multiplicity as the thought it expresses and the reality it represents (4.04). "That is to say, a sign-language that is governed by logical grammar—by logical syntax" (3.325).

"Once we have a sign-language in which everything is all right, we already have a correct logical point of view" (4.1213). "It follows from this that we can actually do without logical propositions; for in a suitable notation we can in fact recognize the formal properties of propositions by mere inspection of the propositions themselves" (6.122).[4] Philosophy will then have served its purpose, which is the logical clarification of thought. "Without philosophy thoughts are, as it were, cloudy and indistinct: its task is to make them clear and to give them sharp boundaries" (4.112).[5]

II. No Meaning Outside Use

Two great principles guided Wittgenstein in his inquiry into the meaning of everyday expressions, though they are so intimately connected with each other that we might almost call them one and the same. In strictly logical order,[6] the first is this: "An expression has meaning only in a proposition" (3.314). For instance, "Only in the nexus of a proposition does a name have meaning" (3.3).[7]

This seems a hard saying. Mustn't words have meaning before they are used? (NB 64) Isn't that why we understand the new combinations in which they are used? (4.024; 4.03) What do definitions do if not give words meaning? (4.025; 3.261)

As both Frege and Russell said quite similar things, a study of their reasons may supplement the rather meagre remarks in the *Tractatus*, and help in their interpretation. Not only was their influence on Wittgenstein great, but what they had already said and said well Wittgenstein could take for granted and might feel no need to repeat.

A. *The Principle in Frege*

In Frege's writings we find the same problem—or rather a similar one, since the system in which it arises affects the sense of the expressions used, which are very similar to those of the *Tractatus*. For instance: "We ought always to keep before our eyes a complete proposition. Only in a proposition have the words really a meaning. . . . It is enough if the proposition taken as a whole has a sense; it is this that confers on its parts also their content."[8] As in the *Tractatus*, this needs to be reconciled with a statement such as the following: "The definition of an object does not, as such, really assert anything about the object, but only lays down the meaning of a symbol."[9] How is this sort of pre-established meaning compatible with Frege's previous statement according to which signs acquire their meaning in propositions?

Frege did not answer this question directly, but he did suggest repeatedly, if not very fully, the reason for his view. The fullest exposition is in the introduction to *The Foundations of Arithmetic*:

> In the enquiry that follows, I have kept to three fundamental principles:
> always to separate sharply the psychological from the logical, the subjective from the objective;
> never to ask for the meaning of a word in isolation, but only in the context of a proposition;
> never to lose sight of the distinction between concept and object.
> In compliance with the first principle, I have used the word "idea" always in the psychological sense, and have distinguished ideas from concepts and from objects. If the second principle is not observed, one is almost forced to take as the meanings of words mental pictures or acts of the individual mind, and so to offend against the first principle as well.[10]

It seems probable that the anti-psychological bias evident here and amply illustrated in the rest of Frege's writings was extremely important for the development of Wittgenstein's thought. It probably accounts in part for his early avoidance of psychological investigations. And in much of his later criticism of such explanations, he repeated what Frege had stressed before him, making the same distinction between "concept" and "idea" and taking the latter as an image or other psychological phenomenon. So it may well be that the same reason motivated him as motivated Frege to insist that signs have meaning only in propositions.

However, it is easier to understand the psychological-linguistic alternative presented by Frege than it would be to understand the same alternative in the *Tractatus*. In the *Tractatus*, meanings are absolutely simple (2.02; 3.203) and so we might well wonder why a simple cannot have a name given to it outside a proposition. In Frege's system, on the contrary, meanings can be exceedingly complex and even contradictory.[11] For instance, "square circle" is, according to Frege, a genuine concept, which can become the meaning *(Bedeutung)* of an expression if we care to talk *about* the concept.[12] Obviously we can form no mental image of this concept, that is, no image which falls under it. Neither experience nor imagination reveals it.[13] But language does. And so it is with all difficult concepts, especially the complex, abstract notions of mathematics. We could never have arrived at them without the help of language.[14] If we would become familiar with a mathematical object like $\sqrt{-3}$, we must look to the mathematical propositions in which its sign occurs. No amount of experience or introspection will reveal the meaning of this sign. Language—the world of propositions—is its habitat.

Other reasons and supporting examples could easily be found in Frege's writings, but this is all he alleged explicitly in defense of his view.

B. *The Principle in Russell*

I have not found any such general principle in those of Bertrand Russell's writings which may have influenced the *Tractatus*.[15] But something very similar could be worked out from the doctrine of *Principia Mathematica*. Let us consider the principal types of signs recognized there.

On page 66, a general division is suggested between "incomplete symbols" and "what (in a generalized sense) we may call proper names: 'Socrates,' for example, stands for a certain man, and therefore has a meaning by itself, without the need of any context. If we supply a context, as in 'Socrates is mortal,' these words express a fact of which Socrates himself is a constituent: there is a certain object, namely Socrates, which does have the property of mortality, and this object is a constituent of the complex fact which we assert when we say 'Socrates is mortal.' " "Incomplete symbols," on the other hand, are "not supposed[16] to have any meaning in isolation." Thus, for instance, all phrases (other than propositions) containing the word *the* (in the singular) are incomplete symbols: they have a meaning in use but not in isolation. For "the author of Waverley" cannot mean the same as "Scott," or "Scott is the author of Waverley" would mean the same as "Scott is Scott," which it plainly does not; nor can "the author of Waverley" mean anything other than "Scott," or "Scott is the author of Waverley" would be false. Hence "the author of Waverley" means nothing.[17]

But what of "Scott" and what of "Socrates"? Do such proper names have meaning independently of use, "in isolation"? They are doomed by this general principle:

> Whenever the grammatical subject of a proposition can be supposed not to exist without rendering the proposition meaningless, it is plain that the grammatical subject is not a proper name, i.e., not a name directly representing some object. Thus in all such cases, the proposition must be capable of being so analysed that what was the grammatical subject shall have disappeared.[18]

By this disappearing act all the proper names in use turn into incomplete symbols which have the meaning determined by their context, and none outside a context.

Thus the only signs that might possibly have meaning independently of a context are "genuine proper names" for objects whose existence is assured. Since no proper names have ever been invented for the sort of "individuals" Russell and Whitehead had in mind, it would seem that the sum total of words and other signs in existence belong to the category of "incomplete signs." We may say of them all that they have no meaning in isolation, but only in the context of a proposition.

There are many resemblances between these views of Russell and Whitehead and those of the *Tractatus*; so the arguments in *Principia Mathematica* may throw some light on Wittgenstein's universal principle that expressions have meaning only in the context of a proposition. He certainly accepted Russell's analytic ideal and analytic technique, which made ordinary expressions disappear, revealing the true names and other expressions hidden in them (3.325; 4.0031).

C. *The Principle in the* Tractatus

If we could suppose that Wittgenstein was talking about ordinary, analyzable names when he said that names have no meaning outside of propositions, then the explanations in *Principia Mathematica* would suffice to explain his view. However, shortly before the passage quoted (3.3), he made quite clear what he meant by "names": they were genuine names, the names resulting from complete analysis (3.2-3.203). It is also clear that such names would have to be included among the "expressions" referred to in 3.314.[19]

Various explanations might be constructed which would be more or less in accord with the rest of what Wittgenstein said in the *Tractatus*,[20] but there is good evidence that Wittgenstein himself had the following reasons in mind.

Number 5.4733 is suggestive:

Frege says that any legitimately constructed proposition must have a sense. And I say that any possible proposition is legitimately constructed, and, if it has no sense, that can only be because we have failed to give a *meaning* to some of its constituents. (Even if we think that we have done so.) Thus the reason why "Socrates is identical" says nothing is that we have *not* given any *adjectival* meaning to the word "identical."

At first glance this passage might seem to contradict 3.314. It does not suffice to use the word "identical" in grammatical fashion with other words (as a complement with "is") for it to acquire a meaning; the supposed proposition cannot give it a meaning. It must have that already, prior to its use.

However, Wittgenstein did not say that a proposition determines the meaning of an expression (3.263), but rather that expressions have no meaning outside of propositions. And that is something quite different. His point is clear from the present case. Does the word "identical" have meaning? Well, it may or it may not. It depends on how you use it. In "Socrates is identical" it has none, for "Socrates is identical" does not qualify as a proposition. It does not qualify because it has not been determined what meaning the word "identical" would have *in such a combination.*[21]

The same reasoning would apply to any sort of expression, including genuine names. Even though it had been determined what object the sign *"a"* referred to, the sign would have no meaning in a combination such as *"(a)fx"* (NB 115). In general, if a sign has been "given a meaning," this means that it is capable of having such a meaning. But that it does not always have this meaning and of itself, is clear from the fact that there are many combinations in which it has no meaning (NB 115).[22]

Besides this line of explanation, in the sayings of both Frege[23] and Wittgenstein there are indications of a quite different reason—a practical view of language and certain general principles in which the viewpoint is expressed. In saying "Socrates is identical," we do not merely violate or exceed a rule. We fail to do something. We fail to do what language does, and therefore our name or other expression is not part of language; it is a mere scribble or sound.[24] The elements of a picture have "feelers," but a name by itself has no feelers; it does not reach out and touch reality (2.1514). Words may appear by themselves, but they cannot appear in two different *roles*, by themselves and in propositions (2.0122). If they appear by themselves, they have no role, they do nothing. But, "if a sign is put to no use, it is meaningless" (3.328).[25] If nothing behaves as if a sign has meaning, then it has no meaning (3.328). Certainly such an idle sign is not a name, for a name is defined in the *Tractatus* as a simple sign employed in a proposition (3.202). The conclusion from all the foregoing would seem to be that the modifier ("employed in a proposition") in this definition of a name should be understood as a restrictive modifier. And this is no idle stipulation; there is all the difference in the world between a mere sound or scratch and one that is being used as a sign. This is a point stressed both in the *Tractatus* and in Wittgenstein's later writings.[26]

III. Meaning Revealed by Use

It seems rather obvious that "identical" in "Socrates is identical" has no meaning. But how are we to tell? What is our criterion? If we decide the matter according to our success in imagining an identical Socrates, we are falling back into the deep abyss of psychologism that Frege warned against. Russell might have ruled the construction out *a priori*, for the sake of his system, as he ruled out the propositions which gave rise to the paradox of classes. But Wittgenstein's reply was: "If everything behaves as if a sign had meaning, then it does have meaning" (3.328).

Similarly, to learn *what* the meaning is, we should again consult the use of a sign.[27] "In philosophy the question, 'What do we actually use this word or this proposition for?' repeatedly leads to valuable insights" (6.211). "What signs fail to express, their application shows. What signs slur over, their application says clearly" (3.262).

Consultation of use is not only helpful; it is necessary. Consider the case of primitive signs: "The meanings of primitive signs can be explained by means of elucidations. Elucidations are propositions that contain the primitive signs. So they can only be understood if the meanings of those signs are already known" (3.263)—known, that is, by observation of their use, not by definition. Wittgenstein generalized this conclusion, saying, "In order to recognize a symbol by its sign we must observe how it is used with a sense" (3.326).

The distinction between symbol and sign is itself the fruit of applying this principle. For it comes from noticing that one and the same sensible sign can be used to designate quite different things (3.322) or in still more differing ways (3.323) and that quite different signs may serve the same purpose (3.341). Thus we can distinguish between the accidental features of a symbol and what is essential. Accidental features are those that result from the particular way in which the propositional sign—what can be perceived of a symbol (3.32)—is produced (3.341). "What is essential in a symbol is what all symbols that can serve the same purpose have in common" (3.341).

So Wittgenstein's aim in the *Tractatus* might be expressed as a search for the symbols expressed by signs and for a notation which would clearly reveal them.

IV. The Picture Theory of Meaning

The manner in which Wittgenstein distinguished between signs and symbols is characteristic of his whole approach to language in the *Tractatus*. Just as he asked what was the "essence" of a symbol, so he asked what was the essence of language. Just as the essence of a symbol was what many symbols had in common (3.341; 3.344), so the essence of language was what all use of signs, all language, had in common. And just as observation of signs' use revealed the common essence of symbols, so the observation of the way language is employed revealed the essential thing common to all language (§§ 65, 92, 97).

For Wittgenstein, studying language meant studying propositions (5.4711), for language consists of propositions (4.001). "My whole task," he said in one of his notebooks, "consists in the explanation of the proposition" (NB 39).

Professor von Wright tells how the secret of language, its essential function, was revealed to Wittgenstein:

> He was in a trench on the East front,[28] reading a magazine in which there was a schematic picture depicting the possible sequence of events in an automobile accident. The picture there served as a proposition; that is, as a description of a possible state of affairs. It had this function owing to a correspondence between the parts of the picture and things in reality. It now occurred to Wittgenstein that one might reverse the analogy and say that a *proposition* serves as a *picture,* by virtue of a similar correspondence between *its* parts and the world. The way in which the parts of the proposition are combined—the *structure* of the proposition—depicts a possible state of affairs.[29]

This then is what language does, this is its essence, this is what all propositions have in common. All language is propositions, and all propositions are logical pictures in which "one name stands for one thing, another for another thing, and they are combined with one another. In this way the whole group—like a *tableau vivant*—presents a state of affairs" (4.0311).[30] The proposition says: "This is how things stand" (4.5).

It not only presents a possible state of affairs. It says: "This is how things stand." This addition is important. It seems to lay Wittgenstein wide open to his later fundamental objection against the *Tractatus,* that it overlooked the diversity of language.[31] If all language is *Sätze,* and all *Sätze* are statements of fact, what becomes of questions, commands, jokes, and the rest? Aren't they language?

If, as James Griffin says,[32] in the *Tractatus Satz,* means "sentence," then there might seem to be no problem. For questions, commands, and the rest are of course sentences. However, Griffin does not mean these sorts of sentences. Furthermore, his translation of the term is based on what seems a faulty interpretation of a sentence in 3.13: "A *Satz* does not actually contain its sense, but does contain the possibility of expressing it." He takes this to mean that a *Satz* is a mere sentence, not a sentence with the determinate sense it acquires in actual use. Since in the *Tractatus* account the *Sinn* of a statement is the possible state of affairs it pictures (2.221: "What a picture represents is its sense"), and since this state of affairs is of course not contained in the statement of it, Griffin's interpretation seems unnecessary. It seems more natural to suppose that in the sentence quoted from 3.13, and in the sentences which precede it, Wittgenstein is making a point which he needed to make: a *Satz* does not actually contain the state of affairs it asserts (*das Projizierte*)—and therefore it may be false (2.173). But it is a statement for all that,[33] and not merely a sentence.

Miss Anscombe has suggested[34] that (in 4.001) Wittgenstein was using the term *Satz* much as we often use "proposition," for instance when we speak of a proposition that is asserted or denied. His definition of language as *Sätze* could then be interpreted as meaning that in all meaningful expressions a possible situation is asserted, denied, questioned, commanded, or merely presented for our amusement; that therefore expressions of whatever sort are pictures with a *Sinn*. This is their essential function, the function that interests logicians. The rest can be left to psychologists.

It is clear that the word *Satz* often occurs in this sense in the *Tractatus*. For instance, when Wittgenstein says *Der positive Satz muss die Existenz des negativen Satzes voraussetzen und umgekehrt* (5.5151), he certainly is not talking about sentences, nor does he mean that someone must be asserting the other proposition. However, it was inevitable that the word *Satz* be used in this sense in the treatment of complex statements (what other word was available?), whereas Wittgenstein was not forced to say in the earlier sections, on atomic propositions and propositions in general, that *Sätze* assert the situations they picture. But he did.[35] And it is in this earlier part that he asserted: "The totality of propositions (*Sätze*) is language" (4.001).

For this and other reasons,[36] I prefer to believe that Wittgenstein, with his scientific and mathematical background, with his interest in logic (as traditionally conceived), simply disregarded (not overlooked) all but the assertive, fact-stating uses of language. Commands, questions, jokes or exclamations simply did not interest him. So he used the word *Sprache* much as we shall see him using the word *Bedeutung*: he had it mean what seemed important.[37]

To repeat, then, a proposition is an assertion of fact by means of a representation, a picture. But this insight does not get us very far. In an ideal notation, what sort of things will need to be named and how? The two main principles considered so far give no answer. One ("To find meaning, study use") presupposes a system of signs already established and in use. The other merely tells us that these or any other signs have no meaning except when they are used.

V. Occam's Razor

But the second principle may easily be made to yield a third, to serve as guide in the construction of an ideal notation. If a sign given no function in a sentence has no meaning in the sentence (3.328), likewise a sign which has no function and is therefore unnecessary in the language as a whole has no meaning in the language and so should be eliminated. Occam's razor removes it.

> Occam's maxim is, of course, not an arbitrary rule, nor one that is justified by its success in practice: its point is that *unnecessary* units in a sign-language mean nothing.
>
> Signs that serve *one* purpose are logically equivalent, and signs that serve *none* are logically meaningless (5.47321).

To those familiar with the metaphysical version of Occam's maxim, Wittgenstein may seem to have forced an alien meaning on the schoolman's words. However, J. S. Mill claimed in his *Examination of Hamilton* that "The Law of Parsimony . . . is a purely logical precept."[38] At any rate, the words usually used by Occam suggest Wittgenstein's view to perfection: *Pluralitas non est ponenda sine necessitate.* A great deal in the *Tractatus* may be explained in terms of this principle and the general attitude, the general mentality, it expresses.[39]

Wittgenstein's mentality was that of a craftsman, a maker. He turned his hand to many things—engineering, music, architecture, tinkering, sculpture. And all his efforts revealed his preference for classic simplicity. In fact his whole life—not only the mansion he designed for his sister and the head he sculptured,[40] but his personal dealings with people, too,[41] and the furnishings of his room[42]—was shorn of ornamentation, of the superfluous. For Wittgenstein, *simplex sigillum veri* (5.4541) was more than a principle of logic.

But it was that too. Wittgenstein's model notation is a realm subject to the same law (5.454). It is characterized by *pure* symbolism, that is, by symbolism in which everything signifies, in which there is no excess, no unnecessary ornamentation.

Consequently, as will be shown in detail in the following pages, Wittgenstein tended to eliminate signs of many familiar sorts from his ideal notation. At the same time another tendency is also evident, which will receive detailed attention later, the tendency to multiply signs, in accordance with the principle already mentioned: "In a proposition there must be exactly as many distinguishable parts as in the situation that it represents" (4.04).

There is no obvious conflict between the two tendencies. For it is the *sorts* of signs which are decreased and the *number* of similar signs which is increased. And the whole program follows the principles Heinrich Hertz laid down for the construction of symbolic models:

> Two permissible and correct images of the same external objects may yet differ in respect of appropriateness. Of two images of the same object that is the more appropriate which pictures more of the essential relations of the object—the one which we may call the more distinct. Of two images of equal distinctness the more appropriate is the one which contains, in addition to the essential characteristics, the smaller number of superfluous or empty relations—the simpler of the two.[43]

The rest of this chapter will deal with Wittgenstein's answers to the questions raised by Hertz's program: First, what need not and cannot be represented by signs, and second, what can and must be represented by signs?

Wittgenstein envisaged the basic states of affairs to be pictured in an analytic notation much as Russell had envisaged them when he said in the *Principles of Mathematics:* "In every case of analysis, there is a whole consisting of parts with relations; it is only the nature of the parts and the relations which distinguishes different cases."[44]

Wittgenstein conceived of the world as a totality of complex facts, made up of simple objects in conjunction. The relations realized in facts and expressed by propositions are external[45] and therefore non-necessary,[46] and must be carefully distinguished from the so-called relations holding between objects in virtue of their intrinsic properties (4.122).[47] The simplest facts are mirrored by the simplest propositions—elementary propositions. And in these there are no signs except names. Occam's razor eliminates all others.

A. *Predicates and Signs for Relations*

First, there are no signs for (external) relations between objects. "The fact that the elements of a picture are related to one another in a determinate way represents that things are related to one another in the same way" (2.15). There is no need for signs to express the relations.[48]

Neither are there signs for internal relations between objects or for internal properties. For if analysis is complete, the objects named are simple yet different, somewhat as crimson is different from magenta. To illustrate the point, let us leave out of consideration all variations of shade and intensity and suppose that both magenta and crimson are perfectly precise qualities. Then just as no adjective is needed to describe crimson or magenta, since the names suffice, so no adjectives are necessary to describe the simple objects *a* and *b*, since their different names suffice (3.221; 3.26). The difference in the letters *shows* the difference in the objects—their difference and their multiplicity. Neither the difference nor the multiplicity can be expressed; they can only be shown. It would be nonsensical to say that *a* and *b* are two, or that they are different. What such statements try to say is already evident from the symbolism (4.1272).

Thus Wittgenstein's position is not as crudely physicalistic as it might appear at first view. When he says that relations are to be pictured, he is not overlooking relations like identity and difference, or the complex relations of mathematics. Such "relations" he does not consider to be genuine relations (4.122; NB 115-116) such as need to be pictured by propositions. The only relations of which we need to be informed by propositions are those which might be otherwise than they are without changing their terms.[49] "Relations" of the other sort—"internal relations"—are invariably "shown," and so do not need to be "said." Since the relations are "internal" to their terms, they are automatically expressed the moment their terms are expressed (4.122).

Identity, for instance, or difference cannot be better or more accurately expressed than by identity or difference of sign. "Identity of object I express by identity of sign, and not by using a sign for identity. Difference of objects I express by difference of signs."[50]

So long as he did not know the exact analysis of any proposition (5.55), Wittgenstein could not give any sample layout of names and had to be content with such notations as *aRb* or *fx*. But in a fully analytic notation no internal or external property would be expressed by a functional sign like *f* and no internal or external relation would be expressed by a relational sign like *R*. On that level there would be nothing corresponding to "Gold is yellow" (internal property) or "John is rich" (external property), on the preanalytic level, nor to "Gold is heavier than water" (internal relation) or "John is standing by Jim" (external relation).

Nor would there be anything corresponding to "John is a man." For substantives such as "complex," "fact," "function," "number," and so on all signify formal concepts (4.1272) and "a formal concept is given immediately any object falling under it is given" (4.12721). If only men were called "John," it would be nonsense to say that John is a man. Likewise, that an object is an object is obvious from the sign for an object expressing it; that a proposition is a proposition is obvious from the propositional sign expressing it. So any attempt to say these things, already shown, would be nonsensical. The words "object" or "proposition" would be superfluous, so meaningless. And a proposition using meaningless signs is nonsensical.

It would be equally nonsensical to say that an object exists, for in naming the object one points to it, mentally and grammatically. The very use of a name already indicates the existence of an object, and so the predicate "exists" would be superfluous (4.12721).[51]

But what if we used other signs, leaving out all names for objects? Might we then represent form without content? Might we speak directly about the forms of things, that is, give them their own signs, and not merely "show" them? No, for even in a generalized expression the x's and y's stand for (unnamed) objects, not forms (3.24). There can be no signs for forms. For all the signs we use are objects in the world—sounds, scratches, images and the like (2.13-2.151). Being objects they have the forms of objects, the logic of objects, and so could not possibly stand for forms, which have a different logic.[52] To find signs with the forms of forms, we should have to seek outside the world of objects; we could not use, for instance, marks on paper.[53] To understand this reasoning more perfectly, let us consider its most important applications.

B. *Logical Constants*

It has been shown that names are the only signs in elementary propositions.[54] Words such as "object" or "relation" have been ruled out as superfluous, on the grounds that the names and their arrangement would already show what these words were meant to say. But it has not been determined whether what is thus shown is an objective entity of some sort, whether for instance the name of an object shows an objective essence as well as naming a particular. Wittgenstein was particularly anxious to show that it does not.[55]

For otherwise logic, which speaks of such things—objects, propositions, arguments, functions, relations, and the like—would be just like any other science. As physics treats of electrons and their orbits, as zoology treats of animals and their habits, so logic would treat of logical constants and their relations. But already in 1912 Wittgenstein felt sure that logic was of a "totally different kind than any other science"; and that meant there must be no "logical constants."

Though he wavered at first in this conviction (NB 14-15), the *Tractatus* is unequivocal: "My fundamental idea is that the 'logical constants' are not representatives; that there can be no representatives of the logic of facts" (4.0312; cf. 5.4).

Here it is obvious that by "logical constants" Wittgenstein meant certain signs, which might be thought to stand for objects. At other times when he spoke of logical constants he meant objects for which such signs would stand.[56] Logical constants are whatever is constant in the logic of propositions.[57] "Wherever there is compositeness, argument and function are present, and where these are present, we already have all the logical constants. One could say that the sole logical constant was what all propositions, by their very nature, had in common with one another. But that is the general propositional form."[58] The world of logic is thus reduced to the general propositional form.

But this little realm is not a world of logic, for two reasons: first, it is not a world, it is no thing or combination of things; and secondly logic does not speak about it, or express it.

"There is no *thing* which is the form of a proposition, and no name which is the name of a form" (NB 99). A form is a possibility, not a thing (2.151; 2.0141). For logic, which deals with general forms, deals not with facts but with possibilities (2.0121). "In logic nothing is accidental: if a thing *can* occur in a state of affairs, the possibility of the state of affairs must be written into the thing itself" (2.012; 2.0121). The possibilities written into things are their forms (2.0141). So objects, the substance of the world (2.021), are form and content (2.025; 2.0231). They are themselves and they are the possibility of states of affairs in which they may occur. Likewise a state of affairs, a configuration of objects, has a form and a content; the particular things in the state of affairs show and contain the possibility of these things' being in such a combination. The same possibility is shown by a proposition about the state of affairs; the possibility is the sense of the proposition.[59] And what is true of names and propositions is true of any expression that characterizes the sense of a proposition: "An expression is the mark of a form and a content" (3.31).[60]

Since it is the sign for both, no new representative sign is needed or possible for just the form. Not that the original sign points out two *things,* one the content, the other the form. The form is no thing, but only a possibility. So it cannot be pointed to, referred to; it can only be shown. And it is not possible to show a possibility without pointing out that which makes it possible, namely the contents of the possible state of affairs. It is not possible to show the genuine possibility *aRb* without naming, pointing to, *a* and *b*. But the signs *a* and *b* already do this, and thereby show the possibility of *aRb*. Any other signs which did the same thing would differ only accidentally from *a* and *b*; they would be the same expressions, serving the same purpose (3.341).[61]

The same reasoning holds true for general forms; a proposition (e.g., *aRb*) which shows the possibility of *a* state of affairs (e.g., *aRb* or *bRa*) at the same time shows the possibility of *states of affairs*. This possibility is shown by all propositions; it is the general form common to them all (5.47). Or, if we include affirmation with the sense affirmed, we may say: "The general form of a proposition is: This is how things stand" (4.5). This is *the* logical constant.

Now all such constant forms are represented in logic by variables. Variables are signs for the formal concepts (pseudo-concepts) of logic.[62] For instance, "the variable name *x* is the proper sign for the pseudo-concept *object*" (4.1272). Such variables may be useful in logic, but of course they have no referents, and in that sense no meaning.

C. *Signs for Operations*

From 5.47 it seems clear that Wittgenstein would include negation, disjunction, conjunction and the like among "logical constants." For these are operations (5.2341) and he says there that all logical operations are already contained in the simplest propositions. This is explained in two ways.

First, the various operations are contained as possibilities in every proposition. For instance, if the positive fact *fa* is given, then so is the possibility of (x) fx, $\sim$ (Ex) fx, $\sim$ fa (NB 27). "The possibility of negation"—and therefore of all other operations—"is written into affirmation" (5.44).

Secondly, any proposition as it stands can be considered as the result of logical operations. For instance, p can be considered as a double negation of p, with the negations cancelling one another (5.253). In fact, Wittgenstein says that all propositions *are* the results of operations.[63]

Neither of these reasons, as presented, suggests the need of any signs for operations in a completely analytic language. In so far as an operation is merely possible, is it not *shown,* like forms? And though p may be represented as $\sim$ $\sim$ p, aren't these negation signs quite superfluous?

However, if more than a single elementary proposition is to be expressed, signs for operations—disjunction, conjunction, implication, or at least negation—would seem to be necessary. Even when all signs for functions, relations, logical forms, and properties are eliminated from the notation, signs for operations must remain if other than elementary propositions are to be expressed.

For all other propositions are the *result* of operations performed on elementary propositions. An operation sign does not merely draw attention to a difference shown by other signs. It makes the difference.

The point can be understood by considering negation. For, as Peirce and Sheffer had shown[64] and as Wittgenstein mentioned in the *Tractatus* (5.5), all other operations can be replaced by negation. In fact the general form of all propositions can be expressed as the result of repeated negations (6-6.001).

If we consider the difference between p and $\sim$ p, it is obvious that p does not express the negation. Negation is not contained in p save as a possibility. And of course to this possibility there may correspond an actuality—actual negation. And this actuality is expressed by the curl added to p; p alone does not suffice.

But what is this actual negation expressed by the negative sign? Is it a logical object, or a fact? No, the negative sign simply reverses the sense, that is, the direction, of the proposition p. It points the other way.[65] If p says "This is how things are," $\sim$ p says, "This is how things are not." It excludes a possibility, the same possibility as that affirmed by p. It does not point to any extra thing, any constituent of a state of affairs; rather it points away from the same possible state of affairs.[66]

If the sign for negation has no referent, then of course neither do any of the other signs for operations. For they can be replaced by the joint negation sign (5.5); they are equivalent to a certain number of negation signs. And these have no referents.[67] Signs for operations do not even designate forms, much less objects. They are signs only for differences between forms, for the internal relations between forms (5.24; 5.241).

Therefore, though they do pass the test of Occam's razor since they are necessary in all but the most elementary propositions, signs for operations do not have *meaning, Bedeutung*, in the sense of *Principia Mathematica*, which is the sense the word has in the only place where Wittgenstein gave it a clear sense (3.203) and which seems paradigmatic in the *Tractatus*.[68] In this sense only names have meaning.

VI. *Sinn* AND *Bedeutung* IN THE *Tractatus*

Names are necessary for language, any language, and only they are. With names, you can say something. Without them you can't.

The important thing about names is that they have reference. Wittgenstein called the referent of a name its *Bedeutung* (3.203), a word which has been translated in the English version of the *Tractatus* as "meaning."[69] The important thing about propositions is that they show possible states of affairs. These Wittgenstein called the *Sinn*, or "sense," of the propositions (2.202, 2.221).[70] Thus in the *Tractatus* (though not consistently in the notebooks), there is a clear double distinction between *Sinn* and *Bedeutung*. *Bedeutung* is real, actual; *Sinn* is not; it is a mere possibility.[71] And whereas names have *Bedeutung* but not *Sinn*, propositions have *Sinn* but not *Bedeutung*.

These distinctions correspond neither to ordinary German usage, nor to the usage of Wittgenstein's great predecessor, Frege. Nor is there anything corresponding to them in ordinary English usage.

In one all-important respect, though, the *Tractatus* terminology does resemble Frege's. In both, the *Bedeutung* is a referent, an object of some sort. And this explains in large part why Wittgenstein introduced the distinction he did. His departure from Frege's terminology was not accidental; it reflected a basic divergence in views, the elimination by Occam's razor of a wide range of supposed objects.

He objected in particular (3.143; 5.02) to Frege's view that propositions are complex names for objects called truth-values;[72] for it slurred over a number of basic distinctions. Calling a proposition a name made a fact look comparable to an object. But not only is a fact most unlike an object; the difference is of the greatest importance for logic. For logic deals with the necessary, the unalterable,[73] and objects are unalterable,[74] whereas facts are not (1.21). Furthermore, propositions may therefore be true or false, whereas names cannot be. This is another basic distinction ignored when propositions are called names.[75]

This disagreement with Frege is reflected in Wittgenstein's use of *Sinn* and *Bedeutung*. To speak of a proposition's as well as of a name's *Bedeutung* would be as misleading as to speak of a proposition as a name. The *Bedeutung* of a name is an object; but a proposition does not designate an object.

VII. The *Tractatus* Meanings

In order to appreciate just what definition of meaning Wittgenstein later criticized and rejected, it will be necessary to consider more carefully just what sort of objects the *Tractatus* "meanings" were, and Wittgenstein's reasons for supposing their existence and for saying that they alone were the meanings of words. Their nature will become clear from the reasons.

Wittgenstein reasoned from this premise: propositions are pictures of reality (4.021). But they are pictures which may be either true or false, either accurate or inaccurate.[76] And this raises a problem. For if a picture is false it pictures that which does not exist. That is, it is not a picture of reality. Wittgenstein's answer to this difficulty was the distinction between objects and their relations. A false proposition is one which pictures existing objects in relations they do not have (2.221-2.224). The objects exist, but the relations do not. Propositions say only how things are, not what they are (3.221).[77] But what sort of objects are thus pictured in relation? For a while Wittgenstein couldn't make up his mind whether complex objects could be the things named in propositions.[78] In the *Tractatus* he decided they were not.

"What lies behind the idea that names really signify simples?" Wittgenstein asked later.[79] His answer:

Socrates says in the Theaetetus: "If I make no mistake, I have heard some people say this: there is no definition of the primary elements—so to speak—out of which we and everything else are composed; for everything that exists in its own right[80] can only be *named*, no other determination is possible, neither that it *is* nor that it *is not* . . . . But what exists in its own right has to be . . . named without any other determination. In consequence it is impossible to give an account of any primary element; for it, nothing is possible but the bare name; its name is all it has. But just as what consists of these primary elements is itself complex, so the names of the elements become descriptive language by being compounded together. For the essence of speech is the composition of names."

Both Russell's "individuals" and my "objects" (*Tractatus Logico-Philosophicus*) were such primary elements (§ 46).

Now this gives us a good idea of Wittgenstein's earlier view, but it does not go very far toward explaining it. For, granted that simples can only be named, what is to prevent us from naming things which might also be described, through the combination of names for simples? What is wrong with our ordinary names?

One is tempted to make an objection against what is ordinarily called a name. It can be put like this: *a name ought really to signify a simple*. And for this one might perhaps give the following reasons: The word "Excalibur," say, is a proper name in the ordinary sense. The sword Excalibur consists of parts combined in a particular way. If they are combined differently Excalibur does not exist. But it is clear that the sentence "Excalibur has a sharp blade" makes *sense* whether Excalibur is still whole or is broken up. But if "Excalibur" is the name of an object, this object no longer exists when Excalibur is broken in pieces; and as no object would then correspond to the name it would have no meaning. But then the sentence "Excalibur has a sharp blade" would contain a word that had no meaning, and hence the sentence would be nonsense. But it does make sense; so there must always be something corresponding to the words of which it consists. So the word "Excalibur" must disappear when the sense is analysed and its place be taken by words which name simples. It will be reasonable to call these words the real names (§ 39).

This is how Russell thought[81] and this is how Wittgenstein thought when he wrote the *Tractatus*.[82] In 3.24 there is a clear echo of such reasoning: "A complex can be given only by its description, which will be right or wrong. A proposition that mentions a complex will not be nonsensical, if the complex does not exist, but simply false." If we make explicit the alternative to each of these two statements, the reasoning given in the *Investigations* reappears. For if a complex were not given by a description it would be given by a name (NB 52). But then if the complex did not exist, the "proposition" would be nonsensical, for the name would have no meaning, no referent. But a proposition does make sense. So " ' A *name* signifies only what is an *element* of reality. What cannot be destroyed; what remains the same in all changes' " (§ 59).

In 2.021-2.0211 Wittgenstein says: "Objects make up the substance of the world. That is why they cannot be composite. If the world had no substance, then whether a proposition had sense would depend on whether another proposition was true." Here the reasoning is similar. If there were no indestructible simples, then every name for an object would be a proposition in disguise, a proposition giving the composition and construction of the complex designated by the name. In that case any proposition, since it would contain such names, might suddenly become senseless, according to the caprice of nature. But this would obviously be the undoing of all language.

This argument highlights the most important characteristic of *Tractatus* objects: their simplicity. The nature of the argument demands that this simplicity be absolute. An electron will not do. A speck of color will not do.[83] For even if such physical or empirical elements were indivisible and so indestructible, it is quite conceivable that they should not exist. It is quite conceivable, for instance, that a certain spot which at the present moment is blue should not be blue, that is, that there should be no such empirically simple, logically complex phenomenon as this blue-here-now. But the non-existence of the *Tractatus* objects must not make sense. They cannot be problematical the way contingent complexes are.

Though empirical objects are thus ruled out as *Tractatus* objects, it does not follow that *Tractatus* objects are never empirical. For if we analyze a blue-here-now into its logical components, do we not arrive at an object —blue—and its relations, here and now? Blue cannot be destroyed, but can only be removed from a certain spot at a certain instant. Its relations to other objects alter, the fact perishes, but not the color. The whole visible scene might conceivably be analyzed into a complex of such color atoms, with their various spatial relations.

Wittgenstein's later criticisms of the *Tractatus* position suggest that his thinking may sometimes have tended in this direction, toward simple sense qualities as ultimate objects (§ 57). But in the *Tractatus* we are told that a color is in the same class as a place or an instant. Color, time and space are forms of objects; and particular colors, positions, and instants are accidental facts, not the substance of the world (2.0131; 2.0232; 2.0251). This being the case, I think we are justified in saying that the *Tractatus* objects were not empirical. An object which acquires color as a fact extrinsic to it is not anything that can be seen. Only the fact, the state of affairs, is visible.[84]

If the first argument for atomic meanings is expressed as the demand that there *be* objects represented by words, a second argument might be termed a demand for *precise* objects. Wittgenstein could not say that propositions "reach out" and "touch" reality (2.1511; 2.15121), by means of names and their "feelers" (2.1514), and then say that the feelers touch no precise object, not this object or that object. No, if the world is made up of simple objects *a, b, c, d* . . . (as indicated in the first argument),[85] then any proposition that reaches right out and touches reality touches objects *a, b, c* . . . or *c, d, e* . . . or some other equally definite group. Its sense must be determinate (NB 64).

If we forget the feelers and think of truth, we reach the same conclusion (the necessity of atomic meanings). "A proposition must restrict reality to two alternatives: yes or no. In order to do that, it must describe reality completely" (4.923). The connection may be shown by examples. "When I say, e.g., that the table is a yard long, it is extremely questionable what I mean by this. But I presumably mean that the distance between THESE two points is a yard, and that the points belong to the table" (NB 68). If I did not know what precise points are included in the table and which not, and if these points were not included in the meaning of my statement, then it would not be clear what states of affairs are ruled out by the proposition and which permitted (4.463). It is evident from such an example that "the requirement that simple signs be possible is the requirement that sense be determinate" (3.23); and sense must be determinate in order that truth and falsehood be determinable. "I must, whatever *is the case,* be able to say whether the proposition is true or false" (NB 67).[86]

VIII. The Act of Meaning

Such a requirement raises obvious difficulties. "When I say, 'The book is lying on the table,' does this really have a completely clear sense? (An EXTREMELY important question)" (NB 67). "To anyone that sees clearly, it is obvious that" such a sentence "contains a lot of indefiniteness, in spite of its form's being completely clear and simple in outward appearance" (NB 69).[87]

At this point Russell would start to work on a new, super-precise notation to replace our present "inadequate" ones. And in fact he attributed this aim and this attitude to Wittgenstein.[88] But Wittgenstein chose a different solution.

His solution is clearest in the *Notebooks*. "It seems clear," he says, "that what we MEAN must always be 'sharp'" (NB 68). "The sense must be clear, for after all we mean something by the proposition, and as much as we certainly mean must surely be clear" (NB 67).[89] "It is then also clear to the *uncaptive* mind that the sense of the sentence 'The watch is lying on the table' is more complicated than the sentence itself" (NB 69). "There is enormously much added in thought to each sentence and not said" (NB 70).[90]

Similar reasoning (minus the objectionable idea that a sentence says less than it means) can be found in the *Tractatus*. There is, for instance, this problem about the mere signs in speech: "At first sight a proposition—one set out on the printed page, for example—does not seem to be a picture of the reality with which it is concerned" (4.011). But neither does musical notation at first sight seem to be a picture of music (4.011). Yet "there is a general rule by means of which the musician can obtain the symphony from the score" (4.0141). And we are operating a similar calculus when we utter a sentence and mean or understand it (§ 81). It is the act of meaning which makes our sentence a picture of reality (4.021). To become a thought, a proposition (4), the propositional sign must be applied and thought out (3.5).[91] "We use the perceptible sign of a proposition (spoken or written, etc.) as a projection of a possible situation. The method of projection is to think out the sense of the proposition" (3.11).

So the problem of discrepancies between signs and meaning is solved in similar fashion in both *Tractatus* and *Notebooks*: by the connecting *act* of meaning the signs.[92]

When Wittgenstein said later, "Let's not imagine the meaning as an occult connection the mind makes between a word and a thing, and that this connection *contains* the whole usage of a word as the seed might be said to contain the tree" (BB 73-74), he may very well have had his former views in mind. True, he had never said that this all-important act *was* the meaning of a word. And he steered clear, in the *Tractatus* days, of psychological questions and all introspection. But this showed no depreciation of the meaning act, or disbelief in its existence. His attitude is explained satisfactorily by what he said later: he thought of the acts as "occult." So, had he investigated the mental phenomena connected with speech and thought, he would not have found what he wanted, but would have gotten bogged down in non-essentials (4.1121). He neither knew nor cared to know the observable mental constituents of thought (NB 130), for they were of no more importance than the accidentals of notation (4.1121; 3.34).[93]

Thus the comparison of seed and tree is apt. Who would advise the minute examination of an acorn as the best way to discover its potentialities? Far better to let it grow. It seems that the author of the *Tractatus* felt the same way about introspection. Looking into one's mind and observing what goes on there appeared as promising a way to discover meaning as would be the dissection of acorns for the study of oaks. So let the thought grow. See the consequences of the sign and you will learn its meaning.[94] See how the sign is used. Both words and mental phenomena disguise thought. But what they fail to reveal, their application shows; what they slur over, their application says clearly (3.262). So look at the tree and not the seed.

Yet for young Wittgenstein the meaning was all there in the seed, specified by the mental act. He was still far from saying that meaning *is* the use.

IX. CONCLUSION

The aim of this chapter has been to trace the beginnings of what Wittgenstein said later about the meaning of words. So I have been careful to pick out and stress any themes with a future. At the same time I have had to present views with no later importance save as familiar and important errors in opposition to which Wittgenstein's later views took shape. Now which are which?

Separate lists of the main section headings in the present chapter will give a first indication of what points had future importance, whether negative or positive. Themes with a future: 1) The search for meaning; 2) no meaning outside use; 3) meaning revealed by use; 4) Occam's razor. To these one might add the basic distinction between saying and showing. The following had no future, save as errors to be refuted or maladies to be cured: 5) the picture theory of meaning; 6) *Sinn* and

Bedeutung in the *Tractatus*; 7) the *Tractatus* meanings; 8) the act of meaning.

According to the *Tractatus*, philosophy is an activity. The activity is analysis, analysis of language, since the purpose of the activity is the clarification of confusions and the cure of false problems arising from the misunderstanding of language. To see what is really done by words, we must watch them when they are at work, not when they are idling. Since a sign has no meaning outside its use, its meaning can be discovered only by observing its use. The use observed is no thing, so it cannot be given a name, but can only be shown. Thus philosophy, which studies the uses of signs, does not provide philosophical propositions or propositions about a realm of its own, but opens our eyes to the actual workings of everyday expressions. It does this largely by showing that philosophy does not have a special realm of its own, that a wide variety of sublime and mysterious entities which some have thought language revealed or required are really quite superfluous and mythical.

To all of this the later Wittgenstein would subscribe.

But the *Tractatus* also said that any complete expression we may examine will surely turn out to be a logical picture. That is, the ultimate elements of which it is composed are so articulated that, while pointing to objects, they show a possible state of affairs. This possibility is the proposition's sense, and the referents pointed to are the meanings of the signs. Logical analysis like that in the *Tractatus* reveals them to be absolutely simple, non-sensible objects. Just what objects they are depends on the way the signs are meant by the speaker, the system of projection employed. It is the philosopher's job to analyze the systems used and to set forth his findings in a perspicuous notation mirroring reality as closely as possible in the number and basic variety of the signs used. Every object must have its sign, but only an object may have a sign. Thought will thus be clarified and false problems will be avoided.

With none of this did Wittgenstein later agree. Let us see why.

Chapter III

WITTGENSTEIN'S REJECTION OF UNITARY MEANINGS

ON THE FLYLEAF OF MORITZ SCHLICK'S COPY OF THE *Tractatus* WITTGENSTEIN wrote, "Every one of these sentences is the expression of an illness."[1] We might take this to mean that in the *Tractatus* many sicknesses appear and that each sentence is the expression of one or the other of them. One would be the illness Wittgenstein diagnosed thus, when he had recovered from one of its more virulent forms: "You say: the point isn't the word, but its meaning, and you think of the meaning as a thing of the same kind as the word, though also different from the word. Here the word, there the meaning. The money and the cow you can buy with it" (§ 120).

In this sick view, a meaning is like a word in that it too is, as it were, a logical point. "Here the word, there the meaning." It is a simple, single entity—something you can point to, at least with your attention. It differs from the word because it is, for instance, a different sort of object in the world, as in the *Tractatus* account, according to which a meaning did not need to be spatial in order to be represented by a spatial sign nor audible in order to be represented by an audible sign (2.171-2.18). If this account runs into difficulties, one may fall back, in the case of at least many words, on image meanings, and in the case of other words on feelings or private meaning experiences. Wittgenstein's therapeutic attentions to each of these forms of the illness will be described in successive sections of the present chapter—one on object meanings, one on image meanings, and a final section dealing with feelings or private experiences as the meanings of words. Only in the first is there a close connection with what Wittgenstein said in the *Tractatus* (though all three views, being basically similar, are rejected for much the same reasons). For Wittgenstein had never supposed that an image or a feeling was the meaning of a word.

We might also take Wittgenstein's remark on the flyleaf to mean that the *Tractatus* as a whole and every one of its statements reveal *one* illness:

its author's whole pathological state of mind. This would perhaps be more accurate. The errors of the *Tractatus* are not distinct maladies, but so many symptoms of the patient's mental condition. For instance, what Wittgenstein said about meanings was intimately connected with those basic infections, the picture theory and logical atomism. The disappearance of this symptom, his definition of meaning, cannot be explained without recounting his recovery from these more basic ideas. I will describe first his deliverance from the idea that all language consists of propositions that picture reality.

I. A Wider View[2]

Wittgenstein's criticism of the picture theory is not systematic and explicit. But from the start of the *Investigations* it is obvious that sledgehammer blows are being directed at the very foundations of the *Tractatus* theory of language. By page 12 a major criticism has been fully developed and is finally formulated thus: "It is interesting to compare the multiplicity of the tools in language and of the ways they are used, the multiplicity of kinds of word and sentence, with what logicians have said about the structure of language (including the author of the *Tractatus Logico-Philosophicus*)" (§ 23).[3] In defining language as propositions and reducing propositions to pictures, to combinations of names mirroring the world, the *Tractatus* ignored the great diversity of language, of the uses of words (PI 224).

At best, then, the picture theory is a partial account of language; it covers only statements of fact. But is it even that? Does it represent even them correctly? Countless remarks in the later works might be shown to invalidate the picture theory of statements. To see which are the most damaging, it is a help to remember that only the idea of projection made the picture theory tenable—that is, the idea of complicated hookups effected somehow by the mind between signs and reality, according to regular patterns. Wittgenstein had believed that "if anyone utters a sentence and *means* or *understands* it he is operating a calculus according to definite rules" (§ 81).

Now he decided that all this thinking-out is a myth, that language is no such calculus—in fact, that it is not a calculus at all. First, the mind does not project signs; there is no such conscious act. Under the influence of Frege, Wittgenstein had disdained psychological investigations; just how projections are effected on various occasions could be left to scientists to determine. In his second period Wittgenstein took a closer and wider look at what actually happens in communication with words. The *Blue Book* is full of what he found—and especially what he did not find. He did not find a mental process of thinking which parallels speech and makes all the connections.[4] He did not find a miraculous act of meaning hooking up object and sign (BB 73-74).

The supposition that sentences are projections of facts according to precise projective laws appeared still more gratuitous when Wittgenstein realized that language is not *any* sort of calculus. Not finding a conscious act of projection, he might have remembered the *Tractatus* illustration of musical score, symphony, and record (4.014) and so have proposed the projective theory in some other form, relying less on conscious acts. However, it finally dawned on Wittgenstein "that in philosophy we often *compare* the use of words with games and calculi which have fixed rules, but cannot say that someone who is using language must be playing such a game" (§ 81).[5]

Wittgenstein must have reached this realization shortly before dictating the *Blue Book*. For in the lectures Moore attended, though Wittgenstein recognized that propositions are not pictures in any ordinary sense of the word (M[1]12), he still defended the substance of the picture theory, the projective relationship between propositions and reality (M[1]12; M[2]292). In the *Blue Book,* however, there is a full critique of the calculus view of language. Wittgenstein says, for instance:

> This is a very one-sided way of looking at language. In practice we very rarely use language as such a calculus. For not only do we not think of the rules of usage—of definitions, etc.—while using language, but when we are asked to give such rules, in most cases we aren't able to do so. We are unable clearly to circumscribe the concepts we use; not because we don't know their real definition, but because there is no real "definition" to them. To suppose that there *must* be would be like supposing that whenever children play with a ball they play a game according to strict rules (BB 25).

In the *Blue Book* there is no tombstone, as it were, showing where the picture theory lies or marking the precise moment of its demise; but there is no doubt that it lies there, somewhere, interred. Only in the

Investigations is atomism dealt with as thoroughly, leaving the *Tractatus* definition of meaning exposed and defenseless. A few words (§ 40) then dispose of it.

II. MEANINGS ARE NOT OBJECTS

In the full-scale criticism of the *Tractatus* which Wittgenstein finally made in his *Philosophical Investigations,* his first direct criticism of the *Tractatus* argument (§ 39) for atomic, objective meanings goes as follows:

> Let us first discuss *this* point of the argument: that a word has no meaning if nothing corresponds to it.—It is important to note that the word "meaning" is being used illicitly if it is used to signify the thing that "corresponds" to the word. That is to confound the meaning of a name with the *bearer* of the name. When Mr. N.N. dies one says that the bearer of the name dies, not that the meaning dies. And it would be nonsensical to say that, for if the name ceased to have meaning it would make no sense to say "Mr. N.N. is dead" (§ 40).[6]

This is a good, common-sense argument which would be effective with the ordinary person, and would no doubt make him hesitate to call an object the meaning of a name. However, the argument would be effective only because the ordinary person would think of Mr. N.N. as the object in question. The author of the *Tractatus* did not. Like Russell before him, he considered the perishability of ordinary objects a strong reason for distinguishing between the simple objects referred to by names and accidental complexes like Mr. N.N., and between real names for these simples and apparent names like "Mr. N.N." That such atomic meanings as these had never occurred to most people or that they had not yet been identified by either him or Russell did not trouble Wittgenstein when he wrote the *Tractatus.* He aimed at giving a scientific account of language, and what scientist can be content with pre-scientific conceptions or terminology?

Early in his second period of philosophizing, Wittgenstein came to regard such fascination with scientific method as the bane of philosophy (BB 18; M³27). For philosophy as he had always conceived it was an analysis of language, and it now appeared to him ever more obvious that language did not obey precise and unvarying laws capable of scientific formulation, but was rather a free, spontaneous creation of human beings, who might disregard the rules of speech or make them up as they went along (BB 25; § 83).

Language, therefore, does not *have* to point at things. There is no model that language must conform to under pain of excommunication. In some propositions there are words which name or "stand for" things, in others are none (§§ 3-4). As for the words which do name things, Wittgenstein questioned whether there are any which name atomic objects of the sort described in the *Tractatus*. For neither he nor Russell had succeeded in producing a single "atomic" proposition. This indicated that something was wrong with their theory, but what? (M³1)

Two things, principally. In the *Tractatus*, Wittgenstein had considered it intuitively obvious that complex things are made up ultimately of simple things; therefore there were atomic objects. Furthermore, every statement had to be perfectly precise; therefore the atomic objects were meanings. Wittgenstein now found both conclusions unacceptable, because he rejected both premises.

First, according to G.E. Moore, in the lectures of 1932-1933 Wittgenstein had already concluded "that it was senseless to talk of a 'final' analysis" (M³2). The same view is developed in the *Investigations*. By suggesting the various senses which "composite" and "simple," and therefore "analysis," might have, Wittgenstein showed that in the *Tractatus* the nature of "complete analysis" is left so vague that the theory of atomic objects has no meaning, and so must be rejected (§ 47).[7]

Secondly, he decided that the supposed precision of language, like its supposed regularity, is a myth.

> When I give the description: "The ground was quite covered with plants" —do you want to say I don't know what I am talking about until I can give a definition of plant?
>
> My meaning would be explained by, say, a drawing and the words "The ground looked roughly like this." Perhaps I even say "it looked *exactly* like this."—Then were just *this* grass and *these* leaves there, arranged just like this? No, that is not what it means. And I should not accept any picture as exact in *this* sense (§ 70).

This sense, rejected here and elsewhere,[8] is the *Tractatus* sense, the sense that required atomic meanings. Wittgenstein's disagreement with this view of exactness, like his criticism of "complete" analysis, brings us back to grass, leaves, ground and the like. Such things are the meanings of our words, if any objects are.

Such objects can obviously perish, as can Mr. N.N. None of them satisfies the *Tractatus* requirement of indestructibility. For though they may be simple, like the color red, they may nevertheless cease to be, leaving the word which refers to them without any referent, yet still meaningful (§ 57; BB 31). Nor will it do to say that "we bear in mind the colour (for instance) that a word stands for"; that even when externally destroyed, it is there in the mind. For this need not always be possible (BB 31; § 56). If we still insist that the combination of a name with the verb "exists" is nonsensical, we are not saying something metaphysical, we are not describing language; we are merely expressing our determination to use words in a certain way (BB 31; § 58).

These basic criticisms give the first arguments mentioned (§ 40) their validity. If the objects in question are not the mysterious, undefined simples of the *Tractatus*, reasoned to *a priori* rather than observed; if they are not Russell's empirical simples; if they are instead the ordinary objects which we observe, then objects cannot be identified as the meanings of proper names.[9]

It may seem strange that the only sort of objective realities Wittgenstein considered as possible "meanings" were concrete particular objects, corresponding to proper names. For, after all, proper names are not generally said to have any "meaning," save in so far as they are more than mere names, having been derived from a word of some other sort. But general terms do have "meaning." So one might expect Wittgenstein to give at least a nod to the hypothesis that the meanings of words—nouns, verbs, adjectives, adverbs—are objective essences, whether unique or plural, immanent or Platonic.

There are a number of reasons why he did not. For one thing, it was too obvious that the meaning of, say, the word "dinosaur" is no immanent essence, unique or plural, in any existing things; for no dinosaurs exist. Such "meanings" are too easily ruled out by the argument already mentioned. Words can have meaning even though the things referred to do not exist. As for separate, Platonic "meanings," Wittgenstein was not the one to suppose their existence.

In the *Tractatus* he sought to avoid these difficulties for objective meaning by resorting to atomic meanings corresponding to proper names. If words were to have objects as their meanings, they would have to be

objects which avoided all such eventualities as the extinction of dinosaurs. That is why Wittgenstein later thought it sufficient to consider the
Tractatus hypothesis, the hypothesis of object meanings for proper names,
in order to eliminate all objective meanings.

Another reason too was undoubtedly important. Had Wittgenstein
thought that the activities or objects or properties referred to by general
terms all had some common essence, he might have considered seriously
the possibility that such essences are the meanings of general terms. However, as will be explained shortly, he was convinced that general terms do
not imply the existence of such essences and that in fact essences cannot
generally be found which are common to all the things referred to by a
general term (BB 130).

III. MENTAL MEANINGS

When object meanings fail, mental meanings are likely to take their
place. Wittgenstein suggested and answered a number of general reasons
for theories of this sort, of which I will mention only three principal
ones.[10]

A favorite bête noir with Wittgenstein was the idea, which he held to
be common (M¹7), that in the case of a substantive like "the meaning"
you have to look for something at which you can point and say "This is
the meaning" (BB 1, 5, 36, 47). "You say: the point isn't the word, but
its meaning, and you think of the meaning as a thing of the same kind
as the word, though also different from the word. Here the word, there
the meaning" (§ 120). But where the meaning? Well, if not in the world,
at least in the mind (BB 47). Wittgenstein himself had not taken this step
in the *Tractatus*, for at that time he was still satisfied with object meanings. But he understood the basic error and knew where it led.

His objections against the *Tractatus* picture theory are also objections
against this notion of universal referring. Both the general theory and the
particular theory overlook the great variety of ways in which we use
words. It simply is not true that every word either needs or has a referent.
We are free to use words in any number of ways, and we do (§§ 11-14).

Another source of error is the tendency to consider the mind a sort of
reservoir or warehouse from which all our various activities are derived
(BB 40, 143).

The fault which in all our reasoning about these matters we are inclined to make is to think that images and experiences of all sorts, which are in some sense closely connected with each other, must be present in our mind at the same time. If we sing a tune we know by heart, or say the alphabet, the notes or letters seem to hang together, and each seems to draw the next after it, as though they were a string of pearls in a box, and by pulling out one pearl I pulled out the one following it.

Now there is no doubt that, having the visual image of a string of beads being pulled out of a box through a hole in the lid, we should be inclined to say: "These beads must all have been together in the box before." But it is easy to see that this is making a hypothesis. I should have had the same image if the beads had gradually come into existence in the hole of the lid (BB 39-40).

Of course in speech the word itself is not always there in the mind before it is spoken. But surely there is some reason for the word's being used, and this word rather than another. Well, what sort of reason? A cause? Then let us consider the following example:

In 1)[11] B learnt to bring a building stone on hearing the word "column!" called out. We could imagine what happened in such a case to be this: In B's mind the word called out brought up an image of a column, say: the training had, as we should say, established this association. B takes up that building stone which conforms to his image.—But was this *necessarily* what happened? If the training could bring it about that the idea or image—automatically—arose in B's mind, why shouldn't it bring about B's *actions* without the intervention of an image? This would only come to a slight variation of the associative mechanism (BB 89).

By many such arguments Wittgenstein tried to remove the prejudice that there *must* be mental events preceding or accompanying words (BB 41).

"The proposition that your action has such and such a cause, is a hypothesis. The hypothesis is well-founded if one has had a number of experiences which, roughly speaking, agree in showing that your action is the regular sequel of certain conditions which we then call causes of the action" (BB 15).[12] As we shall see, Wittgenstein considered it a gratuitous and ill-founded hypothesis to suppose that each word is thus constantly associated with some conscious mental experience.

However, there is a sort of reason which seems far less conjectural. We have *motives* for our actions; we are not mere automata, mere talking machines (BB 16). And of our motives we are immediately and infallibly aware (BB 15).

In this and a thousand similar cases, said Wittgenstein, we have the idea that "something must make us" do what we do (BB 143). We are misled, perhaps, by a confusion between motive and cause (BB 143). If we realized that the chain of *actual* motives has a beginning, we would no longer be revolted by the idea of a case in which there is *no* motive for what we do. "A reason [motive] is a step preceding the step of the choice. But why should every step be preceded by another one?" (BB 88) We are kept from seeing this by the fact that when the chain of motives has come to an end and still the question "why?" is asked, we are inclined to give a cause instead of a motive (BB 15).

A third major reason for mental theories of meaning is closely connected with the one just mentioned. As we have reasons but a machine does not, so too we *think* whereas a machine does not. And the way we use this verb "think" gives the impression that thinking must be something which goes on side by side with speech. We say: "Think before you speak!," "He speaks without thinking," "What I said didn't quite express my thought," "I didn't mean a word of what I said," "The French language uses its words in that order in which we think them" (BB 148). Such expressions lead us to suppose that thinking *accompanies* speaking (Ibid.).

Wittgenstein considered this a needless duplication (§§ 327-332). Speaking itself is a sort of thinking. For "we may say that thinking is essentially the activity of operating with signs." Such activity may be performed by the hand, when we write, or by the mouth and larynx, when we use vocal signs. Or it may be performed interiorly by imagining signs or pictures; for, as we shall see, mental pictures may be signs, of much the same sort as sensible signs. But this latter is not the only sort of thinking, nor need it accompany the former when we are writing or speaking (BB 6, 15, 16). Asides need not accompany all lines spoken on the stage (BB 35).

These general considerations suggest two strands of argument that interweave in Wittgenstein's more detailed treatment of mental meanings, each reinforcing the other: sometimes he questions the actual occurrence of such "meanings," sometimes their necessity. Because the definition of meaning as a mental event—an image, feeling, or idea—would give the impression that these things are both necessary and constantly associated with words, Wittgenstein was opposed to any such definition. For he believed that they were neither necessary nor specially characteristic of words' use.

IV. MEANINGS ARE NOT IMAGES

Russell once said: "When we ask 'What does such and such a word mean?' what we want to know is 'What is in the mind of a person using the word?' "[13] Later, in *The Analysis of Mind*, he became more specific about the mental contents in question. "The use of words in thinking," he said, "depends, at least in origin, upon images, and cannot be fully dealt with on behaviorist lines."[14]

> The essence of language lies, not in the use of this or that special means of communication, but in the employment of fixed associations (however these may have originated) in order that something now sensible—a spoken word, a picture, a gesture, or what not—may call up the "idea" of something else. Whenever this is done, what is now sensible may be called a "sign" or "symbol," and that of which it is intended to call up the "idea" may be called its "meaning." This is a rough outline of what constitutes "meaning."[15]

Long before, Augustine had said similar things. Thus, in the *Confessions*, with which Wittgenstein was familiar, he says in one place that when I speak of pain, I am not in pain, yet the image of pain is in my memory. Were it not I wouldn't know what I was saying nor would I be able to distinguish pain from pleasure when discussing pain. The same is true, he says, of bodily health. Unless the image of health were supplied by the memory, we would not know what the word "health" meant, nor would sick people know what had been said when health was spoken of.[16]

Wittgenstein's discussion of image meanings is aimed at just such views as these.[17] Neither Russell nor Augustine pretended to have carried out a statistical survey revealing the universal association of images with words. They were saved the trouble of investigating by the supposed necessity of such images. So it is the necessity of images that Wittgenstein questioned more insistently than their non-occurrence, though of course their non-occurrence would indicate that they can be done without.

Wittgestein's main arguments against the image theory of meaning are aimed at destroying the idea that images *must* accompany words, that words would be dead and useless without them. He felt that when people turn to the image theory they are not relying on the evidence of their own experience, but are the victims of a common prejudice regarding the workings of language. Since image meanings are not objects of perception but creatures of prejudice, Wittgenstein would destroy the prejudice.[18]

A. Sentence Pictures

Wittgenstein criticized images both as the meanings of individual words and as the meanings of sentences. I will start with the latter discussion and its implications for word meanings.

In the *Blue Book* he considered at length the sample proposition "King's College is on fire." Once a person realizes that in thinking this he is not thinking a fact, that the fact need not be present to be thought as an object needs to be present to be seen, he is likely to suppose that the object of his thought is a shadow of the fact (BB 32). "The shadow would be some sort of a portrait of the fact." That is, it would be similar to the fact.[19] "However, it is quite clear that similarity does not constitute our idea of a portrait; for it is in the essence of this idea that it should make sense to talk of a good or a bad portrait. In other words, it is essential that the shadow should be capable of representing things as in fact they are not" (just as it is essential for a meaningful sentence to be capable of stating a falsehood) (BB 32). But what makes a picture the portrait of a given person or thing if it does not resemble the thing it portrays?

If it is suggested that a picture is a portrait of a particular object because of some intrinsic, projective relation it has with the object (as in the *Tractatus* account), this is true of the words as well. So "the interpolation of a shadow between the sentence and reality loses all point. For now the sentence itself can serve as such a shadow" (BB 37).[20]

In other words, as a picture is the portrait of someone for reasons quite extrinsic to the picture itself (in virtue of a name-tag, for instance, or the painter's intention) (§§ 683-684), so too a mental shadow would be the picture of a given fact only for reasons extrinsic to the shadow itself—reasons of a sort which might apply equally well to the words of the proposition. So the supposed shadow meaning is quite superfluous. It is a gratuitous assertion in need of Occam's razor.[21]

In this line of argumentation, the conclusions regarding individual words remain implicit. But they are rather obvious. Suggesting that images are the meaning of a sentence is not the same thing as suggesting that images are the meanings of individual words; one or two images might do for the whole sentence or for several sentences. Yet there is a close enough connection between the two suggestions so that to rule out images as the meanings of sentences in the way Wittgenstein does is at the same time to rule out image meanings for individual words.

Thus if we are trying to defend this latter position, it appears in the first step of Wittgenstein's argument that at least some of the words in the proposition must express images that are both pictures of something and yet perhaps inaccurate pictures. The expression "King's College," for instance, may correspond to an image of a building engulfed in flames when, as a matter of fact, King's College is giving forth no flames. We naturally wonder, therefore, what makes this an image of King's College. And we will be hard put to find anything *in* the image which makes it surely and unmistakably the image of King's College and no other. But once we recognize this, the supposition of an image appears pointless. The spoken expression may be a sign for the thing in the same way that an image would be. It may be related to an object in the same complex, extrinsic fashion. Wittgenstein makes this line of argumentation explicit in his comments on individual words and their supposed image meanings.

B. *General Images*

The image theory of word meanings takes special forms when the word to be explained is a general term.

There is a tendency, says Wittgenstein in the *Blue Book,* rooted in our usual forms of expression, to think that the man who has learnt to understand a general term, say, the term "leaf," has thereby come to possess a kind of general picture of a leaf, as opposed to pictures of particular leaves. He was shown different leaves when he learnt the meaning of the word "leaf"; and showing him the particular leaves was only a means to the end of producing "in him" an idea which we imagine to be some kind of general image. We say that he sees what is in common to all these leaves; and this is true if we mean that he can on being asked tell us certain features or properties which they have in common. But we are inclined to think that the general idea of a leaf is something like a visual image, but one which only contains what is common to all leaves. (Galtonian composite photograph.)[22] This again is connected with the idea that the meaning of a word is an image, or a thing correlated to the word (BB 17-18).

The view mentioned here is not refuted by introspection, but by countless studies of objects or activities designated by general terms in which Wittgenstein failed to find any common essence. He recognized common features. Leaves, for instance, all have certain features or properties in common (BB 18). They are all visible, they are all colored, all three-dimensional, and so on. But so are many other things. What Wittgenstein failed to discover was a set of properties common to all the things called by a common name, and common to them alone, so that we might point to the set and say, "This is the reason for using the word; this is its meaning." As early as the lectures of 1932-1933,

> He illustrated this problem by the example of the word "game," with regard to which he said both (1) that, even if there is something common to all games, it doesn't follow that this is what we mean by calling a particular game a "game," and (2) that the reason why we call so many different activities "games" need not be that there is anything common to them all, but only that there is "a gradual transition" from one use to another, although there may be nothing in common between the two ends of the series (M³ 17).

Since the word "game" is typical of other general terms,[23] there is no need for introspection to decide whether as a rule general ideas are suggested by general terms and are their meanings. When there are no general essences, no sets of common properties, for general ideas to mirror, such ideas are clearly impossible.

C. *Particular Images*

However, particular ideas or images are possible in all cases. And Wittgenstein frequently considered the hypothesis that such pictures are the meanings of words. Moore suggests Wittgenstein's early concern with this theory and the line of argumentation he always opposed to it:

> He also insisted on three negative things, i.e. that three views which have sometimes been held are mistakes. The first of these mistakes was the view that the meaning of a word was some image which it calls up by association—a view to which he seemed to refer as the "causal" theory of meaning. He admitted that sometimes you cannot understand a word unless it calls up an image, but insisted that, even where this is the case, the image is just as much a "symbol" as the word is (M¹8).

Moore explains elsewhere (M¹11) that for Wittgenstein whatever was necessary to give a sign significance was a part of the "symbol," so that where, for instance, the "sign" is a sentence, the "symbol" is the sign plus everything which is necessary to give the sentence sense. In the case just envisaged by Wittgenstein the word needs completion by at least an image in order to be a symbol, in order to have meaning. In comparing the image with the word and saying that it too is a symbol, Wittgenstein is therefore arguing that the image does not suffice by itself, that it too needs something besides itself if it is to have meaning, if it is to be the image of this or that. Finding an image does not end the search for a meaning. Thus in the same lecture he said, "You can't give any picture which can't be misinterpreted" (M[1]14). There is nothing in the image itself which makes it infallibly the sign of this or that. Of an image "meaning" Wittgenstein would therefore say what he said of a "shadow" sense for a sentence: "it would be susceptible of different interpretations just as the expression is" (M[1]14).

For instance, let us suppose the word "green" suggests not an impossible general idea of green, but a particular shade, pure green, and that the word "leaf" begets in one's mind the image of a leaf with a particular shape. This is quite possible. But for such a leaf-shape to be understood as a general sample and not as the shape of a particular leaf, and for a slip of pure green to be understood as a sample of all that is greenish and not as a sample of pure green—this in turn resides in the way the samples are used. It is not intrinsic to them. So anyone who hears a word and gets such an image is no better off than he would be with just the word. The image by itself does not give him the meaning (§ 73).[24]

"Ask yourself this: what shape must the sample of the colour green be? Should it be rectangular? Or would it then be the sample of a green rectangle?—So should it be 'irregular' in shape? And what is to prevent us then from regarding it— that is, from using it—only as a sample of irregularity of shape?" (§ 73)[25]

But can't the image fit the sense of a sentence that I understand? (§ 138) For instance, someone uses the word "cube" in a sentence. He says "Point to a cube." When I hear the word "cube," the drawing of a cube comes to my mind. Now if that picture occurs to me and I point to a triangular prism for instance, and say it is a cube, then this use of the word doesn't fit the picture.

"Doesn't it fit?" asks Wittgenstein. "I have purposely so chosen the example that it is quite easy to imagine a *method of projection* according to which the picture does fit after all" (§ 139). The picture of the cube may indeed suggest a certain use to us, but it is possible for us to use it differently. Not all images must be used as we use onomatopoeic words. "What is essential is to see that the same thing can come before our minds when we hear the word and the application still be different. Has it the *same* meaning both times? I think we shall say not" (§ 140).

> Suppose, however, that not merely the picture of the cube, but also the method of projection comes before our mind?—How am I to imagine this? —Perhaps I see before me a schema showing the method of projection: say a picture of two cubes connected by lines of projection.—But does this really get me any further? Can't I now imagine different applications of this schema too? (§ 141)

Yes, we can. We can go on adding picture to picture. We can picture the application of the picture, and picture the application of the pictured application, and so on, just as we may add gestures to a spoken order (§ 433). But neither addition is necessary. The words may seem incomplete, but the pictures will be incomplete in precisely the same way. So what good are they? If the verbal signs are not enough, then neither are the mental ones (BB 34).

And suppose we put the picture outside, where we can see it more clearly. Won't the visible picture serve just as well as the mental picture? Yet would we call such a visible picture the meaning of the word it accompanies?

For instance, suppose I give someone the order "Fetch me a red flower from that meadow." How is he to know what sort of flower to bring, as I have only given him a *word*? The answer one might suggest is that he goes looking for a flower carrying a red image in his mind, and compares it with each flower in order to see which has the color of the image. Now there is such a way of searching, but it is not at all essential that the image used should be a mental one. Wouldn't a picture in his hand do just as well? (BB 3) And would such a picture be the meaning of the word "red"?

Once we make this supposition, and put the image in the hand rather than in the mind, it is obvious that the image has no special importance (BB 5). I might tell a person to bring me a red flower, and put in his hands the picture of a yellow tulip. He will then go off, perhaps admiring the picture I have given him, and come back with a *red* flower—maybe a red tulip, if he understood me that way.

Now is there a collision between the picture and the application here? "Can there be a collision between picture and application? There can, inasmuch as the picture makes us expect a different use, because people in general apply *this* picture like *this*" (§ 141).

This is a matter of habit, and applies as well to words as to images. And that explains why the image, though sometimes useful, is often quite superfluous. The association may be made directly, without the intermediary of an image (BB 89). Thus it may be that when told to fetch a red flower, "we go, look about us, walk up to a flower and pick it, without comparing it to anything" (BB 3). Images do not, as a matter of fact, always accompany words (BB 41).

"To see that the process of obeying the order can be of this kind, consider the order 'imagine a red patch.' You are not tempted in this case to think that *before* obeying you must have imagined a red patch to serve you as a pattern for the red patch which you were ordered to imagine" (BB 3).[26]

It might be questioned whether obeying is possible in this case. We could not obediently call forth an image which the order had already brought to our minds, any more than we could obey the order to stand up when already standing. However, if it be granted that no such thing ordinarily happens and that we can call forth the requested image, then we have at least one example of an order obeyed without previous imagining of the action. We therefore see the possibility of the same thing's occurring in other cases (BB 12). Since in any such case we would have understood the order and it would have meaning, its meaning would not be an image.

V. MEANINGS ARE NOT FEELINGS

As a defendant of referent meanings may retreat from object meanings to images, so too he may retreat from these to "feelings" or other mental "experiences" when the image theory begins to look implausible. For instance:

> When someone asks me "What colour is the book over there?", and I say "Red," and then he asks "What made you call this colour 'red'?", I shall in most cases have to say: "Nothing *makes* me call it red; that is, no reason. I just looked at it and said 'It's red.'" One is then inclined to say: "Surely this isn't all that happened; for I could look at a colour and say a word and

still not name the colour." And then one is inclined to go on to say: "The word 'red' when we pronounce it, naming the colour we look at, *comes in a particular way"* (BB 148-149).[27]

And so a new hypothesis is introduced, vaguer and broader: the fact that a word has meaning must consist in some special feeling or experience that accompanies it.

In many cases we would not think of assigning an image meaning to a word, but would have recourse immediately to this vaguer account. It is natural that images should be suggested as the meanings of substantives like "chair" or adjectives like "red," whereas a private experience of some other sort will have to be found for words like "not" and "if." It is not easy to imagine a not or an if. This difference is reflected in the fact that whereas words for visible objects and properties dominated in the preceding section, here syncategorematic, emotive, and other non-visual terms take first place.

The nondescript collection of supposed mental contents corresponding to this nondescript assortment of words were vaguely referred to by Wittgenstein as "feelings," "sensations," "experiences" (*Fühlen, Empfindungen, Erlebnisse*). His loose terminology resembled that of Russell and William James. "The mental states usually distinguished as feelings," said James,[28] "are the *emotions* and the *sensations* we get from skin, muscle, viscus, eye, ear, nose, and palate." As though this were not broad enough, he elsewhere instances "psychic overtones, halos, suffusions, or fringes."[29] As for Russell, "When I speak of a feeling of belief," he says, "I use the word 'feeling' in a popular sense, to cover a sensation or an image or a complex of sensations or images or both; I use this word because I do not wish to commit myself to any special analysis of the belief-feeling."[30] Such are the "feelings" discussed in this section.

Wittgenstein was very familiar with the works of James and seems often to have had his views in mind when discussing this question of word feelings.[31] For James, the meaning of each word is "an altogether specific affection of the mind"[32] accompanying the word. This view he clearly distinguished from an image theory of meaning. Like Wittgenstein, James attributed the image theory to the misleading influence of language.[33] Like Wittgenstein, while recognizing the occurrence of images, he denied that there is a constant flow of them accompanying speech or that when they do occur, they have any special importance.[34] Like Witt-

genstein, he drew a parallel between images and words, saying that both
had meaning in the same way, not intrinsically, but through something
extra. But his extra something was very different from Wittgenstein's.
James explains:

> Every definite image in the mind is steeped and dyed in the free water that
> flows round it. With it goes the sense of its relations, near and remote, the
> dying echo of whence it came to us, the dawning sense of whither it is to
> lead. The significance, the value, of the image is all in this halo or penumbra
> that surrounds and escorts it,—or rather this is fused into one with it and
> has become bone of its bone and flesh of its flesh; leaving it, it is true, an
> image of the same *thing* it was before, but making it an image of that thing
> newly taken and freshly understood.[35]

It is quite possible, James said, like Wittgenstein after him, to think in
images. This is how a deaf-mute is likely to think to himself.[36] But for
the ordinary person it is handier to think in words, with verbal imagery.[37]
It makes little or no difference, though

> in what sort of mind-stuff, in what quality of imagery, his thinking goes on.
> The only images *intrinsically* important are the halting-places, the substan-
> tive conclusions, provisional or final, of the thought. Throughout all the
> rest of the stream, the feelings of relation are everything, and the terms
> related almost naught. These feelings of relation, these psychic overtones,
> halos, suffusions, or fringes about the terms, may be the same in very dif-
> ferent systems of imagery.[38]

This, then, is the view or the sort of view Wittgenstein often criticized.
It is summed up beautifully when James says of a certain expression: "We
must mean *that* by an altogether special bit of consciousness *ad hoc*."[39]
This special bit of consciousness is the meaning of the expression.

Naturally, such a theory does not stand alone. What James said about
words was intimately connected with what he said about whole statements. Similarly, Wittgenstein's criticism of the theory about words does
not stand alone; it is supported by his criticism of the sentence theory.
So this theory too needs to be mentioned. Further reference to James will
illustrate the sort of sentence theory Wittgenstein had in mind.

According to James, the meaning of a sentence is a "single pulse of
subjectivity, a single psychosis, feeling, or state of mind."[40] It is not a

chain of feelings, one succeeding the other for each word.[41] Were we to slice out any section of the thought stream that accompanies a sentence, we would find the whole sentence there.[42] "It is the overtone, halo, or fringe of the word, *as spoken in that sentence.*"[43] Yet the section that coincides temporally with any given word is unmistakably *its* meaning. *Its* feeling is then most prominent—even though it be but an "and" or an "if" or a "but."[44] Thus if we divided a sentence into time parts thus: "The pack / of cards / is on / the table," and were able to examine any corresponding section of the thought stream, the whole thought would be found present in each section; yet in the second section the cards would be the object most emphatically present to the mind and in the final section the table feeling would be most prominent.[45]

It follows that any objection calling in question the whole unitary impulse also calls in question the moments corresponding to individual words. So two lines of criticism were open to Wittgenstein, one directed against word feelings, the other against sentence feelings. As in the previous section, the sentence theory will be considered first.

A. *Sentence Feelings*

Wittgenstein did not attack this theory head-on, but went to its roots. One principal answer took this form: "The meaning of a word is not the experience one has in hearing or saying it, and the sense of a sentence is not a complex of such experiences" (PI 181). It is true that the meaning of a sentence is, in a sense, a function of its words' meanings.[46] So if we think of these meanings as feelings, we will end up with a feeling theory of sentence meanings (PI 181). To disprove the word theory is, therefore, to remove one reason for holding the sentence theory. Since we are interested only in the reverse process, by which word feelings are disproved, this line of argumentation is not as interesting as the following ones, which provide independent support for Wittgenstein's direct attack on the feeling theory of word meanings.

The idea that sentences are accompanied by an appropriate aura, atmosphere, or feeling is suggested too by the recollection of other words with other meanings or other ways of saying the same words. I might, for instance, have said them as a quotation rather than as a question, or as a joke, as practice in elocution, and so on (§ 607). Reflecting after I have asked a question, I am inclined to say that I must after all have *meant* the words somehow specially—differently, that is, from in those other cases. The picture of a special atmosphere forces itself on me; I can see it quite clear before me (so long, that is, as I do not look at what my memory tells me really happened) (§ 607). And so it seems quite incredible—afterwards—that all I did was open my mouth, or frown, or raise my voice, or say to myself beforehand, "I wonder if breakfast will be on time." *Afterwards* no such description satisfies me. True, I don't remember anything else. Yet I feel that there must have been something else, something hidden and difficult to catch sight of (§§ 19-21).

The villain in this piece is the word "mean" (*meinen*). According to Wittgenstein, what tempts us most of all to think of the meaning of what we say as a process essentially of the sort James described is the analogy between the forms of expression "to say something" and "to mean something" (BB 35; § 358). "It is such phrases as 'He said it and meant it' which are most liable to mislead us" (BB 146). The similarity in the external form of these expressions suggests that speaking is one sort of activity, a visible kind, and meaning is another sort—nowhere to be seen, and therefore no doubt spiritual, mental. " 'Meaning it' is something in the sphere of the mind. But it is also something private! It is the intangible *something*; only comparable to consciousness itself" (§ 358). This something accompanies the spoken expression.

Wittgenstein's varied criticisms of such a view can be summed up by saying that he was opposed to its generalities. The characteristic features of meaning an expression are not *always* mental. Inner experiences which are characteristic of a certain expression are not *always* present when it is uttered and meant, nor always absent when it is not meant; there is no constant correlation. And the characteristic features of meaning an expression are not *always* simultaneous with speaking the words. In fact, Wittgenstein put his objections more strongly than this.[47] But he did not defend the opposite generalities. He did not deny that inner feelings are characteristic of meaning some expressions, or that these expressions are sometimes accompanied by these characteristic feelings, or that features typical of meaning an expression are sometimes simultaneous with its utterance. He was opposed to the generalities as generalities.

His own view was that many different criteria distinguish, under different circumstances, cases of meaning what you say from those of not meaning what you say.[48] Often gestures, tone of voice, accentuation, facial expression, and the like and the sensations connected with such externals distinguish meaning what you say from not meaning it.[49] Sometimes other sensations do (BB 144; § 677). And "sometimes what distinguishes these two is nothing that happens while we speak, but a variety of actions and experiences of different kinds before and after" (BB 145). If we took a slice out of the experiences that accompany the words, as James suggests, we might find nothing characteristic of meaning the words.[50] Some examples:

> Compare meaning "I shall be delighted to see you" with meaning "The train leaves at 3:30." Suppose you had said the first sentence to someone and were asked afterwards "Did you mean it?", you would then probably think of the feelings, the experiences, which you had while you said it. And accordingly you would in this case be inclined to say "Didn't you see that I meant it?" Suppose that on the other hand, after having given someone the information "The train leaves at 3:30," he asked you "Did you mean it?", you might be inclined to answer "Certainly. Why shouldn't I have meant it?" (BB 146).

Here we have a case in which no inner feelings are characteristic of meaning an expression, and another in which such sensations do occur. But even in this latter case, where meaning what one says may actually consist in having these experiences (BB 147), we must not be misled into supposing that these are all there is to meaning the expression or that having this experience would in all circumstances guarantee that one had meant the expression. The instances of meaning any given expression form a family of cases.

> To understand this family of cases it will . . . be helpful to consider an analogous case drawn from facial expressions. There is a family of friendly facial expressions. Suppose we had asked "What feature is it that characterizes a friendly face?" At first one might think that there are certain traits which one might call friendly traits, each of which makes the face look friendly to a certain degree, and which when present in a large number constitute the friendly expression. This idea would seem to be borne out by our common speech, talking of "friendly eyes," "friendly mouth," etc. But it is easy to see that the same eyes of which we say they make a face look friendly do not look friendly, or even look unfriendly, with certain other wrinkles of the forehead, lines round the mouth, etc. Why then do we ever say that it is these eyes which look friendly? Isn't it wrong to say that they characterize the face as friendly, for if we say they do so "under certain circumstances" (these circumstances being the other features of the face) why did we

single out the one feature from amongst the others? The answer is that in the wide family of friendly faces there is what one might call a main branch characterized by a certain kind of eyes, another by a certain kind of mouth, etc.; although in the large family of unfriendly faces we meet these same eyes when they don't mitigate the unfriendliness of the expression (BB 145).

In exactly similar fashion,

> It is even possible while lying to have quite strong experience of what might be called the characteristic for meaning what one says—and yet under certain circumstances, and perhaps under the ordinary circumstances, one refers to just this experience in saying, "I meant what I said," because the cases in which something might give the lie to these experiences do not come into the question. In many cases therefore we are inclined to say: "Meaning what I say" means having such and such experiences while I say it (BB 146).

But this would be a multiple mistake. For these cases are not all cases. In others actions may be characteristic, or circumstances, rather than subjective experiences. Or the characteristic experiences, of whatever sort, may not occur while one speaks.[51] And in any case a characteristic experience is not simply identical with meaning a given expression; for the experience is only *characteristic*, in the manner explained. Only in certain circumstances is having this experience the same as meaning this expression.[52]

That "mere" externals are, in general, quite as characteristic of meaningful discourse as are images or feelings is a purely statistical observation (§ 35), and so might be compared by proponents of mental meanings with the observation that as often as not the oysters brought up by divers contain no pearls. This does not prevent us, they might argue, from characterizing the divers' occupation as diving for *pearls*. Neither does the prevalence of external characteristics prevent us from recognizing the inner occurrence as essential in speech. Wittgenstein repeatedly contested this qualitative primacy of the inner.[53] He observed:

> It has sometimes been said that what music conveys to us are feelings of joyfulness, melancholy, triumph, etc., etc. and what repels us in this account is that it seems to say that music is an instrument for producing in us sequences of feelings. And from this one might gather that any other means

of producing such feelings would do for us instead of music.—To such an account we are tempted to reply "Music conveys to us *itself!*" (BB 178)

Later Wittgenstein wondered out loud what this might mean (§ 524), but made much the same point[54] by means of a comparison with painting:

> When I look at a genre-picture, it "tells" me something, even though I don't believe (imagine) for a moment that the people I see in it really exist, or that there have really been people in that situation. But suppose I ask: "*What* does it tell me, then?"
> I should like to say "What the picture tells me is itself." That is, its telling me something consists in its own structure, in *its* own lines and colours (§§ 522-523).

The same is true, in much the same way, of sentences.[55] "Understanding a sentence, we say, points to a reality outside the sentence. Whereas one might say 'Understanding a sentence means getting hold of its content; and the content of the sentence is *in* the sentence'" (BB 167).

So James was doubly wrong when he attributed to the stream of inner feelings all "significance" and "value." For one thing, the stream does not flow as steadily as he thought. Nor is it the center of interest in speech. Externals are in every way quite as important, especially words themselves. He was wrong, too, in identifying meaning as a process accompanying the statements we mean; for meaning what we say is not an activity of the same logical form as saying the words. Rather it is a pattern woven into our lives, in and around and before and after the expressions we utter. In this varying pattern many strands appear and disappear—gestures, tones, actions, thoughts—and not just inner feelings.

B. *Word Feelings*

Wittgenstein's reasons for denying that the meaning of a word is a feeling or experience accompanying it include those we have already seen for denying that the meaning of a sentence is the experience or experiences that accompany it. They are not terribly complicated. But the denial is established and illustrated by such a bewildering wealth of examples, comparisons, and random remarks that the outlines of Wittgenstein's argument had better be roughly sketched at the start. His viewpoint may be summed up by saying that a definition, such as the definition of meaning, is to be judged by its success in getting us to see the facts as they are.[56] But a definition such as "A word's meaning is the feeling or experience which accompanies it" would mislead us both as to: 1) what actually happens; and as to 2) the part played in language by such feelings and experiences. For it would suggest: 1) that whenever a word is uttered in ordinary discourse, one characteristic feeling is invariably present; and 2) that if a word is not regularly accompanied by its special feeling, it cannot serve its purpose, its foremost purpose supposedly being to beget this experience in somebody else's mind (BB 185; § 363) and thereby achieve its other purposes.[57]

1. What Happens

It would also mislead us by suggesting the wrong sort of experiences as most characteristic of words. The feelings and experiences considered by Wittgenstein are of two principal sorts: those that might accurately be said to accompany words, and those which should not be so described, since they are inseparable from the experience of seeing or hearing the words they characterize. This distinction will be made clear by examples of both sorts. Here a general notion of the difference may be suggested by the case of a picture puzzle in which one is to pick out faces hidden amidst a maze of lines. When one notices a face, this is a new experience, but an experience inseparable from seeing the lines one was already looking at. The glad feeling, however, which perhaps accompanies this experience is an experience one might have had without looking at the lines. One might have the identical feeling when checkmating an opponent in chess.

Wittgenstein recognized that feelings and sensations of this separable sort often do accompany words. Furthermore, certain such feelings might even be called characteristic of certain words (BB 65, 78). But they are characteristic only in the sense that they *often* accompany this or that word. The association is not constant, or if it is, we are not aware of the fact (BB 159). For instance, "are you sure that there is a single if-feeling, and not perhaps several? Have you tried saying the word in a great variety of contexts? For example, when it bears the principal stress of the sentence, and when the word next to it does" (PI 181-182). And "does a person never have the if-feeling when he is not uttering the word 'if'? Surely it is at least remarkable if this cause alone produces this feeling."

So "the if-feeling is not a feeling which accompanies the word 'if'"
(PI 182). It cannot be so defined. For, so far as we know, it does not
accompany all and only uses of the word "if." "And this applies generally
to the 'atmosphere' of a word;—why does one regard it so much as a
matter of course that only this word has this atmosphere?" (PI 182).[58]

If we turn from separable "halos," "atmospheres" and the like to "the
sensations we get from skin, muscle, viscus, eye, ear, nose, and palate,"[59]
we reach the same conclusion.

> William James speaks of specific feelings accompanying the use of such
> words as "and," "if," "or."[60] And there is no doubt that at least certain
> gestures are often connected with such words, as a collecting gesture with
> "and," and a dismissing gesture with "not." And there obviously are visual
> and muscular sensations connected with these gestures. On the other hand it
> is clear enough that these sensations do not accompany every use of the
> word "not" and "and" (BB 78-79).

For of course the gestures which give rise to these sensations do not always
accompany the words.

Emotive expressions might seem to lend at least some support to the
feeling theory. For instance, when longing makes one cry out "Oh, if only
he would come!" surely there is feeling then. And mightn't we call this
feeling the meaning of the words?

"But does it give the individual words their meanings?" Wittgenstein
asks (§ 544). Is there a feeling for each word as well as for the sentence,
or does just one feeling of hope do for the whole expression? If there
is just one feeling for the many words, then the meaning of each word is
not a feeling.

So a defendant might change the example: When one says "I *hope*
he'll come," doesn't the feeling give the word "hope" its meaning? The
meaning of at least this word is a feeling.

No, not even of this word, replies Wittgenstein. For "What about the
sentence 'I do *not* hope for his coming any longer'?" (§ 545) Is this too
accompanied by a feeling of hope? If not, is the word "hope" meaningless,
or has it changed its meaning?

It should be noted, furthermore, that even when a characteristic feeling
is associated somehow with a word, "the mental attitude doesn't 'accompany' what is said in the sense in which a gesture does" (§ 673). The
attitude may accompany the word as my good wishes accompany a man

who is traveling alone (*Ibid.*). It may come before or after the word. For "does one say, for example: 'I didn't really mean my pain just now; my mind wasn't on it enough for that'? Do I ask myself, say: 'What did I mean by this word just now? My attention was divided between my pain and the noise—'?" (§ 674) Pain or attention to pain need not coincide with my use of the word "pain" in order for the word to be meaningful. " 'I meant *this* by that word' is a statement which is differently used from one about an affection of the mind" (§ 676).

We may illustrate the true situation, or feelings in general (§ 596), by considering the feeling of familiarity, which Wittgenstein characterizes, in James's words,[61] as a feeling of "intimacy and warmth" (BB 181). For clarity's sake, it will be best to consider familiar objects other than familiar words. Yet the illustration will be more than a comparison, for words too are familiar and our encounter with them may involve feelings of familiarity (BB 156, 182; § 167).

Feelings of familiarity are most varied. For instance:

> If a boulder lies on the road, we know it for a boulder, but perhaps not for the one which has always lain there. We recognize a man, say, as a man, but not as an acquaintance. There are feelings of old acquaintance: they are sometimes expressed by a particular way of looking or by the words: "The same old room!" (which I occupied many years before and now returning find unchanged). Equally there are feelings of strangeness. I stop short, look at the object or man questioningly or mistrustfully, say "I find it all strange" (§ 596).

"But the existence of this feeling of strangeness does not give us a reason for saying that every object which we know well and which does not seem strange to us gives us a feeling of familiarity" (§ 596). "My room," for instance, "with all the objects in it, is thoroughly familiar to me. When I enter it in the morning do I greet the familiar chairs, tables, etc., with a feeling of 'Oh, hello!'?" (BB 182) No. "Asked 'Did you recognize your desk when you entered your room this morning?'—I should no doubt say 'Certainly!' And yet it would be misleading to say that an act of recognition had taken place. Of course the desk was not strange to me; I was not surprised to see it, as I should have been if another one had been standing there, or some unfamiliar kind of object" (§ 602). Yet "no one will say that every time I enter my room, my long-familiar surroundings, there is enacted a recognition of all that I see and have seen hundreds of times before" (§ 603).

And so it is with words. We do not have a familiar feeling for every one of them, even though they are all familiar. If they are misspelled, misplaced, or misused, we are startled, disturbed (§ 167). But this does not mean that on all other occasions we have that feeling of fittingness of which James speaks[62] (BB 156-157).

Yet, to continue the comparison, "We think that, as it were, the place filled by the feeling of strangeness must surely be occupied *somehow*. The place for this kind of atmosphere is there, and if one of them is not in possession of it, then another is" (§ 596). James had the same idea about words. If certain feelings characterize the use of meaningful words, then *some* such feelings must always be present when we say a word and mean it. His view and all such views are included in this blanket judgment: "When we do philosophy, we should like to hypostatize feelings where there are none. They serve to explain our thoughts to us. 'Here explanation of our thinking demands a feeling!' " (§ 598).[63]

Wittgenstein showed much greater positive interest in the second, nonseparable sort of word experiences. This interest accounts in large part for the amount of attention he paid to experiences such as seeing a drawing in this or that way, or hearing a musical phrase in a certain way—as a conclusion (PI 182) or as an introduction (PI 202), as a march or a dance.[64] Wittgenstein gave innumerable examples of this sort of thing and repeatedly indicated, either directly or indirectly, that the interest of his examples lay in the light they threw on the manner in which we experience words.[65]

Though he had this comparison in mind, Wittgenstein left to his readers the job of determining to what extent the comparison holds good. He did not draw up a list of respects in which the verbal experiences resemble the non-verbal.

This is worth doing. For one thing, a long list of similarities culled from Wittgenstein's remarks about both sorts of experiences will provide further evidence that he considered them comparable. More importantly, such a list will give a rather full idea of just what sort of experiences Wittgenstein considered most characteristic of words, and thereby reveal the basis of his objections to identifying even such experiences as the meanings of words. There follows such a list:

1) First, experiences of both sorts have some practical importance; they have consequences. On the one hand,

> There is such a thing as seeing in this way or that: and there are also cases where whoever sees a sample like *this* will in general use it in *this* way, and whoever sees it otherwise in another way. For example, if you see the schematic drawing of a cube as a plane figure consisting of a square and two rhombi you will, perhaps, carry out the order "Bring me something like this" differently from someone who sees the picture three-dimensionally (§ 74).[66]

In like manner, our feelings for words are manifested by the way we choose and value them (§ 530; PI 218).

2) In both cases one and the same object of perception may be experienced in different ways. Thus Jastrow's duck-rabbit drawing can be seen now as a duck, now as a rabbit (PI 194). The sketch of a cube can be seen now as a glass cube, now as an open box, now as a wire frame (PI 193). The sketch of a triangle can be seen as a triangular hole, as a solid, as a geometrical drawing (PI 200). A smile can be seen now as a kind one, now as malicious (§ 539). So, too, we can "mean" words one way or another. We can "mean" the word "till" as a proposition or as a verb (PI 214). We can say the word "March" and mean it one time as an imperative, at another as the name of a month (PI 215). And here to "mean" differently means to have a different experience.

3) Such examples suggest a third similarity. Such variation of "meaning" is obviously subject to our will. And the same is true of seeing an aspect (§ 536; PI 213).

4) Yet a "meaning" may be fixed by a context. The same is true of aspect-seeing (PI 195, 206). "The aspects in a change of aspects are those which the figure might sometimes have *permanently* in a picture" (PI 201). No doubt this fact is explained by a further parallel:

5) A peculiarity which distinguishes such experiences, such non-separable "halos," from "the sensations we get from skin, muscle, viscus, eye, ear, nose, and palate" is their dependence on training, custom, or previous experience (PI 209). For instance, you only see Jastrow's duck-rabbit drawing (PI 194) as a duck or as a rabbit if you are already acquainted with the shapes of these two animals (PI 207). Similarly, when you look at a certain painting and say, "That glass has fallen over and is lying there in fragments," custom and upbringing probably had a hand in this reac-

tion (PI 201). Likewise, someone who has only just met the concepts of apex, base, and so on will not see now this as apex, now that as base in the picture of a triangle (PI 208, 203, 209). Something similar is true of words. Thus if one agrees to use new signs in place of familiar ones, it will take time for these signs to be experienced as were the old (§§ 508-509).

6) This connection with former experience would seem to account for still another similarity: as we cannot see things as anything we please, so too we cannot experience words in any way we please. For instance, we can picture "Beethoven writing the ninth symphony," but not "*Goethe* writing the ninth symphony" (PI 183). Neither can we see just any face as courageous; for sometimes "we should, as it were, not know how to lodge courage in these features" (§ 537). Similarly, in the case of words, we cannot for instance say "bububu" and mean "If it doesn't rain I shall go for a walk." It is only in language that we can have the experience of meaning something, and "bububu" happens not to be part of our language (PI 18).

7) This connection with the past should not, however, lead us to suppose that a conscious connection or comparison is made with the past when we have this sort of experience. A further similarity between the verbal and non-verbal experiences under discussion is the absence of any element called up from the past. The experience of one who has had the requisite preparation is not the experience of one who lacks such preparation, plus an added element distinguishable from the rest of the experience. It is just one simple experience, a different one. For instance, in looking at a sketch of a face,

> one feels that what one calls the expression of the face is something that can be detached from the drawing of the face. It is as though we could say: "This face has a particular expression: namely this" (pointing to something). But if I had to point to anything in this place it would have to be the drawing I am looking at. (We are, as it were, under an optical delusion which by some sort of reflection makes us think that there are two objects where there is only one. The delusion is assisted by our using the verb "to have," saying "The face *has* a particular expression." Things look different when, instead of this, we say: "This *is* a peculiar face." What a thing *is*, we mean, is bound up with it; what it has can be separated from it.) (BB 162)

Likewise, " 'seeing dashes as a face' does not involve a comparison between a group of dashes and a real human face; and, on the other hand, this form of expression most strongly suggests that we are alluding to a comparison" (BB 164).[67]

A similar conclusion with regard to words is implicit in much that has been said already—about the absence of images and the interest which words have *in themselves*, and about the general similarity between inseparable aspects and word experiences. Wittgenstein makes the point explicit, in the first part of the following passage, when he says:

> Now we have used a misleading expression when we said that besides the experiences of seeing and speaking in reading there was another experience, etc. This is saying that to certain experiences another experience is added.— Now take the experience of seeing a sad face, say in a drawing,—we can say that to see the drawing as a sad face is not "just" to see it as some complex of strokes (think of a puzzle picture). But the word "just" here seems to intimate that in seeing the drawing as a face some experience is added to the experience of seeing it as mere strokes; as though I had to say that seeing the drawing as a face consisted of two experiences, elements (BB 168).[68]

Much later Wittgenstein was still insisting on this point: "Above all do *not* say 'After all my visual impression isn't the *drawing*; it is *this*—which I can't shew to anyone'" (PI 196). He had always been opposed to such multiplication of entities through the trickery of language. And this particular misconception would provide meaning theorists with the discrete and detachable referents they sought.

As Wittgenstein apparently sensed, the danger was especially acute here. For he was conceding that such experiences really do characterize our use of words, that they make the difference between thinking of what one says and speaking thoughtlessly (PI 197). So it was important that they be understood correctly. But his remarks about them could easily be misconstrued. For instance, "The expression of a change of aspect," he said, "is the expression of a *new* perception and at the same time of the perception's being unchanged" (PI 196). To a mathematical mind this would mean only one thing: new plus old equals two. There must be two experiences, the old and the new, side by side. And in the case of words, one of them will do quite well as the "meaning."

If, however, we recognize that the experience is simple and cannot be distinguished from the word itself, we will not be tempted to say that the experience is the word's meaning. Word and experience are one. This is one reason for Wittgenstein's assertion: "The meaning of a word is not the experience one has in hearing or saying it" (PI 181).

8) A second reason is this final similarity between word experiences and the duck-rabbit sort: in neither case is the experience constant. It is not invariably connected with the word or thing.

The importance of this point may be indicated by means of Jastrow's duck-rabbit drawing. It seems unlikely that any person familiar with ducks or rabbits would ever look at this drawing without seeing it either as a duck or as a rabbit. The same might be true of words. We would not necessarily take the word this way rather than that, but we would always experience it in one characteristic way or another. This experience would determine its meaning, either for the speaker or for the hearer. In fact, the experience would be the meaning. So runs the hypothesis.

Since this theory is suggested by a non-verbal analog, let us consider some more examples of the same sort to see if they support the hypothesis. For instance, "I meet someone whom I have not seen for years; I see him clearly, but fail to know him. Suddenly I know him. I see the old face in the altered one" (PI 197). For a moment at least, I fail to have the aspect experience even though the requisite object is present to my view. Similarly it is possible to see a smile and not recognize it as such (PI 198). Or consider the case of photographs: though we often regard a photograph—that is, see it—as a human being, it may be that we only see it this way when we are actually concerning ourselves with the picture as the object depicted (PI 205). The same might be true of some arbitrary cipher. One can see it in various aspects according to the fiction one surrounds it with. These aspects too last only as long as one is occupied with the object in a particular way. "Ask yourself 'For how long am I struck by a thing?'—For how long do I find it *new*? The aspect presents a physiognomy which then passes away. It is almost as if there were a face there which at first I *imitate*, and then accept without imitating it" (PI 210).

"Here there is a close kinship with 'experiencing the meaning of a word'" (PI 210). Word aspects behave in similar fashion. For instance, if we repeat words often enough they become mere sounds (PI 214). If we pronounce the salutation "Hail!" while thinking of hailstones, its sense seems to disintegrate (PI 175-176). We can play a somewhat similar game with the word "March," meaning it in different ways and seeing what experiences we have. But this game should not mislead us regarding the ordinary occurrence of words. "If a sensitive ear shows me, when I am playing this game, that I have now *this* now *that* experience of the word—doesn't it also show me that I often do not have *any* experience of it in the course of talking?" (PI 215-216; BB 159)

So "the meaning of a word is not the experience one has in hearing or saying it" (PI 181). For the experience may fail to occur and the word still have meaning.

The same dissociation of meaning and experience appears perhaps more clearly still in the case of new-coined words. Though meaningful, these are not familiar, and so are not yet experienced in a characteristic way. For instance: "Suppose I had agreed on a code with someone: 'tower' means bank. I tell him 'Now go to the tower'—he understands me and acts accordingly, but he feels the word 'tower' to be strange in this use, it has not yet 'taken on' the meaning" (PI 214).

A third reason for rejecting the identification of meaning with any sort of experience remains to be considered under a separate heading. Here we have been considering only what happens—what sort of feelings and experiences actually occur when words are used, and how often. We have seen, first, that the experiences most characteristic of words' use cannot be said to "accompany" words at all; they are not distinct or separable from hearing or seeing the words. We have seen too that there is no constant correlation between such experiences and words, or between words and any external or internal experiences which might more properly be said to accompany words.

These are the plain facts, minus all theory. By themselves they suggest how misleading it would be to identify the meaning of a word as some feeling which accompanies it or even as a characteristic experience had when it occurs.

2. The Role of Private Feelings or Experiences

Besides blinding us to the facts, to what happens, such a definition (of meaning as a feeling) would also mislead us into supposing that feelings or experiences play a part in language which they do not and cannot play. It would suggest that language could not work, that words would be useless, without these special feelings or experiences. Yet no particular experiences are indispensable for the effective employment of words.

The pragmatic argument regarding personal feelings can be divided into two parts: first, words can be understood without them by those who are addressed; secondly, such experiences do not constitute a person's ability to use signs meaningfully. Both on the receiving and on the sending end, communication can go on without them. Receiving will be considered first.

> . . . we are so much accustomed to communication through language, in conversation, that it looks to us as if the whole point of communication lay in this: someone else grasps the sense of my words—which is something mental: he as it were takes it into his own mind. If he then does something further with it as well, that is no part of the immediate purpose of language (§ 363).

The answer to this conception of the finality and functioning of language cannot consist in a comparison showing the absence of any parallel between the speaker's and the hearer's experiences. No such comparison is possible, nor is it seriously attempted. The assumption of an exchange of mental experiences is therefore gratuitous. Let us suppose that "every familiar word, in a book for example, actually carries an atmosphere with it in our minds." "This simply goes for us. But we communicate with other people without knowing if they have this experience too" (PI 181). "If in some language the word 'but' meant what 'not' means in English, it is clear that we should not compare the meanings of these two words by comparing the sensations which they produce. Ask yourself what means we have of finding out the feelings which they produce in different people and on different occasions." And think of yourself. "Ask yourself: 'When I said, "Give me an apple *and* a pear *and* leave the room," had I the same feeling when I pronounced the two words "and"?'" When you have such difficulty knowing what you yourself experienced, how can you possibly discover what another person experienced? (BB 79) Understanding certainly does not consist in conjectures about another person's feelings or personal experiences. And the hypothesis that the transfer takes place automatically, by a sort of pre-established harmony, has no evidence to support it.

The hypothesis of transferred or apprehended feelings seems improbable as well as gratuitous. For suppose I "mean" a phrase in the wrong way and feel that its sense disintegrates. In that case "I feel it, but the person I am saying it to does not. So what harm is done?" (PI 176).[69]

Not only is there no such communication of feelings, but the feelings, like images, would be of relatively little interest even if they were regularly transmitted from person to person.[70] "What if I said 'I believe it will rain' (meaning what I say) and someone wanted to explain to a Frenchman who doesn't understand English what it was I believed?" "Even if my words had been accompanied by all sorts of experiences, and if we could have transmitted these experiences to the Frenchman, he would still not have known what I believed." "We should say that we had told the Frenchman what I believed if we translated my words for him into French. And it *might* be that thereby we told him nothing—even indirectly—about what happened 'in me' when I uttered my belief" (BB 147). Perhaps if God Himself had looked into my mind at the moment I spoke, He would not have seen there what it was I believed (PI 217).[71]

In contrast to the interpretation of understanding as a single event in the mind, Wittgenstein offered his own much larger view. "We refer by the phrase 'understanding a word' not necessarily to that which happens while we are saying or hearing it, but to the whole environment of saying it" (BB 157). "Understand" is one of a large class of psychological terms —terms like "grief" and "hope" and "expect"—which refer not to any single event but to "a pattern which recurs, with different variations, in the weave of our life" (PI 174).[72]

But are there not at least certain cases in which feelings are uniquely important for understanding words, namely those cases where the words name sensations? When, for instance, a person speaks of pain, mustn't I at least *have experienced* pain in order to understand him, and don't I perhaps experience a shadow-pain, as it were, when he speaks of pain? How else would I know what he is talking about—his private feeling?

To get rid of this idea of a private object essential for speech (PI 207), "Imagine a person whose memory could not retain *what* the word 'pain' meant—so that he constantly called different things by that name." One time he has a dry feeling in his mouth (no pain) and speaks of his pain, and another time feels warm, yet speaks of his feeling as pain. But suppose that nonetheless he used the word in a way fitting in with the usual symptoms and presuppositions of pain, and in this sense used the word as we all do. His warm feeling, for instance, coincides with his being burned, and the dry feeling in his mouth occurs as a dentist is drilling in one of his teeth. Now in such a supposition, will the machinery of language break down for lack of the appropriate feeling communicated from one person to another? Will the word work any differently than it ordinarily does, or have different consequences? No. And so of the missing sensation we can say: "a wheel that can be turned though nothing else moves with it, is not part of the mechanism" (§ 271).

The following comparison makes much the same point:

> Suppose everyone had a box with something in it: we call it a "beetle." No one can look into anyone else's box, and everyone says he knows what a beetle is only by looking at his beetle. Here it would be quite possible for everyone to have something different in his box. One might even imagine such a thing constantly changing.—But suppose the word "beetle" had a use in these people's language?—If so it would not be used as the name of a thing. The thing in the box has no place in the language-game at all; not even as a *something;* for the box might even be empty.—No, one can "divide through" by the thing in the box; it cancels out, whatever it is (§ 293).

That is, the pain is not denied, but its supposed role in the language-game is. It might be that a causal connection, an association, has been established so that I use certain words in connection with certain sensations which I experience. But the words will produce the same effect on my hearer regardless of what sensation I have or whether I have any sensation at all—not, however, regardless of the linguistic contexts and total situation in which I use the words.

Unimportant for the ability to understand, inner experiences are equally unimportant for the ability to use signs. On the sending as on the receiving end communication can go on without them.

The point may be made both negatively and positively. On the one hand, what would you be missing if you did not have any feeling for a word? You might use it nonetheless (PI 214). On the other hand, suppose that you could react with a characteristic feeling to a word—say, the word "till." Even so, "if you were unable to say that the word 'till' could be both a verb and a conjunction, or to construct sentences in which it was now the one and now the other, you would not be able to manage simple schoolroom exercises. But a schoolboy is not asked to *conceive* the word in one way or another out of any context, or to report how he has conceived it" (PI 175).

> How should we counter someone who told us that with *him* understanding was an inner process?—How should we counter him if he said that with

him knowing how to play chess was an inner process?—We should say that when we want to know if he can play chess we aren't interested in anything that goes on inside him.—And if he replies that this is in fact just what we are interested in, that is, we are interested in whether he can play chess— then we shall have to draw his attention to the criteria which would demonstrate his capacity, and on the other hand to the criteria for the "inner states."

Even if someone had a particular capacity only when, and only as long as, he had a particular feeling, the feeling would not be the capacity (PI 181).

The difference between a feeling and an ability is of the same sort as the difference between a feeling and understanding (PI 59), and is suggested in similar fashion: "Suppose it were asked: *When* do you know how to play chess? All the time? or just while you are making a move? And the *whole* of chess during each move?—How queer that knowing how to play chess should take such a short time, and a game so much longer!" (PI 59).[73] How queer, too, that the use of most words should be so complicated and yet be crammed into a single sensation at the moment of use!

The ability to use a word, like the ability to use a formula, is not a "process occurring behind or side by side" with that of saying the word. If there has to be anything "behind the utterance of the word" it is *particular circumstances*, which justify me in saying I can go on (§§ 154, 155). For in both cases there is a rule to be followed, and such rules need to be learned (§ 249). What I acquire in the training is not a feeling; but it is the ability. This shows the difference.[74]

So "where is the connexion effected between the sense of the expression 'Let's play a game of chess' and all the rules of the game?—Well, in the list of rules of the game, in the teaching of it, in the day-to-day practice of playing" (§ 197), not simply in or by a sensation or miraculous feeling. The same is true of words and their use. In general,

> the criteria which we accept for "fitting," "being able to," "understanding," are much more complicated than might appear at first sight. That is, the game with these words, their employment in the linguistic intercourse that is carried on by their means, is more involved—the role of these words in our language other than we are tempted to think (§ 182).

From what has already been said about the experience that a person has when using words, it is clear that the following remarks on the connection between a formula (a closely related case) and its use suggest quite accurately what Wittgenstein held regarding the experience we have of a word and our ability to use it:

> It is clear that we should not say B had the right to say the words "Now I know how to go on," just because he thought of the formula—unless experience showed that there was a connexion between thinking of the formula—saying it, writing it down—and actually continuing the series. And obviously such a connexion does exist. . . . The words "Now I know how to go on" were correctly used when he thought of the formula: that is, given such circumstances as that he had learnt algebra, had used such formulae before. . . . We can also imagine the case where nothing at all occurred in B's mind except that he suddenly said "Now I know how to go on"—perhaps with a feeling of relief; and that he did in fact go on working out the series without using the formula. And in this case too we should say—in certain circumstances—that he did know how to go on (§ 179).

Neither causally nor conceptually is there a necessary connection between the thought of the formula and the ability in question. Since characteristic feelings or experiences, too, are sometimes missing when we use words, they too cannot be accounted necessary conditions for using words.

This is a general conclusion regarding all words, but may there not be exceptions? There are cases in which we might seem to be specially dependent on private feelings and experiences for the correct use of words. It might be conceded that in general the use of words does not require an accompanying sensation or experience, but that the correct use of psychological terms requires both acquaintance with and recognition of psychological phenomena. For in psychological discussions it is such things that we are talking about.

If the "psychological" terms in question are words like "expect," "understand," "hope," "believe," what has just been said about "understanding" suggests already the objection Wittgenstein would make to the idea that recognition of private experiences is required in such cases. Such terms do not refer to single events, but rather to "a pattern which recurs, with different variations, in the weave of our life" (PI 174). Terms for feelings, sensations, and the like require closer attention, though, and Wittgenstein gave it to them.

There is a general theory about such words which accords to private experiences a key role in their use. A feeling, it is said, cannot be defined.

It is something special and indefinable (PI 185), indescribable (§ 610). That is why words for feelings can be taught only indirectly (§ 362), and why each person can learn their meaning only from his own experience (§§ 293, 315). Only from pain can one learn what the word "pain" stands for, and the only pain each one can feel is his own (BB 48, § 253). Once you know that—*what* the word stands for—you understand it, you can use it (§ 264). You can use it, that is, according to this criterion, to refer to the same thing. Examining your sensations thereafter, you apply this criterion in judging whether to use the word "pain," or some other word. Your feeling is the criterion which enables you to make a correct identification.

Wittgenstein's criticisms of this general conception are profuse. He objected, for instance, that often, as in the first-person expression "I am in pain," the psychological term is not being used to identify anything. *No* criterion is applied, no description given, no identification made—any more than when a baby wails. It would be better to say that such an expression is learned pain-behavior (§§ 244, 289-290; PI 187).

If the use of sensation words is governed by criteria (and it sometimes is), these criteria cannot be merely the sensations to which the words refer. An "inner sensation," like an "inner process," stands in need of outward criteria (§ 580). This is a point Wittgenstein developed at length.[75] Suppose, for instance, that someone does not know what the English word "pain" means. How should we explain it to him? Perhaps by means of gestures, or by pricking him with a pin and saying: "See, that's what pain is!" (§ 288). This is how it is done. So we might perhaps say, "Pain is what you feel when a pin is stuck in you." But now suppose that each time a pin is stuck in you, you feel something different. Will you call all these things pain? "Certainly not!" But why not? Weren't you taught to call such things (pin-prick feelings) "pain"? Consider a word like "color," which is used for a much wider range of things than "turquoise" or "red." What would narrow the range of "pain"? How would you know beforehand that you should call only *this* "pain" and not the other feelings you have when the demonstration is repeated? (§ 377) No, pain is not a certain special something (§§ 261, 304, 308), specified by itself and nothing else. If pains are all closely similar, this is an accident of nature and not something foreordained by language or by the manner in which the word "pain" is learned. We fix the criteria (§ 322), in this case by means of public use and public demonstrations. The gestures and the pricking and the whole linguistic context are part of the definition, and not mere accessories (§§ 354-356), helping one to *guess* the essential thing.[76]

The very complex workings of ordinary language may obscure this truth. So let us isolate the hypothesis of the all-important sensation (BB 17); let us imagine a simple language-game (§§ 243, 258) in which all these supposed "inessentials" are eliminated or reduced to a minimum, and let us see how well it operates in this condition. All ties with the ordinary language-game are cut.[77] We fix the meanings ourselves, simply by fixing our attention on the sensation and engaging to use a certain sign for this sensation in the future. The sensation alone is our criterion. We now have all that is essential in the ordinary language-game after we have managed by hook or by crook (the manner doesn't matter, so long as it succeeds), to connect a word with the proper sensation. We have the word, and the criterion for its proper use.

But what use is proper, what use is correct? Won't any use we make of the sign be equally correct? For when we engaged to use the sign thus or thus, what did that effect? Was the future use somehow precontained in this decision? And even if it was, won't any new decision have equal force, be equally legitimate? Doesn't this private sign mean just what we want it to mean? Aren't we the absolute masters of this language? So there is no right or wrong here. "Right" is merely what we choose to say (§§ 258, 262-263; PB 104; LC 18, footnote 5).

But suppose that a criterion had somehow been established; the sign "S" is correctly applied to just *this* range of feelings, as the word "red" is correctly applied to just a certain range of colors.[78] How would this criterion be applied by the individual? To check on our identification of red, independent corroboration is possible. Of course we never do have misgivings about our memory of red. ("Let me see, now, is this color called 'red' or is it called 'blue'?") But if our memory did go bad and we needed to check, we could do it. We could look up a color chart or ask someone else. Here, though, in our private language, no such check is possible. Sensations cannot be labeled and laid aside for consultation. We would have only our own memory to go by, and that is what is in question. So once again, whatever we think is the experience "S," for all practical purposes is S. The "correctness" does not matter. It really makes no difference what happened inside us (§§ 270-271).

If one is still convinced that the feeling is the essential thing and that we cannot use a sensation word correctly until it has been connected with a particular feeling, it may help to reflect that "the essential thing about private experience is really not that each person possesses his own exemplar, but that nobody knows whether other people also have *this* or something else. The assumption would thus be possible—though unverifiable—that one section of mankind had one sensation of red and another section another" (§ 272).[79] The same goes for pain or any private sensation. It is obvious, therefore, that in connecting up just *this* sensation with the word and regarding it as essential, "we as it were turned a knob which looked as if it could be used to turn on some part of the machine; but it was a mere ornament, not connected with the mechanism at all" (§ 270). The same point appears in still other ways.

For instance, "We do not say that possibly a dog talks to itself" (§ 357).[80] Why not? Are we so intimately acquainted with its soul? Is it from observation or experiment that we have come to detect the absence of silent talk in dogs? Obviously not. We do not even consider the hypothesis. It does not occur to us that something which *behaves* as a dog does might be talking to itself. *Grammar*—the complex logic of verbs like "talk" and "pretend"—is the basis of our untroubled conviction (§§ 357, 359-361).

Similarly the real logic of sensation words like "pain" is revealed by the limits of their application. We are quite ready to say that human beings can feel. But we do not say the same of stones, plants, and so on (§ 283). In fact, it is not at all clear what would be meant by saying that a stone has pains (§ 283). We wouldn't know where to put them, as it were, or how they were to be connected with the stone (§ 361). But if we look at a wriggling fly instead of a stone, "at once these difficulties vanish and pain seems able to get a foothold here, where before everything was, so to speak, too smooth for it" (§ 284). For "only of what behaves like a human being can one say that it *has* pains" (§ 283).

Again, this is not a scientific fact, ascertained by introspection into stones or plants (BB 73), but a fact of grammar. Such is the meaning of sensation terms, such their use (§ 281). It is evident that the criteria for their use are not hidden sensations but observable differences such as those between an eggplant and a fly. These observable properties are not mere clues, mere symptoms of the important thing without which we would not think of using the term. Our use is not based on induction but on observation. The complex external phenomena are *ultimate* criteria guiding our use (§ 354).

The primary purpose of Wittgenstein's discussion of sensation words was probably not to rule out exceptions to the denial that meanings are psychological experiences.[81] But this is the effect of his remarks. Even in the grammar of words like "pain" they deny to inner experiences the sort of role which might win them the title of "meaning." We are not uniquely dependent on such experiences, either to use these words effectively or to understand them. What is true in these cases holds *a fortiori* in others. This is a third, pragmatic reason for denying that words' meanings are feelings, experiences. It is somewhat conjectural, questioning the necessity of such feelings, whereas the previous two reasons merely described what happens—the irregular association between word and feeling, the indivisible unity of word and word experience.

To sum up: the comparison with chess, a Wittgenstein favorite,[82] is a good one. First, we are under no delusion that certain inner experiences invariably accompany each type of move made with each type of chessman. Yet of course we intend our moves, we mean them, we make them quite effectively according to the rules of the game, others understand and react appropriately, and so on. Only prejudice or post-factum play-acting could make us suppose that certain experiences are invariably associated with each specific move. If we show little inclination to investigate the matter, this is no doubt due to the realization that whatever we discovered, though it might be of psychological or physiological interest, would be of no interest for the game of chess. We would not thereupon revise all our explanations and definitions of the game, saying for instance: "To checkmate your opponent is to have a sort of triumphant feeling, joined to satisfaction and a certain lessening of nervous tension." No, private experiences form no part of a public game; they are not the important thing about the moves we make. We see this clearly in the case of gestures or facial expressions which, though more apparent and often revealing, are not at all essential to the game. Since all this is true as well of the meaningful use of words, "the meaning of a word is not the experience one has in hearing or saying it" (PI 181).

VI. Conclusion

One after another, Wittgenstein ruled out all simple meanings of words. Meanings are not objects, they are not images, or feelings, or any sort of psychological experiences. His technique in each case was much the same;

of every such item he asked: "Is it always there?" and: "Need it be?" The answer was always negative.

Such arguments are not syllogistic; for nothing but minor premises are given. If someone argues: "These things—these feelings, images, and the rest—are such and so; therefore they are not meanings," he must have a general idea about meanings with which the stated descriptions conflict. Wittgenstein did have a general idea of what meanings are, but his notion generally appears as conclusion rather than as premise of his negative arguments. In these his major premise was very vaguely stated or not stated at all. Meaning was merely the "important thing" about a word. Only his arguments suggest the two ways it should be important: statistically and practically.

Perhaps it is misleading to speak of syllogisms. Wittgenstein had no use for them. He thought that in philosophy as in ethics reasons are "of the nature of further descriptions." You get a person to see what you see, you clear up the circumstances of the activity under discussion, and so win his agreement (M³19). For without this agreement regarding the facts, what good are syllogisms? Your major will be denied. And if there is agreement regarding the facts, what is achieved by a syllogism?

Even so, if someone who is syllogistically inclined still feels a hankering for a major premise, there is something right about his attitude. For Wittgenstein did not merely describe what happens or needs to happen when words are used; he used these facts to eliminate various definitions of meaning. He went beyond the facts to something else. To what? To a conclusion?

According to Moore (M³17) Wittgenstein said of the word "good" that "each different way in which one person, A, can convince another person, B, that so-and-so is 'good' fixes the meaning in which 'good' is used in that discussion." If this was Wittgenstein's attitude in his discussions of meaning, there was no place in them for a major premise.

But if he showed interest in how the word meaning is actually employed, if he meant his discussions of meaning to throw light on the "grammar" of the word "meaning," mere description of language was not enough. Besides describing the way words are used, he needed to describe the way this word, "meaning," is used.

The situation would then be somewhat as follows. If a certain person, A, claimed to "have" many illustrious ancestors and identified them as Q, R, and X, the present tense of "have" might tempt someone to object. The individuals Q, R, and X, he might say, cannot possibly be A's ancestors; for all these people are dead, they no longer exist. This argument would rest on the supposition that the word "ancestor" is used to refer only to actually existing individuals. Similarly, Wittgenstein's negative arguments against objects, images, and feelings seem to presuppose that if a word in a sentence "has" a meaning, this meaning is something present and important. So long as the actual grammar of "meaning" is left unexplored, this supposition may be challenged and with it Wittgenstein's whole argument. It is conceivable that the use of "meaning" resembles the use of "ancestor," which refers to individuals who are neither present when one "has" them nor of any practical importance in the present conduct of most people's affairs.

Now this *is* the situation. For Wittgenstein was interested in the actual use of the word "meaning." This interest will appear in the following chapter, along with positive arguments needed to complete the negative ones given in this chapter. These positive arguments are the only conclusive ones.

Chapter III

THE ORIGINS OF THE LATER DEFINITION

I. The Moment of Transition

Word, thing, subjective feeling or idea—what other possibility is there? Where else is the meaning to be found? As Wittgenstein had stressed from the start, there is the use of the word. It seems most natural for him to conclude, then, after eliminating thing, idea, and feeling, that the meaning of a word is its use. It seems still more natural when we remember that for Wittgenstein the meaning was the important thing about a word, and that the use of words had always seemed most important to him.

So it might seem that after the negative arguments, positive arguments are hardly necessary. The conclusion is implicit in them. Use alone is left. For it is untouched by the arguments against objects or mental states and shadows.

They, objects and shadows, are unnecessary for speech. Use is obviously necessary. A word must be used in a certain way if it is to have meaning, if it is to count as speech rather than mere sounds.

They are sometimes missing; use never is.

Mental pictures are themselves signs; use is not.

Mental events are private; use is not.

It is important to notice also that what Wittgenstein criticized was always an atomic, simplified meaning, an isolated element in the total speech situation. No such item survived criticism. It was not adequate to what is required of meaning. Use, on the other hand, is something complex and varying, and so immune to the same sort of criticism. Because of these contrasts Wittgenstein moved quite naturally from the negation of one to the affirmation of the other; whatever the reason for dissatisfaction with object or idea, use always gave satisfaction.

Thus, when Mr. N. N. dies (§ 40), Wittgenstein still finds use for the expression "Mr. N. N.," and draws a parallel with one of his language games: besides fetching existing tools in response to their names, a person

76

might also have been instructed so that he shakes his head when the name is given of a tool that has been broken. The sign would still have meaning even when its bearer ceased to exist. It might even be imagined that a bearer had never existed and that the name was used as a joke. Use is all that counts. Wittgenstein concludes: "For a *large* class of cases—though not for all—in which we employ the word 'meaning' it can be defined thus: the meaning of a word is its use in the language" (§ 43).[1]

Yet, however natural the transition, it was not immediate. There was a brief transition period, between his rejection of object meanings and his dictation of the *Blue Book*,[2] during which Wittgenstein suggested a definition of meaning different from that in the *Tractatus* or the *Blue Book*. Having dropped atomic meanings, he did not immediately shift to use, but gave instead the following definition: the meaning of a word is its "place" in a "grammatical system" (M^16).[2a] This definition is no longer atomic; word meanings are no longer individual items in the total situation. And "place in a grammatical system" might easily be interpreted in the same sense as "use in the language." But the views which this definition suggests and which it actually expresses are quite different from those which Wittgenstein fittingly condensed in the formula "meaning is use in the language." The distance separating the two definitions can be judged from Moore's explanation of the former:

> About the meaning of single words, the positive points on which he seemed most anxious to insist were, I think, two, namely (a) something which he expressed by saying that the meaning of any single word in a language is "defined," "constituted," "determined" or "fixed" (he used all four expressions in different places) by the "grammatical rules" with which it is used in that language, and (b) something which he expressed by saying that every significant word or symbol must essentially belong to a "system," and (metaphorically) by saying that the meaning of a word is its "place" in a "grammatical system" (M^16).

A study of these two points—"rules" and "system"—will reveal, first, how the former definition differed from the later and, second, how and why Wittgenstein was led to abandon the former definition and to adopt the second. The negative arguments in the preceding chapter narrowed the field of choice, by ruling out unit meanings. The negative arguments of the present chapter limit the field still further, by eliminating certain complex alternatives.

It is as though a microscope were being focused. At first it was badly
out of focus. One turn, and the general outlines became visible: meaning
is nothing simple, no single entity. Another, and the focus will be sharper
still. However, the final adjustment will be made in a second section of
the present chapter, where positive arguments are added to the negative.
It will be possible then merely to look and to describe what is seen.

II. THE DECLINE OF RULES

When Wittgenstein spoke of "grammatical rules" which "constituted"
the meaning of a word, he meant the sum-total of rules followed in its use
—grammatical rules in the ordinary sense,[3] definitions, or rules such as are
implicit in statements such as "This line can be bisected" (M²296) or "I
can't feel his toothache." "Can" and "can't" in such statements do not
refer to physical or psychological powers or their absence, just as statements
about unliftable stones do not indicate divine impotence; in a roundabout
way they indicate rules of language. They reflect our realization that a
statement like "I can feel his toothache" would have no meaning (M³11-15,
BB 55, FM 40, #128).[4]

The important thing to notice is that the rules he had in mind here, as
in the *Tractatus*, are prescriptive, not descriptive. They do not resemble
laws of nature. They are applied, followed, obeyed. They must be obeyed,
if our words are to have meaning. We must "commit ourselves" to follow
them. If we use a word in a certain way we *have* to go on using it in that
way (M¹6-7, M²290-291).

Furthermore, such rules are conceived of as distinct from their applications, that is, from the actual use of words. They are "contained" in the
intention of the one speaking (M¹12). The speaker is like a piano player
who "sees the rule in the score" (M¹13). And Moore reports that Wittgenstein often gave him the impression that "he was giving the name of
'rules' to actual statements that you are allowed or forbidden to use certain expressions—that, for instance, he would have called the statement,
'You can't say "Two men *was* working in that field"' a rule of English
grammar" (M²291). The same viewpoint comes out in Wittgenstein's
reaction to the remark of a pupil. "He said that the student who had asked
him whether he meant that the meaning of a word *was* a list of rules
would not have been tempted to ask that question but for the false idea
(which he held to be a common one) that in the case of a substantive

like 'the meaning' you have to look for something at which you can point and say 'This is the meaning' "(M^{1}7). If the student was tempted to point at the rules of which Wittgenstein spoke and if Wittgenstein thus diagnosed his difficulty, doubtless the rules under discussion were conceived of as more than mere regularities of use, like laws of nature. They were prescriptive and separate.

As I have already mentioned in a general way, the *Blue Book* reveals a distinct change of outlook. For one thing, Wittgenstein there distinguishes carefully between two ways in which a process may be related to a rule. "We must distinguish between what one might call 'a process being *in accordance with a rule,*' and 'a process involving a rule.' "

> We shall say that the rule is involved in the understanding, obeying, etc., if, as I should like to express it, the symbol of the rule forms part of the calculation. (As we are not interested in where the processes of thinking, calculating, take place, we can for our purpose imagine the calculations being done entirely on paper. We are not concerned with the difference: internal, external.) (BB 13)

Now, in practice we very rarely follow rules of language in this second way. We do not think of the rules of usage—of definitions and the like—while using language; rather, even when we are asked to give such rules, in most cases we aren't able to do so.[5]

So much, then, for rules distinct from usage and for their supposed importance in speech. But there is another sort of rule, which we might call "a natural law describing the behavior of people" who follow it, or a sort of "record belonging to their natural history" (BB 98).[6] This sort of rule causes less difficulty for the later definition, for it is practically equivalent to use (PI 147).

Might we define meaning, then, as the rules of a word's use? Why did Wittgenstein say simply that meaning is use, never that it is the rules of use? For one thing the word "rule" would naturally suggest the wrong sort of rule, the sort he was arguing against. And even if it didn't, there were other errors it might easily suggest. For instance, it might seem to indicate that ordinary usage is both simple and perfectly regular, whereas Wittgenstein had concluded that it is neither.

First, it is not simple. "There are words with several clearly defined meanings. It is easy to tabulate these meanings. And there are words of which one might say: They are used in a thousand different ways which gradually merge into one another. No wonder that we can't tabulate strict rules for their use" (BB 28). Furthermore, language is not rigidly regular. Even in the case of words with a few clear meanings, there is no guarantee against variations. "For remember that in general we don't use language according to strict rules—it hasn't been taught us by means of strict rules, either" (BB 25). To suppose that we must follow precise definitions with unwavering fidelity "would be like supposing that whenever children play with a ball they play a game according to strict rules" (BB 25).[7]

Thus by the time Wittgenstein gave the *Blue Book* lectures his old conception of "rules" in language was dead and could no longer conflict with the definition of meaning as use.[8] Not only was usage independent of rules, but in most cases there simply were no rules of the sort he had supposed. Use was the all-important thing.

III. The Decline of the "System"

Simultaneously, Wittgenstein's ideas on language as a "system" were changing sufficiently to remove a second obstacle. The changes took place on two levels, on the level of what Wittgenstein later called "surface grammar" and on the level of what he called "depth grammar" (§ 664). That is, he changed his views on the relation of words to words, and he broadened his view to take in the relation of words to the rest of life.[9] I will consider these two developments separately.

A. *Exceptions in the "Surface Grammar"*

Wittgenstein's sayings regarding "system" had an uncertain sound when Moore attended his lectures (M[1]8). For Wittgenstein's views on this subject too were apparently in transition.

In the analytical language of the *Tractatus*, a word could have no meaning without other signs. For it had no meaning, pointed to nothing, save when used to point, that is, save in a proposition. Furthermore, every proposition, if it was to picture a complex state of affairs, had itself to be complex. It had to be articulated (3.141; 3.1431). A simple sign would not do. In ordinary language a single sign might do, but in an analytic notation this single sign would be revealed as a complex symbol, consisting of more than one name. No name could possibly have meaning by itself. A "real name" was like one of the *Tractatus'* objects for which it stood. Just as such an object is content and form, that is, a thing and its ability to be combined with other things, so too Wittgenstein considered a name as endowed through the rules of syntax with certain powers of combination with other names (3.311-3.312). In virtue of this linguistic form, a name would acquire meaning when combined properly with other names, and used in assertions of fact.

This background makes quite intelligible the statements reported by Moore. Wittgenstein was still thinking of language as one vast, interconnected calculus. He did concede that even a single sign might signify, if this had been provided for in the system (M[1]9). A proposition did not have to be articulated. A certain Neapolitan gesture of P. Sraffa[10] seems to have opened his eyes to this possibility. However, he seemed still to maintain that it is necessary for a sign to belong to the same "system" with other signs. Each word has its "place" in such a system and thereby its meaning. Wittgenstein illustrated this view by saying, "A crotchet can only give information on what note to play in a system of crotchets" (M[1]8).[11]

Such a view could hardly survive the sort of detailed examination of cases Wittgenstein undertook in the *Blue Book* lectures. He still said similar things regarding the meaning of sentences (e.g., BB 42), but never again of individual words. If he was struck by Sraffa's simple but expressive gesture, and reflected on it, he may easily have noticed that it is quite independent of other signs for its meaning. In any case, Wittgenstein's language games were full of equally independent signs.

Already in the lectures Moore reported, Wittgenstein referred to "language games." In the *Blue Book* lectures he started to use them (e.g., BB 16-17, 69), and explained: "We recognize in these simple processes forms of language not separated by a break from our more complicated ones. We see that we can build up the complicated forms from the primitive ones by gradually adding new forms" (BB 17). This additive view of language games, which Wittgenstein made still clearer later on (§ 18)[12] would seem to imply that such a game, even a one-word game, could retain its independence, as it were, even if incorporated within a larger system. The language games he described were not to be regarded "as incomplete parts of language, but as languages complete in themselves, as complete systems of human communication" (BB 81).[13]

Now within these games we see words quite independent of one another. In the *Blue Book* there are few games, but in many suggested in the *Brown Book* it seems quite evident that each word might be used as it is regardless of whether any other words existed. A naming game, for instance, might be carried on with one word as well as with many. Or a person might be taught to fetch just one object and not many, in a system consisting of one word rather than many. Thus Wittgenstein introduces one of his first games with the words: "Let us introduce a new instrument of communication—a proper name. This is given to a particular object (a particular building stone) by pointing to it and pronouncing the name. If *A* calls the name, *B* brings the object" (BB 80). There is no mention of other words.

It makes little difference, really, whether there are self-sufficient words in actual language, similar to the words in such a limited language game, or whether Wittgenstein noticed any such.[14] For once the possibility of such signs is recognized, alone or within a total language of which they form an independent part, one will make no statements such as those Moore reported. And Wittgenstein did recognize this possibility. The requirement that all signs be dependent on other signs for their meaning was irreconcilable at least with the freedom of language, if not also with the facts of language. Even if for some strange reason no such signs figured among the countless sorts of signs in existing languages, still, "this multiplicity is not something fixed, given once for all" (§ 23). There *might* be such signs.

The relevance of this shift in Wittgenstein's thinking regarding language as a "system" may be suggested by a comparison. "What is meant by the *value* of a check?" It seems to me that I would answer such a question less readily than this other: "What is meant by the value of money?" Asked this question, I would probably launch into some definition in terms of *commerce*, whereas I would be likely to answer the first question with something like, "The amount of money that a bank will give you for it." And yet a check can be used in commercial transactions just as money can. Why would I be inclined to leave out the commerce and bring in the bank? Why? Because visions of an empty bank account would make the check's commercial utility seem problematical.

In like manner, it seems, when the "system" was so dominant in Wittgenstein's thinking that it made the usability of any word seem problematical, he brought in the bank—that is, the system—and left out the commerce, the word's employment in language. He said that meaning is a word's place in a grammatical system. That is, he gave a wholly relational definition, relating the word to the all-important thing, the system. When the system seemed somewhat (only somewhat) less important, he brought in the use as well as the system: "The meaning of a word is its use in the language." By thus replacing the word "place" with the word "use," he adapted his definition so as to include all cases, including any where perhaps the word did not get its meaning from its "place in the system," but was simply part of the system.

"Perhaps," Moore wrote, "he only meant, not that for a sign to have *some* meaning, but that for some signs to have the significance which they actually have in a given language, it is necessary that they should belong to the same 'system' with other signs" (M^{1}8). Were that the case, I might seem to have made a mountain out of a molehill. However, in spending so much time on this development I have at least indicated how the closing words of the definition are to be understood. The expression "in the language" means no more than it says. We should not read into these words what is probably true in most cases and what Wittgenstein once extended to all cases: the dependence of the word on the rest of the verbal system. By mentioning the system, "the language," Wittgenstein does justice to the majority of words, whose meaning does depend on the system. By saying "language" instead of "system," and leaving out "place," he makes room for signs like the Neapolitan gesture, or "Hello!", "Goodbye," "Rummy!"

B. *Stress on Wider, Varied "Depth Grammar"*

There is a second, complementary explanation for Wittgenstein's de-emphasis of "system" and emphasis on "use." This one is more important, as it extends to all words and not just to a small minority. It is his increasing awareness of the complex and varied workings of words—their "depth grammar," as he called it.

This "depth grammar" he contrasted with "surface grammar," the aspects of use that are most obvious and strike the eye—the fact, for instance, that a verb has an object in the sentence or is in the present tense. However, this is not the contrast I have in mind here, in the development of Wittgenstein's thought. He always emphasized depth grammar.[15] The picture theory of language was a theory of depth grammar. It is rather the narrowness of the picture theory that I would emphasize, a narrowness that Wittgenstein grew out of only gradually, and that seems still to have characterized his thought, though to a lesser degree, in the first years after his return to Cambridge.

I will mention some of the evidence that gives me this impression, and by contrasting it with later remarks on the same topics indicate more clearly just what trend it is I am associating with the rise of Wittgenstein's final way of speaking about meaning.

In the first lectures Moore attended, Wittgenstein said, "To explain the meaning of a sign means only to substitute one sign for another" (M²310). To know what point Wittgenstein meant to make by this statement, we would need to know what contrasting view he had in mind and meant to eliminate. It is possible that he meant to dispel the idea that definitions express and beget some sort of mental content distinct from words. It seems more likely, though, in the light of things said by those under his influence at this time,[16] that Wittgenstein was contrasting verbal explanations with, say, ostensive definitions. Implicit in such a contrast is a rather impoverished notion of words and their relation to "reality": The only way to break out of the circle of mere words is the ostensive definition; a finger pointed at an object—that does it! It makes contact with reality, establishes the link, in a way mere words could never do. If there was something of this in Wittgenstein's remark, it soon vanished completely, as we shall see shortly.

Another example. In the early thirties Wittgenstein made remarks about changes in "grammar" which greatly puzzled Moore (M²293). He seemed to hold that by a mere *fiat* the speaker may give his words meaning. It will depend on how he means his sentences. He need only project them in some perhaps totally new and original way, and meaningless statements thereby become meaningful ones. Learning, custom, convention —the whole mechanism of social intercourse—these are left out of consideration (M²292; PB 55, #9).

"It's as if we could grasp the whole use of the word in a flash" (FM 40). And yet, asked Wittgenstein a few years later, "are all the rules contained in my act of intending? . . . And if that is nonsense, what kind of super-strong connexion exists between the act of intending and the thing intended?—Where is the connexion effected between the sense of the expression 'Let's play a game of chess' and all the rules of the game?— Well, in the teaching of it, in the day-to-day practice of playing" (FM 40; cf. FM 4, 8). The expression has deeper, broader roots in reality than a mere meaning act projecting the expression towards this or that reality (PB 63), roots not so readily altered at the speaker's whim.

Further remarks reported by Moore, on commands, seem to indicate the same narrow, systematizing outlook. "One of the most striking things about his use of the term 'proposition' was that he apparently so used it that in giving an order you are necessarily expressing a 'proposition,' although, of course, an order can be neither true nor false" (M[1]10-11). I think that we can detect here the sort of view criticized later in the *Investigations* (§§ 21, 24). Wittgenstein did not yet realize that a command is what "has the function of a command in the technique of using the language" (§ 21). As far as the words are concerned, the report "Five slabs" does not differ from the order "Five slabs!" The difference is "the part which uttering these words plays in the language game"—that is, in a game which includes much more than signs or symbols (§ 21).

If we fit these remarks about commands into the larger picture of Wittgenstein's views on language in general, we find the same contrast. A good deal has already been said, in Chapter One, about Wittgenstein's statement in the *Tractatus* identifying speech with statements, propositions. In 1930-1931 he was still saying the same thing: "Speech means the totality of propositions (Sätze). We might say: A proposition is what truth functions may be applied to. Truth functions are essential to *speech*" (PB 113).

This is undoubtedly a very narrow view, a highly abstract and unrealistic view, of language and its varied workings. And it is only partially redeemed by a statement such as: "I will count every fact, whose existence is required for some statement to make sense, as belonging *to speech*" (PB 78). For Wittgenstein still had the limited, picturing view of what it means to make sense, and therefore of the presuppositions belonging to speech.

How different already is his preoccupation in the *Blue and Brown Books* with learning, with training, with following a rule, with playing a game, with giving and obeying orders—with the sort of thing he had so neglected earlier. The clearest indications of his new outlook are the language games in the *Brown Book* and the *Investigations*; here there is no idly sitting down to exchange words, but orders are given (BB 80, 83, etc.), things are fetched (BB 80, 83, etc.), bets are made (BB 110), directions are given (BB 95-99), objects are counted (BB 81, 83, 94), and so on. Words are *used*, not merely meant in different ways. The important thing about them is not their "place" in some simplified logical "system," half abstraction and half fabrication (§ 81), but their life within the whole of life—their "use in the language."

I am aware that passages can be found in the *Philosophische Bemerkung-en* which seem to go counter to some things I have been saying here regarding "rules" and "system." And the unpublished writings from Wittgenstein's transition period may reveal still more. However, currently available evidence does seem to indicate a general trend whose varying aspects I will summarize as follows. In the *Philosophische Bemerkungen* Wittgenstein said: "We can say: The sense of a proposition is its aim. (Or of a word 'its meaning is its purpose.') But logic cannot concern itself with the natural history of a word" (PB 59). The chief difference, perhaps, between the *Tractatus* and the *Investigations* and *Blue and Brown Books* is that in the latter two works Wittgenstein did concern himself with the "natural history," the actual behavior, of ordinary words, and that in the *Tractatus* he did not. It is understandable that during the transition, in the period of unsettled thinking in between, Wittgenstein should speak of a word's meaning *both* as its purpose and as its place in a system of words, understandable too that at the end of such a transition he should consistently prefer the formula: "The meaning of a word is its use in the language."

One of Wittgenstein's typically effective comparisons suggests a variant expression of the same overall contrast and transition between his earlier and later thought. In his criticism of Russell's *Principia Mathematica*, Wittgenstein said (FM 89, #53): "If someone [e.g. Wittgenstein] tries to shew that mathematics is not logic, what is he trying to shew? He is surely trying to say something like:—If tables, chairs, cupboards, etc. are swathed in enough paper, certainly they will look spherical in the end." Likewise, in the *Tractatus* the diverse forms of language were so heavily swathed that they *all* came out looking like pictures, propositions (FM 156, #48). It took Wittgenstein several years to gradually remove all the wrappings—and thereby destroy the "system," and consequently the definition of meaning in terms of the "system."

IV. DEMONSTRATING THE NEW DEFINITION

A. *The General Method*

In the demotion of the word-system and the questioning of rules, as in the negative arguments that preceded, *a priori* reasonings and generalized "intuitions" like the picture theory are rejected and observation takes their place. Observation reveals that words can have meaning when there is no bearer, when there is no shadow, when no rule is obeyed, when the word is independent of other words and operating on its own in the stream of life. Similarly it is observation that shows meaning to be the same as use. Use does not simply win by default, once its rivals are eliminated. The equivalence is established by the only method Wittgenstein considered appropriate to philosophy: the accurate description of concrete cases.[17] A word now on this approach.

Reliance on the description of many and varied concrete cases not only distinguishes the *Investigations*, say from the *Tractatus*; it also, though less obviously, connects the two works. The importance of the "say"—"show" distinction in the *Tractatus* has been stressed. Practically the same distinction dominates the later philosophy of Wittgenstein, quite as much as it did the *Tractatus*. According to the *Tractatus*, words are used for the humble statement of facts and accomplish this task quite satisfactorily without any help from philosophers, even linguistic ones; we all understand *what* words say. But we do not all see how or why they say what they say; we do not all see what the statements only show, namely their grammar.[18] Close observation of their use is required to discover this, and so to avoid philosophical problems, which arise from blindness to the true grammar of words. Closer inspection of cases awakened Wittgenstein later to the fact that *the* grammar of the *Tractatus* is only one possible grammar. But on all the other points just mentioned, his views remained basically unchanged. Understanding what words say is usually no problem;[19] but grasping their grammar requires reflection and close observation.[20] That is why there are philosophical problems; philosophical puzzles arise from misunderstanding the way our language works and the way individual expressions are used.[21]

It might appear that an important difference disturbs this parallel. It might be said that whereas in the *Tractatus* Wittgenstein forbade us to say what the grammar is which we observe, in the *Investigations* there is no such prohibition. However, this objection points mainly to a difference in words. After all, Wittgenstein evidently thought the *Tractatus* worth writing, even though it flagrantly violated "the correct method in philosophy" (6.53). Its sentences might be nonsensical, in the technical *Tractatus* sense, but they served a purpose[22] (6.54).

Furthermore—and this is the point I have been coming to in order to illuminate Wittgenstein's procedure—there is an important sense in which the later Wittgenstein does *not* permit us to "say" what the grammar of an expression is. For saying it would be making a generalization about it, and a generalization is quite likely to mislead rather than to instruct a hearer who is not already acquainted with the grammatical complexity alluded to by the generalization (BB 17-19). If someone has taken to philosophy and is suffering from the philosophical worries brought on by blindness to grammar, the only thing to do is to give him examples, cases—lots of them and as varied as possible.[23] That is, one must *show* him how the expressions are actually used. This is the method Wittgenstein advised for the solution of problems about meanings and about meaning itself. We must see how the word "meaning" is actually used, the sort of thing actually referred to, in concrete cases, when we talk about "meaning."[24]

B. *Applying the Method to "Meaning"*

We would do well to look, for instance, at explanations of meaning. "If you want to understand the use of the word 'meaning,'" said Wittgenstein, "look for what are called explanations of meaning."

Asking first "What's an explanation of meaning?" has two advantages. You in a sense bring the question "what is meaning?" down to earth. For, surely, to understand the meaning of "meaning" you ought also to understand the meaning of "explanation of meaning." Roughly: "let's ask what the explanation of meaning is, for whatever that explains will be the meaning." Studying the grammar of the expression "explanation of meaning" will teach you something about the grammar of the word "meaning" and will cure you of the temptation to look about you for some object which you might call "the meaning."

What one generally calls "explanations of the meaning of a word" can, *very roughly*, be divided into verbal and ostensive definitions. It will be seen later in what sense this division is only rough and provisional (and that it is, is an important point).[25] The verbal definition, as it takes us from one verbal expression to another, in a sense gets us no further. In the ostensive definition however we seem to make a much more real step towards learning the meaning (BB 1).

With an ostensive definition we break out of the circle of words and reach reality. We point to the *thing*. That is how we would like to put it.[26]

But it is not all that easy.[27] Suppose we explain the word "tove" by pointing to a pencil and saying "This is tove." "The definition can then be interpreted to mean: 'This is a pencil,' 'This is round,' 'This is wood,' 'This is one,' 'This is hard,' etc. etc." (BB 2). What is being pointed to? And even if we know what is being pointed to, *what does that tell us about the use of the word?* (§ 49). The whole force of Wittgenstein's argument is here.[28] We think that once we have hooked up a word with a thing or an idea or a feeling, the rest will take care of itself. But in this "we are like people who think that pieces of wood shaped more or less like chess or draught pieces and standing on a chess board make a game, even if nothing has been said as to how they are to be used" (BB 72). With our ostensive definition, for instance, we have put the chess piece on a square. Now what? Wittgenstein asks the same basic question in the following examples.[29]

A simple example: Someone points to two nuts and says, "That is called 'two' " (§ 28). What is called "two"? The color, the shape, the size? Well, if the circumstances and the learner are such that the definition is not understood, the person can say, "This *number* is called 'two' " (§ 29). And that may do the trick. If it does, it is because "the word 'number' here shews what place in language, in grammar, we assign to the word" (*Ibid.*). It gives a general indication of the word's role in the language. Doubtless, then, what is being explained is the specific role of this specific word. That is, an explanation of the meaning is an explanation of the word's use, its role in the language.

The same would be true even if no helping word like "number" were necessary. If such guiding words are not needed, that is because one already has the requisite knowledge of the sort they give. But precisely what sort of knowledge is this? (§ 30).

The statement "This is called 'two' " resembles the statement "This is the king." Neither the chess piece nor the word "two" can yet be used unless one already knows the rules of the game up to this last point: the sound of this word, the shape of the piece (§ 31; cp. PB 328).

For let us suppose that when the nuts are used to define "two" the person does direct his attention to their number. Of what use is this directing of the attention (§ 34) unless he knows he is being given a number, a word with a particular use, as the king in chess has a particular use? What is he supposed to do with this word "two"? What *can* he do with it and be understood? Use it for any number but that of the walnuts? (PI 14). Use it for counting walnuts, but nothing else? Use it as a sort of numerical proper name, for the number of these and only these two nuts? Only if a person has already played the game in which this word is used will the definition be effective, will he learn the meaning. Or, in terms of pure description, only if he now uses the word in a certain familiar way will we say that he knows its meaning. And he only does this if he has already played the game, or, as we would put it, if he has mastered a technique (BB 2, § 31).

Let us consider an even simpler case to illustrate the same point. For Augustine all words were like names. Here the name, there the thing (PI 49). But what makes the word a name? What is the relation between name and thing named? (§ 37). Well, look at the various language games, for instance the game of ordering things by calling out names.

> There you can see the sort of thing this relation consists in. This relation may also consist, among many other things, in the fact that hearing the name calls before our mind the picture of what is named; and it also consists, among other things, in the name's being written on the thing named or being pronounced when that thing is pointed at (*Ibid.*).

"The word 'name' is used to characterize many different kinds of use of a word" (§ 38). And it is all this that we learn when we learn a "name," when we learn the meaning of even the simplest sort of word, a proper name.

But let us simplify still further. Let us consider just one of these cases, that in which the name is written on the thing named.

> Imagine it were the usual thing that the objects around us carried labels with words on them by means of which our speech referred to the objects. Some of these words would be proper names of the objects, others generic names (like table, chair, etc.), others again, names of colours, names of shapes, etc. That is to say, a label would only have a meaning to us in so far as we made a particular use of it. Now we can easily imagine ourselves to be impressed by merely seeing a label on a thing, and to forget that what makes these labels important is their use. In this way we sometimes believe that we have named something when we make the gesture of pointing and utter words like "This is . . ." (the formula of the ostensive definition). We say we call something "toothache," and think that the word has received a definite function in the dealings we carry out with language when, under certain circumstances, we have pointed to our cheek and said: "This is toothache." (Our idea is that when we point and the other "only knows

what we are pointing to" he knows the use of the word. And here we have in mind the special case when "what we point to" is, say, a person and "to know that[30] I point to" means to see which of the persons present I point to.) (BB 69)

The special importance of these examples, and the reason for Wittgenstein's stress on them is clear. If there is any instance in which the meaning of a word might possibly be an object, or an image, or a characteristic experience, if there is any instance which, above all others, suggests such theories to us, it is the case of a *name* that is used to *refer*.[31] So Wittgenstein considers names that refer. If he proves his point even here, then his argument is conclusive and universal. He proves it by pointing out that when we learn the meaning of a name we learn not only that it is a name for *this*, but that it is a *name*. We learn not only *what* it refers to but *that* it refers. We learn not only that it refers to *this*, but that it *refers*. We learn not only that it may refer to this individual thing but that it may refer to other things of the same sort (or that it may not). This is what we learn. And what we learn is the "meaning." The meaning, therefore, is not a thing referred to but the use of the word to refer to such a thing.

And what is true even of a name that refers is true *a fortiori* of other sorts of words. What we learn through an explanation of meaning is not an object, not an idea, not a feeling, but the use of a word. This is its meaning.

It seems that this key point was long obscured by Wittgenstein's picture theory of language, with which he was still wrestling when Moore heard his lectures, and which lingered on in his references to "projection," still very numerous in those first lectures ($M^1$12-13, $M^2$292-293). For in the picture theory *all* (analytical) signs referred. A proposition was like a picture; and in a picture, for instance a painting, each blotch of paint stands for something. Therefore when someone points to a particular blotch and asks, "What is this?" the answer is not, "A blotch of paint that stands for the roof of a house," but simply, "A roof." The referring can be taken for granted (BB 69). That is what Wittgenstein did for a long time. He took the referring for granted. All the signs in the *Tractatus* referred. So referring was hardly what accounted for their difference in meaning. The meaning was what distinguished one sign from another —first the particular object it referred to, then at least its place in the overall system, like the position of a dab of paint in the overall picture. But when Wittgenstein finally awoke to the full diversity of uses, he no longer took referring or any other use for granted. He recognized that this too was something specific about each sign. One sign differed from another not merely because it referred to this thing rather than that, but also because it referred. Others did not.[32] And in each case this was the important thing about the sign: its use.

V.   CONCLUSION

Now what would Wittgenstein say had been accomplished by his definition? He certainly would not say that his arguments and final definition had revealed some new, previously unknown object (§§ 126, 401). "Grammar tells what kind of object anything is" (§ 373), and it shows that meaning is *no* object. He might say that he meant to change our way of looking at familiar things (§§ 401, 305) and to make us duly cognizant of the familiar things whose importance we so often overlook (§ 129). "It is as if one had altered the adjustment of a microscope. One did not see before what is now in focus" (§ 645). But his negative arguments also put his definition in the class with Berkeley's definition of existence or Hume's definition of causality. On page 135 of the *Investigations*, Wittgenstein says: "I shall get burnt if I put my hand in the fire; that is certainty. That is to say: here we see the meaning of certainty (What it amounts to, not just the meaning of the word 'certainty.')" (§ 474).[33] At first sight this last remark is puzzling. How could certainty "amount to" anything but what is included in the correct definition of "certainty"? What distinction does Wittgenstein intend to make?

It is an important one not only in this case, but in many others as well. He means that the definition is not only an accurate account of usage, but also a complete account of the thing in question (§ 126). It has left nothing out. It shows what is really in question. Of course any evident reality left out of one definition is sure to be included in some other; call it Ireland or call it Eire, any map will include the island and give it a name.[34] But if, for instance, the word being defined has suggested a nonexistent entity as its referent, the definition which excludes this entity excludes it not only from the definition, but from being. Doubtless Wittgenstein intended his definition of meaning to be of this sort. Therein lies much of its importance. It is not mere word-mapping, giving a correct view of grammar. It is Occam's razor in action. It helps us see *things* as they are.

A variety of reasons, some of which we have mentioned, might lead philosophers to believe that to any word with meaning there must necessarily correspond some entity—either psychological or objective—which is the meaning. Having denied this necessity, Wittgenstein eliminated the supposed entities from his definition. Implicitly the definition denies that objects, including the mysterious *Tractatus* objects, or mental entities of some characteristic sort are constantly present in speech. Explicitly it denies that there ever exist mental or other entities of the sort sometimes supposed, possessing such marvellous properties that their mere presence gives words meaning (BB 42).[35] So when Wittgenstein defines meaning as use, he means: this is what meaning amounts to.

This is a very interesting result, perhaps, but is it worth all the effort? It might be interesting, too, to know the grammatical difference between "city" and "town" or the general outlines of the concept "picture." But there is no end to such investigations, and no evident utility in them. When a correct definition is found, one will be tempted to say, "So what?"

Such, apparently, was Wittgenstein's reaction to many such investigations.

> He held that though the "new subject" must say a great deal about language, it was only necessary for it to deal with those points about language which have led, or are likely to lead, to definite philosophical puzzles or errors. I think he certainly thought that some philosophers now-a-days have been misled into dealing with linguistic points which have no such bearing, and the discussion of which therefore, in his view, forms no part of the proper business of a philosopher (M³27).

The concept "meaning," however, is one which had led and was likely to lead to philosophical puzzles or errors. That is why Wittgenstein considered it worth his attention. Numerous paradoxes and illusions, some of which have already been mentioned, can be avoided only by getting a clear view of what meaning really is, of the way "meaning" is actually used. In a final chapter I will say more about the therapeutic value of Wittgenstein's definition. But first it will be necessary to see more precisely what meaning—"use in the language"—amounts to.

Chapter IV

THE EXTENSION AND INTENSION OF THE DEFINITION

"FOR A *large* CLASS OF CASES—THOUGH NOT FOR ALL." FOR WHAT CASES? What cases are included and which excluded, and how is the division made? These are the questions to be answered in the first part of the present chapter. "Use in the language" will then be studied in the second part. This order might, of course, be reversed. Not only is it helpful to know instances in order to discover what they are instances of. It is also helpful to know what sort of "use" is meant in order to know when such use is being spoken of. However, the former question happens to be the easier one to answer, especially in the present state of the discussion; so I shall begin with it.

I. THE DEFINITION'S EXTENSION

"It seems," said Wittgenstein at the start of the *Blue Book,*

> that there are *certain definite* mental processes bound up with the working of language, processes through which alone language can function. I mean the processes of understanding and meaning. The signs of our language seem dead without these mental processes; and it might seem that the only function of the signs is to induce such processes, and that these are the thing we ought really to be interested in. . . . We are tempted to think that the action of language consists of two parts; [sic] an inorganic part, the handling of signs, and an organic part, which we may call understanding these signs, meaning them, interpreting them, thinking (BB 3).

A series of passages in Moore's notes, the *Blue Book,* the *Brown Book,* and the *Investigations* reveals that a double use of the words "meaning" and *Bedeutung* corresponds (roughly) to this division. They thus reveal the reason why Wittgenstein restricted his definition on page 20 of the *Investigations* to just a large class of cases, and indicate with increasing clarity what other sorts, or rather, what other sort of "meaning" he recognized. After mentioning the two main positive points Wittgenstein made regarding the meaning of single words (namely that it was determined by "rules" and that other words had to belong to the "system"), and immediately after mentioning his metaphorical definition of meaning as a word's place in a grammatical system, Moore continues:

> But he said in (III)[1] that the sense of "meaning" of which he held these things to be true, and which was the only sense in which he intended to use the word, was only one of those in which we commonly use it: that there was another which he described as that in which it is used "as a name for a process accompanying our use of a word and our hearing of a word" ($M^1$6).

"Another." It does not seem that hereafter Wittgenstein ever envisaged any other sort than these two, the operational and the mental. Objects were already ruled out once for all. However, his understanding of both these senses was still to be modified, clarified, and made more precise, with a consequent narrowing of the area covered by these senses.

In the *Blue Book* his remarks on mental meanings are still very general:

> Now if for an expression to convey a meaning means to be accompanied by or to produce certain experiences, our expression may have all sorts of meanings, and I don't wish to say anything about them. . . . The meaning of a phrase for us is characterized by the use we make of it (BB 65).

Here there is the same contrast as before between two senses of "meaning," between a psychological sense and a non-psychological sense. Once again the non-psychological sense is the only one that interests Wittgenstein and seems important to him. In fact his attitude toward the other use of the word is so negative that one would not expect him to make it his own. No doubt he would have dropped it entirely had he not thought at this time that it was commonly accepted ($M^1$6).

In the *Brown Book* Wittgenstein was readier to discuss the mental sort of "meanings," and his attitude was not so negative. He even suggests a connection between psychological and non-psychological meaning, which might account for the double use of the word:

> We think of the meaning of signs sometimes as states of mind of the man using them, sometimes as the role which these signs are playing in a system

of language. The connection between these two ideas is that the mental experiences which accompany the use of a sign undoubtedly are caused by our usage of the sign in a particular system of language (BB 78).

At this time Wittgenstein was already investigating the sort of experiences actually connected with words in this way (BB 155-185); already he was drawing a parallel between the aspect-seeing type of experience and the experiences characteristic of words (BB 165). But he did not yet speak of experiencing words' meanings, nor refer to such experiences themselves as meanings. These developments came in the *Investigations*, where he put still greater stress on this type of experience.

The distinction between operative and mental meanings appears in the *Investigations* in massive form. Meaning as the role of words is the major theme in the first forty pages of the book; meaning as a psychological experience is the major theme in Part Two. And meaning as use is contrasted with meaning as experience in pages 139-150 and 168-172. No other sort of meaning is mentioned. The *Bedeutung* of a word is either its use, its role in language, or it is the experience of an individual person who means or understands the word. We have already seen in some detail what Wittgenstein considered these experiences to be, and what sort he considered most characteristic. Not even in this second sense did he leave much room for images or sensations. Here "Meaning is a physiognomy" (§ 568). So the separable mental meanings which he chased out through the door do not come back in through the window.

"But the question now remains why, in connexion with this game of experiencing a word, we also speak of 'the meaning' and 'meaning it'" (PI 216). "'How can this be, if meaning is the use of the word?' Well, what I said was intended figuratively. Not that I chose the figure: it forced itself on me.[2] But the figurative employment can't get in conflict with the original one" (PI 215). If I am inclined to say that Wednesday is fat and Tuesday lean, nobody will think the days have bodies. "Here one might speak of a 'primary' and 'secondary' sense of a word. It is only if the word has the primary sense for you that you use it in the secondary one" (PI 216).

Wittgenstein gave more than a hint as to why this second sense should force itself on him. In the *Blue Book* he cites a very similar case:

If one asks what the different processes of expecting someone to tea have in common, the answer is that there is no single feature in common to all of them, though there are many common features overlapping. These cases of expectation form a family; they have family likenesses which are not clearly defined.

There is a totally different use of the word "expectation" if we use it to mean a particular sensation. This use of the words like "wish," "expectation," etc., readily suggests itself. There is an obvious connection between this use and the one described above. There is no doubt that in many cases if we expect some one, in the first sense, some, or all, of the activities described are accompanied by a peculiar feeling, a tension; and it is natural to use the word "expectation" to mean this experience of tension (BB 20).

Now the same sort of connection exists between meaning as use and meaning as an experience. "The mental experiences which accompany the use of a sign undoubtedly are caused by our usage of the sign in a particular system of language." There is no doubt that certain experiences are frequently associated with our use of words (BB 78). So "it is natural" to extend the word to such experiences. This second use "suggests itself" to us because of the first, even though it is "a totally different use of the word."[3]

It is important to notice that the two senses of "meaning" do not divide *words* between them. There are not some words whose meaning is use and others whose meaning is a particular experience. Wittgenstein did not speak in his definition of a large class of words, but of a large class of cases in which we employ the word *Bedeutung*.

Some remarks on page three of the *Investigations* might be misleading in this respect. After attributing to Augustine a certain general view of language in which there figured the opinion that the meaning of a word is the object it stands for (§ 1), Wittgenstein remarks: "That philosophical concept of meaning has its place in a primitive idea of the way language functions. But one can also say that it is the idea of a language more primitive than ours." He then imagines a language "for which the description given by Augustine is right": a builder calls out "block," "pillar," "slab," "beam," and an assistant fetches the items named (§ 2).

We might reword Wittgenstein's remark about "that philosophical conception of meaning" in two ways. Either: "That definition of meaning (as the object referred to) fits a language more primitive than ours"; or: "That philosophical conception of the way words are used (meaning as defined by Wittgenstein) fits a language more primitive than ours." Some authors have understood his words in the first way and so have concluded that in such primitive uses of language, "the meaning of the words is the thing to which they refer."[4] However, I think that Pole[5] and Strawson[6] are clearly right in giving the other interpretation.

It is quite clear that in the shorter version in the *Brown Book* from which this discussion is developed in the *Investigations*, the only respect in which Wittgenstein conceives that Augustine might be right is in his description of what happens. There is no mention of meaning or of a theory of meaning (BB 77).

And in the *Investigations* Wittgenstein points out almost immediately (§ 6) that there is something more involved than a thing and a word; there is the special relation between the thing and the word, there is the word's particular use. Even in the simplest games, the use is the important thing, the meaning.

The inclusion of even Augustine-style word uses in Wittgenstein's definition on page 20 is suggested not only by the intervening twenty pages, with their insistence on the varying uses to which signs are put, so that none will be taken for granted, but by remarks on page 20 itself, where the definition of meaning is elicited by the discussion, not of an advanced and complicated language-game, but of a crudely "Augustinian" one.

Once this possible misunderstanding is removed, it becomes evident that *all* words have the sort of meaning Wittgenstein referred to in his definition. The important thing about any substantive is its use (BB 69), and if this is true of substantives, it is true *a fortiori* of other words. The roles of words are most varied, but each has a use (§§ 11-14).

So Wittgenstein's reservation concerns uses of the word "meaning" and not classes of words. These uses are characterized by different verbs, as can be seen in Wittgenstein's discussions. The meaning which we "learn," "define," "explain," "understand," "know" or "forget" is the word's role. When Wittgenstein spoke of feeling or experiencing the meaning, he was using the word "meaning" in its second, figurative sense. In this sense he even spoke, on one occasion, of the *Bedeutung* of a sentence (§ 540). Now what is it that we learn, define, understand, know? What sort of "use" is meaning?

II. The Definition's Intension

This is perhaps a dangerous question. "A definition," said Wittgenstein on one occasion, "often clears up the *grammar* of a word. And in fact it is the grammar of the word 'time' which puzzles us. We are only expressing this puzzlement by asking a slightly misleading question, the question: 'What is ... ?' " (BB 26). The dots after "is" indicate that such a question is dangerous in other cases as well. And "meaning" is one of them.

> The questions "What is length?," "What is meaning?," "What is the number one?" etc., produce in us a mental cramp. We feel that we can't point to anything in reply to them and yet ought to point to something. (We are up against one of the great sources of philosophical bewilderment: a substantive makes us look for a thing that corresponds to it.) (BB 1)

This is the warning which preceded Wittgenstein's suggestion to study explanations of meaning. "Studying the grammar of the expression 'explanation of meaning,'" he said, "will cure you of the temptation to look about you for some object which you might call 'the meaning'" (BB 1).

These warnings pose a methodological problem. If we must not point to anything, then we can hardly describe anything either. If we may not single out something and identify it as the meaning of a word, how are we to list the characteristics of meaning? How can the intension of a word be given in traditional fashion if the word refers to no thing whose properties may be listed and described?

The proper answer to this problem is suggested by the fact that further on in the *Blue Book* and later in the *Investigations* Wittgenstein did in fact answer the very sort of question he warned against. Whereas he refused to say what time is, he did say what meaning is. He said, "Meaning is use."[7] For use is not an object which can be pointed to. It is neither a material object nor one of the shadowy beings which we create when we wish to give meaning to substantives to which no material objects correspond (BB 36, 47). If it can be called a referent at all, it is certainly not the sort Wittgenstein warned against (§ 370).

A. *Complexity*

Though we can examine (BB 23) and describe it (BB 125), for a number of reasons we cannot point to use. One reason is its complexity. This is a first general characteristic of words' use, one suggested more forcefully by the word "grammar," which, in Wittgenstein's later terminology, was equivalent to "use" (BB 23).

The term "grammar" would most naturally suggest Wittgenstein's earlier views regarding language as a system of signs. And in Wittgenstein's later usage, "grammar" does include the manner of a word's combination with other words, as an important aspect of their "use." For instance, there is strong stress here on the verbal aspect of use:

> There is the statement: "this pencil is five inches long," and the statement, "I feel that this pencil is five inches long," and we must get clear about the relation of the grammar of the first statement to the grammar of the second. To the statement "I feel in my hand that the water is three feet under the ground" we should like to answer: "I don't know what this means." But the diviner would say: "Surely you know what it means. You know what 'three feet under the ground' means, and you know what 'I feel' means." But I should answer him: I know what a word means *in certain contexts*. Thus I understand the phrase, "three feet under the ground," say, in the connections "The measurement has shown that the water runs three feet under the ground," "If we dig three feet deep we are going to strike water," "The depth of the water is three feet by the eye" (BB 9-10).[8]

However, such a tabulation of verbal constructions, though a necessary first step, is a mere preliminary in the study of a word's grammar. The next question is: How are these various combinations used? For instance, the use of the expression "a feeling in my hands of water [sic] being three feet under the ground" has yet to be explained (BB 10).

For the "grammar" of a word is something more than its relationship to other words. For example,

> It is part of the grammar of the word "chair" that *this* is what we call "to sit on a chair," and it is part of the grammar of the word "meaning" that *this* is what we call "explanation of a meaning"; in the same way to explain my criterion for another person's having toothache is to give a grammatical explanation about the word "toothache" and, in this sense, an explanation concerning the meaning of the word "toothache" (BB 24).

Again, we say "This is short" and "Jack is short." We use "this" and proper names in similar phrases, in similar grammatical constructions. But nothing is more unlike than the use of the word "this" and the use of a proper name—that is, the games we play with these words, not the phrases in which they are used. For "This is short" without a pointing gesture and without the thing we are pointing to would be meaningless. "What can be compared with a name is not the word 'this' but, if you like, the symbol consisting of this word, the gesture and the sample" (BB 109).[9]

Similarly, in regard to, say, the word "meaning," we might distinguish "surface grammar" from "depth grammar." What immediately impresses itself upon us about the word "meaning" is the way it is used in the construction of sentences, the part of its use—one might say—that can be taken in by the ear.[10] But if we compare this with the depth grammar of "meaning" we find that this is very different from what the surface grammar would lead us to suppose (§ 664).[11]

The function of a word "can easily be seen if we look at the role this word really plays in our usage of language, but it is obscured when instead of looking at the *whole language game,* we only look at the contexts, the phrases of language in which the word is used" (BB 108).[12] And as we have seen, even in the earliest lectures Wittgenstein recognized that a given word might be used by itself. Thus, though certainly an important aspect of words' use, increasing their complexity, their relationship with other words is not the whole of their "use," nor even the most important aspect.

This fullness and complexity of meaning is the positive truth Wittgenstein had in mind when he rejected isolated objects, images, or feelings as the meanings of words. The important thing about a word is not one item of experience at one moment simultaneous with its production. The important thing about a word is its whole context, including what went before and what follows after.[13]

The following remarks about feelings epitomize what Wittgenstein said in less concise fashion about the meaning of words:

What does it mean to say "What is happening now has significance" [*Bedeutung*] or "has deep significance" [*Bedeutung*]? What is a *deep* feeling? Could someone have a feeling of ardent love or hope for the space of one second—*no matter what* preceded or followed this second?—What is happening now has significance [*Bedeutung*]—in these surroundings. The surroundings give it its importance . . . (A smiling mouth *smiles* only in a human face) (§ 583).

That he thought of meaning in the same way can be seen in a passage like the following:

You say to me: "You understand this expression, don't you? Well then—I am using it in the sense [*Bedeutung*] you are familiar with."—As if the sense were an atmosphere accompanying the word, which it carried with it into every kind of application. If, for example, someone says that the sentence "This is here" (saying which he points to an object in front of him) makes sense [*Sinn*] to him, then he should ask himself in what special circumstances this sentence is actually used. There it does make sense (§ 117).[14]

The illustrative example used here is a proposition, not a word, but it illustrates a principle which applies to all expressions. This is not the principle of the *Tractatus* or of the earliest lectures, that a word has meaning only in a verbal context. But it might be worded in much the same way: "A word has meaning only in a context." It must be understood that this is a vital context, and need not include words. "Only in the stream of *life* does a word have meaning."[15] And it is not the meaning which is in the context, but the word. The context belongs to the meaning.

To say that use includes both the verbal and the non-verbal context does not yet suggest its full complexity. The full, compounded complexity of use is suggested by a remark like the following: "Note, we are not saying '*what a rule is*' but just giving different applications of the word 'rule': and we certainly do this by giving applications of the words 'expression of a rule'" (BB 98). Most words are not worlds to themselves; they are combined in an enormous variety of ways with countless other words, and each resulting expression has its own complex and varied "depth grammar" (BB 23-24), so that we might say of most words what Wittgenstein said of sentences: "To understand a sentence means to understand a language" (§ 199).[16]

B. *Utility and Regularity*

Terms like "function,"[17] "use,"[18] and "role"[19] suggest a second key notion in Wittgenstein's concept of meaning. They suggest that the words are doing something, that they have some effect, that they are of some use.

The usefulness of words was a continuing preoccupation with Wittgenstein. We have seen it in the *Tractatus*. For example, he argued there that certain words are meaningless because they do nothing; whatever they try to say is already shown by other signs. Thereafter he continued to point out cases in which expressions resembling ones used to give information do not actually give any information and so are meaningless (e.g., M²296; BB 65-66, 71-72). But he had made "a radical break with the idea that language always functions in one way, always serves the same purpose: to convey thoughts—which may be about houses, pains, good and evil, or anything else you please" (§ 304). Whereas according to the *Tractatus* all language had been uniformly descriptive, Wittgenstein now insisted that even descriptions vary, not only in their form and object (§ 24), but also in their purpose and consequences:

> What we call "descriptions" are instruments for particular uses. Think of a machinedrawing, a cross-section, an elevation with measurements, which an engineer has before him. Thinking of a description as a word-picture of the facts has something misleading about it: one tends to think only of such pictures as hang on our walls; which seem simply to portray how a thing looks, what it is like (these pictures are as it were idle) (§ 291).

> That is to say: we are so much accustomed to communication through language, in conversation, that it looks to us as if the whole point of communication lay in this: someone else grasps the sense of my words—which is something mental: he as it were takes it into his own mind. If he then does something further with it as well, that is no part of the immediate purpose of language (§ 363).

To remedy this one-sided outlook, Wittgenstein stressed commands. For instance, both in the *Brown Book* and in the *Investigations*, he starts out his language games with a great many commands and instructions. Trainees are told to fetch things,[20] to count (§ 9), to name objects (BB 81-82; § 7), to move according to certain patterns (BB 95-96), to shop with signs.[21] The consequences of words are thus made immediately evident, as they would not be in idle conversations. In this way Wittgenstein stressed the point that words are not idle.

"Without language," he said, "we cannot influence other people in such-and-such ways; cannot build roads and machines, etc." (§ 491). Without language our actions would fall into confusion (§ 207).

All this might be admitted and it still be denied that *individual words* have use in an operative sense. Or, if it be admitted, it might still be claimed that such causal considerations have no place in Wittgenstein's "grammatical" conception of meaning. The formal aspect of use might be equated with meaning.

Let me explain what I mean by the formal aspect of use, the aspect which I shall be contrasting with the operative or functional aspect in the following discussion. If a word is used, obviously it is used in some specific manner, in this or that way. If it is used repeatedly, one manner—specific or general, more or less precise—may be proposed as a rule or model, or may actually be conformed to, giving rise to a regular pattern of usage. Such usage or such rules, criteria, standards, are what I mean by the formal aspect of use. On an individual occasion this aspect may be present as conformity to usage or a paradigm case. In overall usage it may be present as a regular pattern.

To this aspect of a word's use I would contrast the pragmatic, practical aspect. I will be distinguishing between utility and usage, between function and established structure or pattern (§ 93), between how a word is used and what it is used for. The need for distinction is especially great here because the two things can so easily be confused, being closely related. Thus a hammer is habitually used in a certain way because it has a certain utility, was made for a certain purpose; on the other hand, a thing like a dollar bill may be useful precisely because of a custom, an established usage. Yet the two things need not both be present. A newly invented tool, for instance, would have a use, even though it had never been used in any customary way. That is, it would have utility and a purpose. The question now is whether Wittgenstein thought that individual words have use in both these senses or only one. Most of what has been said so far about the general characteristics of a word's use is quite compatible with a merely formal, as opposed to a causal, notion of use. When this question has been answered, it will be time to consider whether Wittgenstein had use in this sense in mind when he defined meaning as use.

Many of Wittgenstein's expressions are ambiguous. For instance, even in context very often the word "use" could be interpreted either way or both ways.[22] The word "role" is likewise indecisive by itself (e.g., § 21), and so is reference to "doing something" with a word (§ 31); I do something with a broom when I wave it idly in the air, but I do something with it in quite another sense when I use it to sweep a room.

But the utility of individual words is clearly stated in many places. The repeated references to their "purpose" (§§ 6, 8) and "functions"[23] seem unambiguous. And words are repeatedly compared with tools, instruments.[24] Something more than mere pattern is suggested when Wittgenstein refers to the role which we see a word play in the life of a tribe (BB 94); when he asks what words are to be "used for" (§§ 96, 363); when he says that "it is the field of force of a word that is decisive" (PI 219);[25] or speaks of expressions' "performing their office" (§ 402). The causal aspect of use is especially evident in BB 67-69, 80-84; §§ 6-11, 22-23.

The formal aspect of use—usage, rules, criteria—is sometimes evident by itself, for instance in BB 104, 115, 125, 135, 170-171; §§ 151, 182, 197, 555, 557, 558, 565, and on page 147 of the *Investigations*, where the connection between meaning and rules is brought out: "There cannot be a question whether these or other rules are the correct ones for the use of 'not.' (I mean, whether they accord with its meaning.) For without these rules the word has as yet no meaning; and if we change the rules, it now has another meaning (or none), and in that case we may just as well change the word too."

Sometimes one aspect appears, sometimes the other—and sometimes both together. Thus in BB 102-103 the effects of a word are listed among the characteristics of the "role" it plays: "whether a word of the language of our tribe is rightly translated into a word of the English language depends upon the role this word plays in the whole life of the tribe; the occasions on which it is used, the expressions of emotion by which it is generally accompanied, the ideas which it generally awakens or which prompt its saying, etc." (BB 103).

A number of passages such as the one just quoted from page 147 of the *Investigations* might easily lead us to define a word's meaning as the rules of its use, and leave it at that. For instance:

What is the use, say, of the words "this" and "that"?—or rather, What are the different uses which we make of them? What we call their meaning is not anything which they have got in them or which is fastened to them irrespective of what use we make of them. Thus it is one use of the word "this" to go along with a gesture pointing to something (BB 170-171).

Here merely being accompanied by a gesture seems to specify a meaning. There is no mention of utility. Again, in the *Brown Book* (BB 124-125) and in the *Investigations* (§ 163) there is a discussion of derivation in which, after Wittgenstein has suggested less and less typical cases, one finally asks, "But where is the dividing line between this procedure and a random one?" (§ 163). Wittgenstein's rejoinder is: "does this mean that the word 'to derive' [*ableiten*] really has no meaning, since the meaning seems to distintegrate when we follow it up?" (§ 163). What has apparently disintegrated is the formal regularity of the concept, and it is this which Wittgenstein seems to call "meaning." Is meaning mere rules, mere regularity in the way pieces are or should be moved in the language game? Is meaning purely formal?

If meaning were defined as rules of use, and merely this were meant (as it often is, when such a formalistic-sounding definition is offered), then the definition would differ from Wittgenstein's thought in a number of ways. He would have a number of objections to it, besides those already suggested in Chapter III.[26]

Just as the significance of an event is its importance, so for Wittgenstein the meaning of a word was, roughly, the important thing about it. And for him this was always what a word *does*. "The service is the point" (PI 178).[27] So in discussing rules of use and the "point" of use, he was treating what I have called the formal and the pragmatic aspects of use. The relation between the two he expressed thus: "if rule became exception and exception rule; or if both became phenomena of roughly equal frequency—this would make our normal language-games lose their point" (§ 142). Words' utility depends on rules, on a certain amount of regularity. This is what gives the rules their importance. In the definition just suggested the rule "stands as it were alone in its glory." But its usefulness must not be left out of account (FM 160). This is one defect of the proposed definition.

Usefulness, in fact, is the criterion for whether a rule belongs to the meaning of a word. "The game," Wittgenstein suggests, using his favorite analog of language, "has not only rules but a point." And one is tempted to say that some rules are essential, some inessential, in so far as they are relevant to the "point" of the game. If we say that the game is defined by rules and leave it at that, then any rule will seem to be an essential part of the game, for instance a rule which prescribes that kings be used for drawing lots before the game begins.

What objection might one make to this? That one does not see the point of this prescription. Perhaps as one wouldn't see the point either of a rule by which each piece had to be turned round three times before one moved it. If we found this rule in a board-game we should be surprised and should speculate about the purpose of the rule. ("Was this prescription meant to prevent one from moving without due consideration?")

If I understand the character of the game aright—I might say—then this isn't an essential part of it (§§ 567-568).

And if it isn't an essential part, then doubtless it isn't part of the meaning; for the meaning is what is important about a sign. This is the conclusion I think we should draw from a passage such as this.[28] It reveals a second defect of a purely formal definition of meaning as "rules of use."

Because its stress on regularity obscures the utility of words, such a definition would falsify Wittgenstein's thought in a third way: it would suggest the possibility of there being meaning where there are rules for the manipulation of signs but not such as give them any utility or application in our lives.

Wittgenstein's contrary view is especially evident in the *Remarks on the Foundations of Mathematics*, where he says for instance: "What Russell's '$\sim f (f)$' lacks above all is application, and hence meaning" (FM 166).[29] This expression obeys rules, but what rules! "The Russellian contradiction is disquieting, not because it is a contradiction, but because the whole growth culminating in it is a cancerous growth, seeming to have grown out of the normal body aimlessly and senselessly" (*Ibid.*). Of mathematical signs he says: "It is essential to mathematics that its signs should also be used in civil life. It is their use outside mathematics, in other words the meaning of the signs, that makes the sign game mathematics" (FM 133).[30] If the mathematical game had nothing but formal rules for the manipulation of signs, if there were no "extramathematical application" (FM 134) to building bridges and keeping accounts, the signs would be meaningless. Mere rules are not enough.

A homely, down-to-earth example reveals the same attitude:

Suppose that the tool with the name "N" is broken. Not knowing this, *A* gives *B* the sign "N." Has this sign meaning now or not?—What is *B* to do when he is given it?—We have not settled anything about this. One might ask: what *will* he do? Well, perhaps he will stand there at a loss, or shew *A* the pieces. Here one *might* say: "N" has become meaningless; and this expression would mean that the sign "N" no longer had a use in our language-game (unless we gave it a new one) (§ 41).

Here nothing has happened to the rules, whether customary or agreed upon. Yet one might say that the word has become meaningless—which one could *not* say if its meaning were simply the rules for its use.

But in this and what follows the importance of rules is also obvious. Wittgenstein stresses that one *might* say that the sign is meaningless, and he immediately adds this second possibility: " 'N' might also become meaningless because, for whatever reason, the tool was given another name and the sign 'N' no longer used in the language-game" (§ 41). The new use, like the old, would depend on rules of some sort. Without them the signs would not have the utility they do have. So the following question arises inevitably: Is not the same thing true of utility as is true of rules? Can there be meaning without regularity any more than there can be meaning without utility? Would some completely irregular use of a word, no matter how effective, deserve to be called "meaning," or to be included in the meaning of the word?

This question must be carefully distinguished from the question whether words may acquire new meanings, gradually or suddenly. They obviously can, either in the way Wittgenstein has just indicated, through agreement on new rules,[31] or by gradual shifts from one related use to another. Wittgenstein's remarks about "family resemblances" in the applications of a word suggest how natural this would be. If, for instance, the things called games only resemble one another more or less, through these or those features, then some new activity never before called a game, with features no game has ever had, if it had a number of familiar game-features might with as much right as existing games be called a game. At the same time other games would be going out of existence, and so the concept would gradually change its content. In general,

> There are . . . countless different kinds of use of what we call "symbols," "words," "sentences." And this multiplicity is not something fixed, given once for all; but new types of language, new language-games, as we may say, come into existence, and others become absolete and get forgotten (We can get a *rough picture* of this from the changes in mathematics) (§ 23).

In the light of statements like these, it seems extraordinary that Wittgenstein is repeatedly accused of having put language in a straightjacket.[32] The real difficulty is just the contrary. There are both statements and examples which give just the opposite impression: that Wittgenstein allowed language too much freedom. Would his critics themselves be willing to call Wednesday "fat" or to give the color of vowels (PI 216)? Wouldn't they perhaps be disconcerted if they reread § 83:

Doesn't the analogy between language and games throw light here? We can easily imagine people amusing themselves in a field by playing with a ball so as to start various existing games, but playing many without finishing them and in between throwing the ball aimlessly into the air, chasing one another with the ball and bombarding one another for a joke and so on. And now someone says: The whole time they are playing a ball-game and following definite rules at every throw.

So we should ask rather: Did Wittgenstein put no limits to meaning? Did he consider any use meaningful so long as it served a purpose, no matter how irregular the use? Is utility necessary, but regularity not, except in the language as a whole?

For instance, the expression "Milk me sugar" will have an effect on the one who hears it. Its effect may be that he stares and gapes, and that may be precisely the effect intended. But will the expression make sense?

Wittgenstein thought not (§ 498). So doubtless he would say that the individual words are meaningless, or rather that their employment here is meaningless, that it does not belong to the meanings of the words.

But why? According to what criterion? How does this use differ from other original uses, that they should make sense and this one be meaningless? When we say that Wednesday is fat and the vowel e is yellow[33] (PI 216), these are certainly original uses of the words. Yet they make sense, whereas "Milk me sugar" does not. Where do we draw the line?

Wittgenstein drew no line. He said of meaning (BB 19) what he said of games: "How is the concept of a game bounded? What still counts as a game and what no longer does? Can you give a boundary? No. You can draw one; for none so far has been drawn." "One might say that the concept 'game' is a concept with blurred edges" (§ 71). Yet "are we to say that we do not really attach any meaning to this word, because we are not equipped with rules for every possible application of it?" (§ 80) "Many words in this sense then don't have a strict meaning. But this is not a defect. To think it is would be like saying that the light of my reading lamp is no real light at all because it has no sharp boundary" (BB 27).

What is true of the particular case is true of words in general: there is no precise criterion to separate the meaningful from the meaningless. We can only say in a general way that even in the most original uses admitted by Wittgenstein, there is a certain minimal similarity between the novel use and some customary one. When we say, "Wednesday is fat," though the depth grammar is very unusual and depth grammar is important, at least the surface grammar is in order, whereas something is obviously awry in the structure of this expression: *Milch mir Zucker. Bring mir Zucker* would be all right, but in *Milch mir Zucker* there is no verb.[34]

But Wittgenstein was not one to consider surface grammar crucial. It is important, therefore, to point out that in the sort of extended language game exemplified by the game of calling days "fat" or "lean," though the depth grammar is quite different from that in the parent game, there is nevertheless enough of a connecting link to suggest what sort of game is being played. Thus the way in which a small girl uses the word "pain" when she is playing and speaks of her doll's pain is very different from ordinary usage, in which the word is reserved for animate objects. But the connection between her language-game and the ordinary one is obvious enough so that this "secondary sense" (§ 282) causes us no problems. Our extended use of the term "is" is quite similar: We point to a picture and say, "This is Lloyd George," though of course in the primary sense of the term it is not Lloyd George (LC 32). The connection is less evident in the language games Wittgenstein introduced with secondary, derived senses of "meaning" and "understand."[35] But both here and in the similar case of calling days of the week "fat" or "lean" he does not leave us completely on our own. He gives us some vague indication at least of what sort of game he intends us to play.

He thereby practiced what he constantly preached. No language-game was too bizarre, no word-use too far-fetched, *provided* the new use was duly explained, its connection with the rest of life duly indicated (BB 65). It was *not* sufficient simply to follow the rules of grammar, to have a verb and a subject and perhaps an object too. Familiar words with impeccable grammar may result in total nonsense. "The mere *ring of a sentence* is not enough to give these connexions of signs any meaning" (FM 54, #20; LC 68).

In some cases the point is obvious, and he meant it to be (§ 464). For instance here: "Certain considerations may lead us to say that 10^{10} souls fit into a cubic centimetre. But why do we nevertheless not say it? Because it is of no use. Because, while it does conjure up a picture, the picture is one with which we cannot go on to do anything" (FM 59, #8). Then there is the person who says, "I can assure you I feel the visual image to be two inches behind the bridge of my nose," and the water diviner who says, "I feel in my hand that the water is three feet under the ground." To this latter statement we should like to answer:

"I don't know what this *means*." But the diviner would say: "Surely you know what it means. You know what 'three feet under the ground' means, and you know what 'I feel' means!" But I should answer him: I know what a word means *in certain contexts*. Thus I understand the phrase, "three feet under the ground," say, in the connections "The measurement has shown that the water runs three feet under the ground," "If we dig three feet deep we are going to strike water," "The depth of the water is three feet by the eye." But the use of the expression "a feeling in my hands of water being three feet under the ground" has yet to be explained to me (BB 9-10).

Suppose now that the diviner said:

"I have never learnt to correlate depth of water under the ground with feelings in my hand, but when I have a certain feeling of tension in my hands, the words 'three feet' spring up in my mind." We should answer "This is a perfectly good explanation of what you mean by 'feeling the depth to be three feet,' and the statement that you feel this will have neither more, nor less, meaning than your explanation has given it. And if experience shows that the actual depth of the water always agrees with the words 'n feet' which come into your mind, your experience will be very useful for determining the depth of water."—But you see that the meaning of the words "I feel the depth of the water to be n feet" had to be explained; it was not known when the meaning of the words "n feet" in the ordinary sense (i.e. in the ordinary contexts) was known (BB 10).

Here Wittgenstein was shadow-boxing, using fanciful cases to teach a lesson. Elsewhere he dealt in the same way with many genuine cases. One example will have to suffice.

According to Moore, "He said that a man who had spent his life in trying to trisect an angle by rule and compass would be inclined to say, 'If you understand both what is meant by 'trisection' and what is meant by 'bisection by rule and compasses,' you must understand what is meant by 'trisection by rule and compasses' but that this was a mistake" (M[3]9). "One supposes that since it is possible to speak of bisection or quadrisection, it is also possible to speak of trisection, just as it is possible to count two, three, and four apples. But trisection—if there is such a thing—

belongs to an entirely different category, an entirely different system from bisection and quadrisection" (PB 334). Of this and many other mathematical statements[36] he would say: "In what practice is this proposition *anchored*? It is for the time being a piece of mathematical architecture which hangs in the air, and looks as if it were, let us say, an architrave, but not supported by anything and supporting nothing" (FM 58-59, #8).

Sometimes, as in the case of the water diviner, the word is actually anchored; there is some connection, which the speaker knows about, because of which he uses the expression in the way he does. He does not sufficiently explain his new usage and so misleads or befuddles people, but Wittgenstein would not call his statements senseless (BB 10). Freud, for instance, really discovered phenomena and connections not previously known, but his manner of speaking, the new use of familiar words by which he expressed his findings, was most misleading (M³15; BB 23, 57-58).

In other cases no connection exists; the word hangs in the air. Then the statement in which it occurs does indeed make no sense. This is frequently the case in philosophy. For the philosopher believes in essences which, like an atmosphere, accompany words wherever they go, no matter how far away from their original applications and contexts.[37]

The results of the investigation in this present section are not surprising: Since Wittgenstein's aim was therapeutic and his later writings largely a reaction to his own and others' errors, he reacted to the exaggerated stress on rules in language by stressing the irregularity of language and to the narrowness and superficiality and formalism of many views of language by stressing the need of connections, especially pragmatic connections. On the one hand, though one feels that rules determine a path for us to follow, even in mathematics the rules do not foretell their application. "If you say 'and so on,' you yourself do not know more than 'and so on' " (FM 116, #8). On the other hand, it is also true that "what belongs to a language game is a whole culture" (LC 8, #26), so that a word not imbedded in a way of life has no role in a language, no meaning. There must be a connection, there must be some continuity, but the connection may be loose and ill-defined.

It is not always easy to reconcile these two contrary tendencies. For instance, the fact that Wittgenstein accepts the water diviner's odd statement as meaningful, even before the new use is explained, may prove disturbing. Isn't meaning use "in the language"? But is the diviner's peculiar use part of any language? We might answer in this particular case that the word "feel" had a meaning, a regular use, in the *diviner's* language, as "unconscious" did in Freud's, though this answer would conflict with the widespread view that Wittgenstein ruled out all private languages. But the difficulty also offers an occasion to make an important distinction which I have ignored till now: the distinction between a word in a language (as when we ask, "What does the German word *gelb* mean?") and a word in a particular statement (or "token," as it is technically termed). We must beware of supposing exact equivalence in what can be said about the meaning of both one and the other. In this latter discussion regarding the need of some regularity, some connection, for there to be meaning, we have had in mind the meaning of words in particular statements, not their overall use in the language. If on some occasion the use of a word is unusual but not so completely disconnected from all previous practice as to render the statement unintelligible, we might grant that the statement makes sense and that therefore the word has some meaning in the statement, yet deny that this meaning, this use, is included in the word's use "in the language." It is not sufficiently common and characteristic for that. For by "language" we naturally understand an institution rather than individual speech acts.[38]

The following passage, though concerned with longer expressions than single words, suggests Wittgenstein's attitude:

The question whether "He can continue . . ." means the same as "He knows the formula" can be answered in several different ways: We can say "They don't mean the same, i.e., they are not in general used as synonyms as, e.g., the phrases 'I am well' and 'I am in good health' "; or we may say *"Under certain circumstances* 'He can continue . . .' means he knows the formula." Imagine the case of a language (somewhat analogous to 49) in which two forms of expression, two different sentences, are used to say that a person's legs are in working order. The one form of expression is exclusively used under circumstances when preparations are going on for an expedition, a walking tour, or the like; the other is used in cases when there is no question of such preparations. We shall here be doubtful whether to say the two sentences have the same meaning or different meanings. In any case the true state of affairs can only be seen when we look into the detail of the usage of our expressions.—And it is clear that if in our present case we should decide to say that the two expressions have different meanings, we shall certainly not be able to say that the difference is that the fact which makes the second sentence true is a different one from the fact which makes the first sentence true (BB 115).[39]

Here Wittgenstein was tempted to leave even certain established features of word use out of account when speaking of meaning. He did not do it. But the temptation suggests how reluctant he would be to include aspects of a word's employment on a particular occasion which are not *characteristic* of its use even "under certain circumstances."

The same viewpoint is suggested by Wittgenstein's advice to see what is learned when meaning is learned. The language games supplied for this purpose make no reference to bizarre or original uses of terms. Meaning is not taught by means of exceptions to the rule.[40] "The children are brought up to perform *these* actions, to use *these* words as they do so, and to react in *this* way to the words of others" (§ 6). This is how they learn the meaning of the words, their "use in the language."

The distinction becomes still clearer.

An important part of the training will consist in the teacher's pointing to the objects, directing the child's attention to them, and at the same time uttering a word. . . . This ostensive teaching of words can be said to establish an association between the word and the thing. But what does this mean? Well, it can mean various things; but one very likely thinks first of all that a picture of the object comes before the child's mind when it hears the word. But now, if this does happen—is it the purpose of the word?— Yes, it *can* be the purpose.—I can imagine such a use of words (of series of sounds). (Uttering a word is like striking a note on the keyboard of the imagination.) But in the language of § 2 it is *not* the purpose of the words to evoke images (It may, of course, be discovered that that helps to attain the actual purpose) (§ 6).

Here at the end the contrast is especially clear between the language and the utterance of someone using it; and between the word's role in the language—its meaning—and the occasional use that may be made of it (here the excitation of an image, as in a piece of impressionistic poetry).[41]

To sum up the argument now: the definition "meaning is rules of use" would tend to obscure the fact that the use *is* effective, that it *must* be effective if the rules are to be included in the meaning, or if there is to be any meaning at all, and that it may be effective and meaningful even though highly irregular. However, it cannot be completely irregular and still be called meaning,[42] especially when the meaning in question is that of the word in the language, as in Wittgenstein's definition.

C. *Abstractness*

The distinction between occasional uses and institutional use makes clear another reason meaning is no referent, no thing we can point to. The uses on this or that occasion are concrete, they have empirical features, whereas the institution is abstract. It is the way a word is used, not any individual employment of it. Stress on learning brings out the same point; for the meaning we learn, the meaning that is explained, is not a concrete instance of a word's use or any number of such instances; it is a general way of using the word. The words Wittgenstein substituted for "use" make the same point. Whereas the word "use" may be taken to refer to actual applications, the abstract (that is, referent-less) nature of meaning is made plain by the terms "role," "function," and "grammar."

Even in particular instances, a word's "role" cannot be identified with any particulars of the situation. When we talk about grammar, meaning, "We are talking about the spatial and temporal phenomenon of language, not about some non-spatial, non-temporal phantasm. But we talk about it as we do about the pieces in chess when we are stating the rules of the game, not describing their physical properties" (§ 108). As for these rules of the game, which we learn when we learn meaning, "A rule *qua* rule is detached, it stands as it were alone in its glory; although what gives it importance is the facts of daily experience" (FM 160).

D. *Openness Versus Obscurity*

One paradox of word use is its regular irregularity, its ordered freedom. Another has now to be investigated: the use of words, Wittgenstein said, is not at all evident; and yet it is open to view. Here we will meet the question of Wittgenstein's rumored behaviorism.

The complexity of even a single word's use has the important consequence that the grammar of words is not immediately evident (§ 664). Even when a word is extremely familiar to us, even when we use and understand it with ease,[43] it may well be that "the part the word plays in our life, and therewith the language-game in which we employ it, would be difficult to describe even in rough outline" (§ 156). "We talk, we utter words, and only *later* get a picture of their life" (PI 209).

"A main source of our failure to understand is that we do not *command a clear view* of the use of our words.—Our grammar is lacking in this sort of perspicuity" (§ 122). "What confuses us is the uniform appearance of words when we hear them spoken or meet them in script and print. For their application is not presented to us so clearly. Especially when we are doing philosophy!" (§ 11). Thus "a philosophical problem has the form: 'I don't know my way about'" (§ 123; FM 104).

> It is like looking into the cabin of a locomotive. We see handles all looking more or less alike. (Naturally, since they are all supposed to be handled.) But one is the handle of a crank which can be moved continuously (it regulates the opening of a valve); another is the handle of a switch, which has only two effective positions, it is either off or on; a third is the handle of a brake-lever, the harder one pulls on it, the harder it brakes; a fourth, the handle of a pump; it has an effect only so long as it is moved to and fro (§ 21).[44]

Though it lacks one sort of perspicuity, words' use has another (FM 104). A better comparison to bring out the sort of obviousness use has is Wittgenstein's remark: "I'm like a guide showing you how to find your way round London."[45] The streets and houses of London are in full view; yet we may not know our way around in them. Likewise, though the whole varied and complex use of a word is not present and evident on any one occasion of its use (BB 42), the use is not anything hidden or hard to get at (§ 435). "It is easy to get into that dead-end in philosophy, where one believes that the difficulty of the task consists in our having to describe phenomena that are hard to get hold of, the present experience that slips quickly by, or something of the kind" (§ 436), whereas "all the facts that concern us lie open before us" (BB 6). "Everything lies open to view" (§ 126), if we will only "take a *wider* look around" (FM 54).

In the *Tractatus*, of course, the meaning of the ultimate signs was nothing perceptible. Such preconceived ideas as that theory of meaning "can only be removed by turning our whole examination round" (§ 108). In the *Investigations*, "We are talking about the spatial and temporal phenomenon of language, not about some non-spatial, non-temporal phantasm[46] . . . we talk about it as we do about the pieces in chess when we are stating the rules of the game, not describing their physical properties" (§ 108).

Reference to language as a "spatial and temporal phenomenon" might suggest behaviorism. And indeed there are the makings of behaviorism in some of Wittgenstein's remarks, for instance in this comparison with chess. The indications might be developed as follows.

Mental acts or psychic phenomena do not enter into the rules of chess. To illustrate this, let us imagine that two people, perhaps with all the appropriate mental accompaniments of playing chess, go through a game of chess translated according to certain rules into a series of actions which we do not ordinarily associate with a game—say into yells and stamping of feet. They yell and stamp instead of playing the form of chess that we are used to; and this in such a way that their procedure is translatable by suitable rules into a game of chess. Should we still be inclined to say they were playing chess, or even that they were playing a game? And yet the only thing changed would be the externals of the game (§ 200).

"Words can in many ways be compared to chessmen," Wittgenstein says. And if we "think of the several ways of distinguishing different kinds of pieces in the game of chess (e.g., pawns and 'officers')" (BB 83-84), we surely are not thinking of what goes on in the minds of those who use them or of their private sensations (§§ 17, 563).

> But it is just the queer thing about *intention*, about the mental process, that the existence of a custom, of a technique, is not necessary to it. That, for example, it is imaginable that two people should play chess in a world in which otherwise no games existed; and even that they should begin a game of chess—and then be interrupted.
> But isn't chess defined by its rules? And how are these rules present in the mind of the person who is intending to play chess? (§ 205)

They are not. "An intention is embedded in its situation, in human customs and institutions. If the technique of the game of chess did not exist, I could not intend to play a game of chess. In so far as I do intend the construction of a sentence in advance, that is made possible by the fact that I can speak the language in question" (§ 337).[47]

The same is true of words. "Suppose we found a man who, speaking of how words felt to him, told us that 'if' and 'but' felt the same. . . . If he *used* the words 'if' and 'but' as we do, shouldn't we think he understood them as we do? One misjudges the psychological interest of the if-feeling if one regards it as the obvious correlate of a meaning" (PI 182).[48]

There is no doubt that in all this Wittgenstein is down-grading the non-external. Yet he does recognize an if-feeling (BB 79, PI 182). He does speak of there being an intention which is imbedded in a situation; there is something more than just the situation (BB 147, 181). He is aware of "appropriate mental accompaniments" during a game of chess (§ 200). And he sometimes includes such accompaniments in the "use" or "role" of words, for example here:

> Now what characterizes an order as such, or a description as such, or a question as such, etc., is—as we have said—the role which the utterance of these signs plays in the whole practice of the language. That is to say, whether a word of the language of our tribe is rightly translated into a word of the English language depends upon the role this word plays in the whole life of the tribe; the occasions on which it is used, the expressions of emotion by which it is generally accompanied, the ideas which it generally awakens or which prompt its saying, etc., etc. As an exercise ask yourself: in which cases would you say that a certain word uttered by the people of the tribe was a greeting; In which cases should we say it corresponded to our "Goodbye," in which to our "Hello"? In which cases would you say that a word of a foreign language corresponded to our "perhaps"?—to our expressions of doubt, trust, certainty? You will find that the justifications for calling something an expression of doubt, conviction, etc., largely, *though of course not wholly*, consist in descriptions of gestures, the play of facial expressions, and even the tone of voice (BB 102-103).[49]

It seems quite safe to pass from remarks like these to the conclusion that inner experiences, psychological events, might qualify for inclusion in meaning. Wittgenstein did not rule them out. For to say that they are included in meaning means merely, in the more appropriate formal mode of speech which Wittgenstein adopted in his definition, that in speaking of words' grammar, their regular use, we would need to speak of such experiences. And Wittgenstein often does mention inner experiences in the account he gives of words (e.g., BB 32, 103, 145; FM 100, #77; 124, #35).

Consider § 6. Wittgenstein there imagines a language in which the purpose of the words would be to bring pictures before one's mind. This would be their regular use. Of course the pictures would not be the meanings of the words. But they would have to be mentioned in an account of their meanings.[50]

Poetical language is somewhat similar to this imagined game. One hears poetical words in a particular sense (§ 534). The thought is not something one might express with other words, but only by these words in these positions (§ 531). Understanding such language means having the experiences Wittgenstein sometimes spoke of figuratively as "meanings" (§§ 530-532).

In everyday language we frequently talk about sensations. Or perhaps it would be better to say that sensation expressions (§§ 244-245) occur in our everyday talk. Saying that we "talk about" sensations would easily suggest that we describe or identify sensations as we describe or identify public objects, using the private sensations as adequate criteria in themselves of whether our statements are true or false (§§ 293, 304; PI 187). But in any case the sensations enter, in one way or another, into the account Wittgenstein gave of such expressions (§§ 244-245, 300; PI 197).

Wittgenstein's position on meaning and the inner can be summarized roughly thus. He was not opposed to the idea of psychological events' playing a part in language games, of their entering into an account of meanings. But they could not monopolize the account; they could never be equated with meaning. Nor could they play the part of adequate, inner criteria of truth; for from that idea famous and vexing problems would arise.[51] In general he felt that the inner had been given undue attention and prominence in the analysis of concepts.

E. *Vagueness*

The use of a word on a particular occasion may, as it were, have sharp contours; its use is quite clear and specific. But the same is not generally true of the "use" mentioned in Wittgenstein's definition of meaning. For the meaning of a word is general; it is the word's use "in the language" and not in this or that sentence alone. And within ordinary language there is great variety and freedom. The consequence is that in most cases concepts—words' uses in the language (§ 532)—have vague, ill-defined boundaries.[52] Some words would seem to have no boundaries at all. (§ 77)

Even if concepts had stable, rather definite boundaries, we probably could not indicate them very accurately; for most concepts are too complex, they make a "tangled impression" (PI 200). And the borders of use are not fixed once for all. No boundaries have been drawn for the use of most words (§ 68), not even by each individual for his own personal use (§ 79).[53] We might as well mark the seas' boundaries with a string as draw sharp lines round such concepts. And even in science, "what today counts as an observed concomitant of a phenomenon will tomorrow be used to define it" (§ 79).

This question of vagueness may be focused more sharply by considering what Ernest Gellner calls "the contrast theory of meaning," "to the effect that any term to be meaningful must allow at least for the possibility of something not being covered by it."[54]

> The argument runs: terms derive their meaning from the fact that there are or could be things which fall under them *and that there are others which do not*. "Apple" has meaning because some things are apples and others are not. "Unicorn" has meaning because something could satisfy the conditions for being a unicorn (though it so happens that nothing does), and there are conditions (in fact satisfied by everything) which warrant the non-application of the characteristic of unicornity.[55]

Gellner lists the contrast theory as one of "Four Pillars of Linguistic Philosophy,"[56] to which category Wittgenstein's philosophy certainly belongs. That Gellner attributes the doctrine to Wittgenstein is also indicated by his reference to "the picture associated with Wittgenstein's approach, of thought consisting of moves within *preexisting* games, and none of them allowing an abrogation of its contrast."[57]

There are indications of such a view in the *Tractatus*, where Wittgenstein insisted that all meaningful propositions have to divide logical space, that there must be conceivable situations in which a proposition would be false as well as situations in which it would be true (4.461, 4.462, 4.463). Moore reported similar views at a later date (M²294). However, only a limited range of utterances—statements of fact, descriptions—were considered on both occasions. So unless Gellner is adopting the arbitrary *Tractatus* viewpoint and limiting language to such utterances, the contrast theory of meaning cannot be inferred from Wittgenstein's remarks. That is, no general theory of meaning, such as Gellner's words indicate, can be derived from Wittgenstein's early treatment of just one sort of meaningful utterance.

Another limited contrast theory does briefly appear, however, in the *Blue Book*. Wittgenstein considers various cases in which words are used "in a typically metaphysical way, namely without an antithesis" (BB 46). For instance, popular scientists tell us "that the floor on which we stand is not solid, as it appears to common sense"; for "it has been discovered that the wood consists of particles filling space so thinly that it can almost be called empty" (BB 47). This is a misuse of language on their part. For now nothing is solid and the word has become useless.

In the *Brown Book* Wittgenstein studies another set of terms and distinguishes between their "transitive" and "intransitive" uses. The former involve contrast, the latter do not. Thus when someone says that the word "red" comes in a "peculiar," "particular" way, he does not intend any contrast. He does not mean, for instance, "It always comes quicker than the word 'two' when I'm counting coloured objects," or, "It always comes with a shock." The person has noted no such contrast between this and other words. Rather he has concentrated on, as it were stared at, his sensations (BB 158-159).

Wittgenstein's attitude here differs from that in the *Blue Book*. There he was dealing with words whose only use in ordinary language is a contrasting one. Here he recognizes that both sorts of use belong to the everyday employment of the terms in question (BB 161). Accordingly, his attitude is one of caution, not of condemnation. True, to the extent that they reveal and express the speaker's confused state of mind, non-contrasting expressions are of course undesirable. Thus when we speak of the "particular" way in which the word "red" comes, "we appear to ourselves to be on the verge of describing the way, whereas we aren't really opposing it to any other way. We are emphasizing, not comparing" (BB 159-160). But Wittgenstein's main point is that these uses exist in ordinary language, just as non-referring substantives do, just as odd-job words do; so we must become aware of these uses, too, if we are to avoid being philosophically misled by them. Wittgenstein warned about odd-job words and about non-referring substantives like "meaning." But he did not call them meaningless. The same is true of words used "intransitively."

The *Investigations* offer still less support for Gellner's interpretation. In fact the passage already cited (§ 77) would seem to rule out any such general theory. Wittgenstein may still have agreed with the *Blue Book* about the contrastless, non-descriptive use of words whose ordinary function is descriptive—words like "solid," "vagueness," and "flux" (BB 46). But his exhortation to bring words back from their metaphysical to their everyday use (§ 116) does not apply to ethical and aesthetical terms, to "beautiful" and "good." For he apparently thought that in their *everyday* use, these terms not only "merge without a hint of any outline," but are used without even ill-defined contrast: "Anything—and nothing—is right" (§ 77).

Admittedly, this view is difficult to reconcile with Wittgenstein's subsequent statement (§ 77) that such terms have a "family of meanings."

For use without any contrast whatsoever suggests the boundless variety of
the human race rather than the limited variations within one human
family. But however we propose to reconcile Wittgenstein's statements,
his analysis of ethical and aesthetical language was consistently so different
from his critical treatment of non-contrasting uses in the *Blue Book*,[58] that
there is little likelihood of a solution which favors Gellner's thesis.[59]

Furthermore, I find no indication in the *Investigations* that Wittgenstein changed his estimate of "intransitive" uses such as the *Brown Book*
studied. Even had Wittgenstein judged some slight contrast to be necessary in the use of ethical and aesthetical terms, these "intransitive" uses
would invalidate Gellner's general thesis.[60] Thus I do not see how a general contrast theory of meaning can be found in Wittgenstein's later
thought.

F. *Variety*

Still another characteristic feature of words' use is variety. The variety
of use is the main point of all the longer passages where Wittgenstein
compares words with tools. "Think of words," he said, "as instruments
characterized by their use, and then think of the use of a hammer, the
use of a chisel, the use of a square, of a glue pot, and of the glue" (BB
67). Then

> imagine someone's saying: "All tools serve to modify something. Thus the
> hammer modifies the position of the nail, the saw the shape of the board,
> and so on."—And what is modified by the rule, the glue-pot, the nails?—
> "Our knowledge of a thing's length, the temperature of the glue, and the
> solidity of the box."—Would anything be gained by this assimilation of
> expressions? (§ 14)

This is Wittgenstein's judgment on any attempt to characterize in any one
formula the way all words are used. "The functions of words are as diverse
as the functions of these objects"—hammer, pliers, saw, screw-driver, ruler,
glue pot, glue, nails, and screws (§ 11). This

> can be understood only if one understands that a great variety of games is
> played with the sentences of our language: Giving and obeying orders;
> asking questions and answering them; describing an event; telling a
> fictitious story; telling a joke; describing an immediate experience; making

conjectures about events in the physical world; making scientific hypotheses and theories; greeting someone, etc., etc. (BB 67-68).

Names, for instance, are just one class among many (§ 383). Yet "there is no one relation of name to object, but as many as there are uses of sounds or scribbles which we call names" (BB 173). Some are used as reminders (BB 173), some as orders (BB 172), some as exclamations (§ 27). Some are proper names, others are names for colors, materials, numbers, points of the compass, and so on, and used accordingly (§ 28). "We call very different things 'names'; the word 'name' is used to characterize many different kinds of use of a word, related to one another in many different ways" (§ 38). If it is so with just one class of words, what chance is there of assigning general traits for the use of all words, as was attempted in the *Tractatus*?

But besides this over-all diversity, besides this diversity within a single class of words, there is still further diversity within diversity. There is the diversity of the individual word.[61] "Composite" and "simple," for example, are both used "in an enormous number of different and differently related ways" (§ 47). There are some words with several clearly defined meanings. But there are also words of which one might say: "They are used in a thousand different ways which gradually merge into one another" (BB 28).

The result is a specific problem regarding the meaning of words, one which gradually merges into a problem already considered—the problem of missing connections—yet is distinct from it, in the ill-defined way Wittgenstein made so much of (FM 163, #5). Consider, for instance, the statement "There are three consecutive 7s in the development of π." In 1930 Wittgenstein couldn't make up his mind whether this made sense or not ($M^3$7-9). It might seem that we have here a case like that of trisecting an angle, or feeling water three feet down in the ground. That is, we might lump together all cases of undetermined sense. However, there is a considerable difference between the need to make a further, more precise connection of a familiar sort with existing usage, because that usage is so various, and the need to specify an entirely new connection with existing thought and practice. In both cases someone might say, "I don't know what you mean," but in one case an example or modifying phrase (e.g., "in the first thousand places") would solve his difficulty, whereas in the other a long explanation, à la Freud or the water diviner, would be required.

The question of precision has already been considered at some length in the preceding section, and the present question has to do with meaning in individual statements rather than meaning "in the language"; so I will not dwell on it, but merely point out that it is a new question, distinct from those already considered, and briefly indicate Wittgenstein's general position.

At first he said the statement about three 7s made no sense, then he said it did. This reversal is not surprising. For his initial judgment showed the influence of the Verification Principle and of the lingering *Tractatus* insistence on precision ($M^3$7-9), and both of these were on the way out. Thereafter Wittgenstein's characteristic approach in *this* sort of case was to point out the need for greater precision, when desirable, and the adequacy of imprecision when precision was not needed (§§ 79, 88), but not to brand an imprecise expression as senseless or nonsensical. He questioned the accuracy and depth of our understanding rather than the credentials of the term or statement in question. For instance:

> When one hears the mathematical axiom that such and such is possible, one assumes offhand that one knows what "being possible" means here; because this form of sentence is naturally familiar to us. We are not made aware how various the employment of the assertion ". . . is possible" is! And that is why it does not occur to us to ask about the special employment in this case. Lacking the slightest survey of the whole use, we are here quite unable to doubt that we understand the proposition (FM 114-115, #6).

Wittgenstein was all too well aware where the alternative approach led: the use of precision as a criterion of meaningfulness, as in the *Tractatus*, led to the conclusion that the expressions of ordinary language, which are the paradigms of meaning and sense, are meaningless (§ 70).

G. A "Family" Word?

Complexity, utility, regularity yet great freedom and consequent vagueness, obscurity and openness to view, variety—these are characteristic features of use in the definition, characteristic, though, somewhat in the manner of "family resemblances" (§ 67), like competition, skill, luck, and amusement in the case of the word "game." "By a family likeness is meant not a single similarity but the combinations of a group of repeatable characteristics taken any number at a time."[62] As I have already gone beyond Wittgenstein's explicit thought in singling out these characteristics of use, perhaps I should not push the comparison. But after such an enumeration as this Wittgenstein himself would certainly point out that many of the features of use that have been mentioned do not characterize all instances of what is referred to as "meaning." For instance, though most meanings are complex and vague, there are also words "with several clearly defined meanings" (BB 28). They "have certain regular functions, functions which can be easily described" (BB 44). Furthermore, though the use of words may be extremely free and varied and consequently quite obscure, in many of the new, scientific boroughs of language the streets are straight and regular and the houses uniform (§ 18). It is easy to see their layout; their grammar is not obscure.

However, it does not appear likely that Wittgenstein would have regarded any words' "use in the language" as either completely useless or entirely irregular. He certainly would have denied that it was "hidden." And changing to the formal mode of speech, as Wittgenstein did in his definition, does not obviously change this situation; it does not eliminate this hard core, as it would were the word "use" still under discussion, rather than "meaning." Let us consider the contrast.

In the material mode of speech Wittgenstein would say that a word's use in the language always has some utility and at least some degree of regularity. But as for the expression "use in the language," this might sometimes refer to utility alone and sometimes to regularity alone, according to the contexts. I have already pointed out such varying contexts in Wittgenstein's own discussions of use. However, I have found no contexts in his writings nor does Wittgenstein mention any customary contexts where reference to the "meaning" of a word would be reference to just the pattern of its use or just what it achieves. Even in interesting instances like § 41, PI 147 (note), § 545, § 556, and § 558, either the senses of "meaning" are not clearly limited to one aspect of use or they are not approved by Wittgenstein and recognized as standard, acceptable usage.

Because of this hard core of important characteristics, I would not venture to say that in Wittgenstein's opinion "meaning" has a family of meanings. In particular contexts it may. Thus if we speak of some particular word rather than of words and their meanings in general, and if the word is one with a family of meanings, in such a discussion the word "meaning" may have a family of meanings. We may speak of this meaning of the word and of that meaning, and the meanings of which we speak form a family. But the same would not be true in the discussion of some other sort of word. And even if all words were words of this sort, it would not follow that between various words or various types of words there is any family resemblance. Wittgenstein insisted on the great variety of word uses. "Assimilating the descriptions of the uses of words in this way cannot make the uses themselves any more like one another. For, as we see, they are absolutely unlike" (§ 10). So in his definition, which applies to all words, "meaning" is not a "family resemblance" word.[63]

III. Conclusion

The definition of meaning described in this chapter may be represented as the terminus of a long line of development stretching back to Frege's definition of meaning and to the view expressed in *Principles of Mathematics*. For Russell then, every word referred to something, and its referent was its meaning. Therefore the word "meaning" had as many referents as all other words put together. Now, in Wittgenstein's final view, though some words do refer, the word "meaning" has no referents whatsoever.

The *Tractatus* stood midway between these extremes. For one thing, only some words (real names) had referents, and these were their meanings. Again, the word "meaning" had as many referents as there were, but there were far fewer. Internal relations, for instance, were not something added to their terms, and general forms were mere possibilities.

There are ways of presenting the *Tractatus* views which make them seem much closer to the *Investigations* than to Frege and *The Principles of Mathematics*, rather than midway in between. For instance, it might truly be said that already in the *Tractatus*, had he been less "scientific" in his terminology, Wittgenstein might have said, "In a large class of cases the meaning of a word is its use in the language." The authors of *Principia Mathematica*, less careful about univocity, had already said something very similar. However, had Wittgenstein said this, both parts of his definition would have required an interpretation drastically different from the one given in the *Investigations*.

First, the large class of cases in the *Tractatus* would have been those cases in which the meanings of non-names were mentioned, for instance of logical particles. For the meanings of names were the objects they re-ferred to. The distinction of cases would thus have been based on a distinction between different sorts of words, whereas in the later works the meaning of all words is their use, the limitation on the extension of the definition coming not from a different class of words but from a different way of discussing the same words.

Secondly, the sort of "use" meant would have been very different—far more rigidly regular and precise, far less varied, and restricted to the sys-tem of words, to the relation of words with words. This last is the principal difference between the use of, say, an operation sign in the *Tractatus*, and the use or meaning of an ordinary word as analyzed in the *Investigations*. The operator was envisaged only in its relation to other signs, whereas "use" in the *Investigations* definition refers to a far larger context than the purely verbal one. Wittgenstein's view had broadened to include a whole new dimension. He now saw language not merely as part of an individual human organism (4.002), but as a "form of life," woven into the whole texture of social intercourse (§ 23), "as much part of our natural history as walking, eating, drinking, playing" (§ 25).

But early and late the important thing for Wittgenstein was a word's use: not a static entity in the mind, nor a static relation between word and thing, but what is done with the sign, its function. And yet under the in-fluence of Russell and Frege he defined meaning as a thing. As their in-fluence waned, his own viewpoint reached maturity and was given defini-tive expression in the definition of meaning as use.

Chapter V

THE DEFINITION'S WORTH

THE TIME HAS COME TO EVALUATE WITTGENSTEIN'S DEFINITION. THIS might be done in many ways. The way I have chosen, one which will, I think, permit me to say most of what should be said on the subject, is to consider the various criticisms that have been made of the definition, whether implicity or explicitly. Here are some main lines which criticism of Wittgenstein's definition might take and has taken.

First it might be claimed that there are important, primary senses of the word "meaning" in which the meaning of a word is not its use, whereas Wittgenstein seemed to envisage only this primary sense of the word. So his definition would have to be enlarged; it is too narrow.

Second, it might be objected that further distinctions are required, either because discussion of a word's use is not always discussion of its meaning, so that the sort of use which is called meaning should be more precisely specified, and distinguished from the other (that is, the definition should be narrowed); or simply because such a general definition, though accurate enough, is still too vague and imprecise.

A more basic misgiving about the definition than doubt about its accuracy would be doubt about its legitimacy. It may be correct, the objection would go, but we cannot know whether it is until it is established by better methods than those Wittgenstein employed.

If Wittgenstein's method can be upheld, in this case at least, it may be through recourse to such arguments and distinctions as make his definition appear quite banal. Squeezed this way and that by critics, it may end up looking the way the principle of verification did—uninteresting, unimportant.

Objections of these sorts will be considered in the order given. But before considering any of these difficulties, I must make one premise clear. Till now I have imitated Wittgenstein in paying little attention to the fact that "meaning" is an English word and *Bedeutung* a German word, and that their uses in the two languages may not be precisely similar. The similarity of what Wittgenstein said about "meaning" in the *Blue and Brown Books* with what he said about *Bedeutung* in the *Investigations* would seem to indicate that Wittgenstein considered their uses to be roughly the same. I think he would have been ready to say about "meaning" whatever he said about *Bedeutung* in the *Investigations*. This is my excuse for having ignored the bothersome distinction this far. But now I have only these alternatives: to answer every objection twice, once for "meaning" and once for *Bedeutung*, since in a critical examination of what Wittgenstein said the interlinguistic equivalence of "meaning" and *Bedeutung* cannot be presupposed; or to simply drop one of the two terms.

I have chosen the latter alternative, for these reasons. First, I do not have the sort of native familiarity with German which would be required in such a close study of usage. Second, Wittgenstein's definition has had far greater impact on Anglo-Saxon philosophy than on Germanic, so that an appraisal of the definition with regard to "meaning" (rather than *Bedeutung*) is at the same time an appraisal of much in present-day philosophy, whereas the same would not be true in the same way of an evaluation of the definition in its German form. Finally, far more has been written about the English form than about the German, with the result that only in considering "meaning" could I follow the procedure which seems to me most profitable—to evaluate Wittgenstein's definition by studying objections actually made against it, rather than all the objections I might think up on my own.

I. Too Narrow?

The criticism of Wittgenstein's definition by L. Jonathan Cohen in *The Diversity of Meaning*[1] is largely implicit; Wittgenstein is meant more often than he is named. But the criticism is the fullest I have come across; so I will spend some time on it. In the following general remark, with which the book opens, Cohen can hardly have intended to exclude Wittgenstein:

> . . . in their general theories about the meaning of words philosophers have tended to treat the concept of linguistic meaning as essentially homogeneous. Meanings, they have said, are subsistent entities, or the causes and effects of speech, as if there is some single, nuclear pattern of discourse about meaning that constitutes the only proper subject-matter for philosophers analysing

the concept of linguistic meaning. No relation theory of meaning will do, they have said, or any adequate theory must be a contextual one, as if there is just one philosophical problem of meaning, not many.

The main destructive purpose of what follows is to show that this has been a mistake, and one of mark.[2]

Certainly he believes that Wittgenstein, along with others whose theories he describes, has overlooked important contexts "in which to ask for the meaning of a word is not to ask in any way at all for its use—neither for a rule of use nor for a regularity of use."[3]

The principal contexts Cohen has in mind are discussions of what he calls "utterance-words" and "saying-words." "However much the functions of language-words and culture-words are illuminated by Wittgenstein's advice to ask for the use rather than the meaning, the position is very different with utterance-words and saying-words."[4]

Examples (my own) will suggest sufficiently for the moment what Cohen means by these four expressions:

Language-word: "liberty" in the English language.[5]

Utterance-word: "liberty" in the Declaration of Independence (the word, not merely the token).[6]

Culture-word: the concept of liberty in Western civilization, instantiated by "liberty" in the Declaration of Independence.[7]

Saying-word: "absence of constraint" in book X as an instance of the "culture-word" liberty.[8]

It may seem strange that I give a concept and a phrase as examples of a culture-*word* and a saying-*word*. But it seems strange to me that Cohen should extend the term "word" to something which "need have no morphological unity or continuity from one place or period to another," and which "is individuated by meaning, not by form"[9]; and just as strange that he should extend it to any expression, no matter of how many words it is composed,[10] which instantiates what he calls a culture-word. In any case, it is not reasonable to object against Wittgenstein's definition, meant for ordinary words, that it does not fit such "words" as these, invented of late by Cohen or other linguists.[11]

As for utterance-words, Cohen shows without difficulty that their meanings are neither rules nor regularities. There is, for instance, no linguistic rule lurking in the Declaration of Independence, telling us how the word is to be used and thereby giving it its meaning. And "where we do speak about the use of an utterance-word or a saying-word, the use does not constitute one of the standing speech-habits that go to make up a language. It is normally just a single event."[12]

Cohen then makes a number of suggestions in behalf of Wittgenstein's view (never clearly stated); but none of them is much to the point. Each shows that the meaning of an utterance-word cannot be equated with this or that sort of use—not with an occasional use, nor with the use of the language word, nor with the use of the language word at the period in question. One is reminded of Wittgenstein's apt simile (BB 125, § 164); Cohen plucks off the leaves of the artichoke one by one and never finds the artichoke—use. He says nothing to show that the meaning of an utterance-word is not the way it is used—use, *tout court*.

Now a second, distinct objection, having to do with language-words as well as utterance-words: "To claim one knows the meaning of a foreign word is very often to claim that one knows in general how to translate it."[13] So one might give "translation" as the equivalent of "meaning" in such contexts, or perhaps "rules of translation," as Cohen suggests.

A concrete case from my own experience may help to illustrate Cohen's point and to decide on its validity. A Spanish friend of mine asked me in French whether I knew the meaning of a certain not-too-familiar Latin word. I said I did. He replied, "What is it?" I groped for an answer, and after a moment he said, "Oh, I see, you didn't know it after all." I rather resented this reply, for I knew the meaning of this Latin word as well as I knew the meaning of many English words without knowing an English (or French) equivalent for them. I just didn't know a French equivalent for the Latin term, or whether there was one, though no doubt there was.

Now who was right, my friend or I? (That is, Cohen or Wittgenstein?) When my friend asked for the meaning and I couldn't give it to him, was this sure evidence that I didn't know the meaning in the sense of "know the meaning" established by the context of our conversation? Or did it merely show my inablity to communicate something I knew? My impression at the time was that he had simply overlooked the language difficulty, taking it for granted that if I knew the meaning I could communicate it in French by means of a French expression with the same meaning. And reflecting on the situation now, I think that this instinctive reaction was well founded. For suppose there had been no French equivalent (or English, for that matter). Suppose that the expression had been one of those expressions which are so proper to a given language that we do not translate them but bring them into our language as they are. In that case what would I have done? How would I have answered? I would have told my friend that there was no equivalent in French and would have proceeded to explain the meaning in a more tedious way, giving examples and suggesting circumstances in which the term might be used. Giving an equivalent term is the usual way of giving the meaning, and a much handier way,[14] but it is not the meaning. The translation or the rules for translating are not the meaning. To say that the translation itself is the meaning of the foreign term would be like saying that the explanation, in the case of an untranslatable foreign term, is the meaning of the term. To say that the rules of translation are the meaning of the foreign term would be like saying that some set of prescriptions on how to give the explanation is the meaning of an untranslatable foreign term. I doubt that anyone would want to assert either equivalence.

I might make the same point in another way. If someone asked for the meaning of *chat*, I would tell him, "It means 'cat.'" If someone asked for the meaning of *esprit de corps*, I would tell him, "It has no English equivalent." That is, there is (to my knowledge) no English translation (and therefore no rules for translating this term into English). Yet even in this context, the sort Cohen has in mind, I would not answer, "It has no meaning of the sort you are talking about." Of course it does; but I will have a harder time than usual teaching him what the meaning is— that is, how the expression is used.

The following objection by M. J. Charlesworth is briefer, but probably more important, since it seems to be based on a very common confusion, one which Wittgenstein himself did not avoid:

> To put this in another way: meaning cannot be defined, as Wittgenstein pretends in the *Investigations,* in terms of linguistic use, as though to mean something were merely to use words in certain ways. For what makes the *use* of certain symbols a linguistic use is precisely that they are used to mean or to *signify* something beyond themselves. In other words, linguistic use is defined in terms of meaning, so that meaning cannot be defined in terms of linguistic use.[15]

It is difficult to see how these several statements form a coherent argument. At the start Charlesworth seems to imply that "linguistic use" is too narrow to be equated with meaning. Then in the second statement he argues that "linguistic use" is really very comprehensive—and apparently includes what Wittgenstein mistakenly omitted in his definition of meaning. That is, the first sentence seems to imply that the definition fails because linguistic use is so narrow, and the second sentence seems to imply just the opposite. And the third sentence adds to the confusion by implying the strange and unacceptable principle that two terms cannot be used in one another's definitions.

What, then, is Charlesworth's difficulty? I venture the guess that it is contained in those words: "as though to mean something were merely to use words in certain ways." He is arguing that for a person to mean what he says is something more than merely to use words in a certain way. And this something more should be included in the definition of meaning. But in the definition of what meaning? The person's meaning, or the words' meaning?

An example may serve to clarify Charlesworth's objection, as I understand it, and my answer. Somebody mutters darkly, "There are people in the government who need watching," and a bystander comments, "He means the Secretary of State." Obviously his words are not *used* to refer to the Secretary of State; yet that is who was *meant*. So use is not meaning. So goes the argument. However, it is the mutterer who "meant" a particular member of the government, not his words. And this shows how mistaken it is to confuse meaning words with the meaning of words, or what people mean with what their words mean.[16]

II. Too Broad?

Wittgenstein's definition is also criticized for taking in too much. Jason Xenakis, for instance,[17] who would like to say that "the meaning of a word is the rule(s) governing its use,"[18] therefore finds mere "use" too broad a definition. He suggests that we might make up a name without giving it a meaning, and concludes: "Moral: contrast between the grammar of 'use' and 'meaning.' "[19]

But of course Wittgenstein did not say that "meaning" and "use" have the same grammar, even when the use and the meaning we are discussing are the use and meaning of words. What he *said* is that a word's meaning —*if* it has one, or is said to have one—is its use. This does not imply that every sound that serves as a sign also has a meaning.[20] So what Wittgenstein *said* is quite correct, at least in this respect.

If, however, we distinguish between the verbal correctness of Wittgenstein's definition and his own application of it, we find that Wittgenstein, though not obliged to do so by anything he said about meaning, did consider meaning and use to be convertible and coextensive to this extent, that all signs with a use, including proper names, he spoke of as having meaning. So in practice he did overextend the definition, taking in verbal uses which should not be included under "meaning." Proper names do have a use, but they are not generally said to have meaning (except by philosophers like Russell and the author of the *Tractatus*). When a proper name does have meaning, that is because it is something more than a mere proper name. And if we ask for the meaning of a name, it is either for this reason, or because we do not know the word is a proper name.[21]

Because Wittgenstein's extension of "meaning" to proper names is mistaken, a criticism by Ernest Gellner misses its mark. Gellner supposes a case of mistaken identity in which a proper name is applied to the wrong person by the whole population.[22] According to Gellner, this supposition shows the error of Wittgenstein's definition. For in his supposition, the meaning of the name would differ from its current use. However, Gellner too has overlooked the fact that a proper name (as such) has no meaning.

He tries again, though, with a word that is not a proper name. He supposes that someone regularly refers to a certain house as "the fifth house in our street," when it is really the sixth. This shows, Gellner argues, that the meaning of "fifth" is not its use; for it is here being used to designate the sixth house.[23]

Wittgenstein's answer to this objection is clear enough. One man's (mis)use of a word does not change its use *in the language*, and it is this which Wittgenstein identified as the meaning of the word.[24] The same distinction would probably answer some brief and not very clear objections by M. J. Charlesworth,[25] L. J. Cohen,[26] M. T. Antonelli,[27] and P. F. Strawson.[28]

Jason Xenakis is quite aware of the distinction Wittgenstein made[29] when he objects[30] that "naming, referring, asserting, describing, prescribing, evincing, expressing, exclaiming, and consequently truth-value, consistency-value, and 'emotive-value' are all functions of the (contextual) *use* of X (words, sentences, or whatnot) and have no direct relevance to the *meaning* of X." He does not answer Wittgenstein's arguments to the contrary, which seem to me adequate. I suspect that Xenakis has been misled by this fact, that such functions are not directly relevant (*de facto*, in our language) to the differences between meanings, nor conseqeuntly to synonymity, ambiguity, univocity, definition, and so on. Practically any word can be used in an expression which names, refers, asserts, describes, and so on. We can take these familiar functions for granted (§ 10). But this does not mean they are irrelevant to meaning, or that they do not constitute part of what we mean by "meaning." Books, magazines, and newspapers are not distinguished from one another, nor reference books from textbooks, by the fact that they are all made of paper, nor would we think to mention this fact when explaining to a foreigner the differences between them. But they are made of paper for all that.

I suspect that J. O. Wisdom should be answered in similar fashion when he complains: "the use of the word 'meaning' has a certain definiteness that the phrase 'the use of' has not. 'Meaning' in a lot of contexts stands for the defining characteristics, at least where there are any, and it does not stand for derivative properties. As the phrase 'the use of' is now used this distinction is completely lost."[31]

Here the "derivative properties" are probably the functions and other properties of which Xenakis speaks. For instance, because (in Wisdom's view) the meaning of a word includes such and such characteristics, it can be used to *describe* such and such things. The describing function is a derivative property. When he speaks of contexts in which "meaning" "stands for the defining characteristics," no doubt he is thinking of contexts such as Xenakis probably had in mind, for instance definitions. Apparently when Wisdom hears a statement like " 'Calumet' means 'a highly ornamented ceremonial Amerindian pipe,' " he takes the listed "characteristics" to be the "meaning" of the word "calumet," overlooking entirely the *use-value* of the words. Money has changed hands, and he took it for pieces of paper. If each of these words did not have the potentialities for describing, referring, naming, and so on that it does have, this transaction could not have taken place. There would have been no equivalence between "calumet" and the words exchanged for it, just as a dollar bill would not be "worth" a hundred cents if suddenly only bills were accepted by banks, or exchangeable for services.

It is probably no accident that Wisdom's colleague in London, Professor Findlay, the most outspoken critic of Wittgenstein's definition, criticizes it for much the same reasons. Addressing the Aristotelian Society in 1961, he said:

The reason why it is absurd to tell us not to attend to the meaning of expressions but to concentrate on their use, is perfectly simple: it is that the notion of use, as it ordinarily exists and is used, presupposes the notion of meaning (in its central and paradigmatic sense), and that it cannot therefore be used to elucidate the latter, and much less to replace or to do duty for it.[32] The notion of use is a *wider* notion than the paradigmatic notion of meaning: it covers many other things beside the meaning of an expression, but the meaning-function in its paradigmatic sense is certainly *one* of the things it covers, and it is not possible to give a clear account of use without presupposing this function.[33]

In this address Findlay did not make clear what he thought the paradigmatic sense of "meaning" to be nor the reasons for his view. An earlier paper is somewhat clearer on these points.[34] The "indispensable, ordinary sense" of the word "meaning," overlaid by definitions like Wittgenstein's,[35] he characterizes thus:

Of the meaning of an expression I shall say nothing more enlightening than that it is the "objective scope" of the expression, that it is all those "aspects" of a possible object or situation, or of possible objects or situations, which the use of the expression is intended to bring to mind. In saying this I take issue with those who have held it to be *wholly* misleading to treat the meaning of an expression as in some sense an *object* connected with it or corresponding to it: this is, in a sense, exactly what it is. While we might, on the analogy of other gerundival words, have used the word "meaning" to stand for the act or function of meaning, we in fact use it to stand for *what* an expression means, in other words for the "object" of the function of meaning, or at least, to use Professor Ayer's term, its accusative. But what an expression means is never, in any ordinary context or situation, the object to which it *refers,* but only at best an abstract aspect or segment of the latter.[36]

Findlay's argument, suggested already in this statement of his view, might be arranged syllogistically:

The meaning of an expression is what the expression means.

But what an expression means is the objects, aspects, actions, or what-not mentioned in the definiens expression of a definition.

So these are the meaning of the expression.

That is, his reasoning is clearly that which I read into Wisdom's remarks.[37] For Findlay the meaning of the word "calumet" is all those characteristics listed in the definition. To make this clear he would refrain from putting the definiens in quotation marks. Quotation marks would suggest that the meaning is the definiens expression, that the expression is being mentioned, whereas it is merely being used to refer to the aspects which are the meaning of the expression being defined.

If it were true that the definiens expression must either be mentioned or be used to mention, Findlay's conclusion would follow; for he is right in saying that the definiens expression is not referred to as the meaning of the definiendum. However, as Max Black has shown,[38] the accusative of a meaning formula designates nothing, or rather, does not designate at all.[39] It is more in the nature of a sample; the meaning of an unknown term is illustrated by means of another expression which has (roughly) the same use. Any expression would do as a sample if it illustrated this same use.

Thus Findlay's minor premise is unacceptable; what an expression means is not aspects supposedly mentioned in its definition. Findlay's major, too, (the statement that the meaning of an expression is what it means) needs attention.

From the fact that the definiens expression of a definition does not mention anything, Black rightly concludes that the verb "means" in a defining formula does not designate a relation between two things—the expression defined and its "meaning." The "act or function of meaning," of which Fidlay speaks, is a myth. So if we accept his statement that the meaning of an expression is what the expression means, we should not understand the words "what the expression means" in the sense of "that which the expression means"—the thing to which it has this relation—but rather as what in Latin grammar is called an indirect question. Thus if one learns and thereafter knows what a word means, this is not to become acquainted for the first time with some thing which the word "means" (a cat, say, or a color) but rather to become acquainted with what-the-word-means. Findlay would say that knowing the thing or aspect meant is knowing the essential thing, the word's meaning in the ordinary, indispensable, paradigmatic sense of "meaning." But, as Black's arguments show (and Wittgenstein's), objects or aspects of objects are not meanings in *any* ordinary sense of the word "meaning."

For quite different reasons, F. Waismann also thought Wittgenstein's definition too broad:

Incidentally, the fact that one can perfectly well know "what time is" without knowing all the idioms of the language is a pointer which suggests that all is not well with the doctrine that "the meaning of a word is the way in which it is used." Indeed, if that was correct, it would only be natural to expect that the adding of *any* new phrase, when it occurs for the first time, such as "time is money," alters something in the meaning of that word: which is obviously far from the truth. Ask yourself whether you are prepared to say that in learning what a number is one has also to learn the use of such phrases as "a number of people," "a small number," "a round number," etc.? Would it be right to say that, if a child is unfamiliar with such expressions, he does not know what a number is? Such examples should make us hesitate to accept the formula "meaning = use."[40]

I will pass over the mistaken implication of the first sentence, that meaning is equivalent to thing referred to, and come to Waismann's two objections, which are independent of this error. It is not difficult to find questions and objections parallel to his which show the unreasonableness of his criticisms. For instance: "Have you ever seen New York? What, you haven't seen all its streets and all its houses? Then you haven't seen New York!" One might prove in this way that New York does not consist of thousands of houses and hundreds of streets. Just as a person who knows, learns, or understands the meaning of a word does not know, learn, or understand all its possible uses, so a person who lives in, visits, sees, remembers, or despises New York does not live in, visit, see, remember, or despise everything in it. So apparently we should conclude that neither is meaning to be identified with use, nor is New York to be identified with the people, streets, parks, and skyscrapers in it! Such a conclusion seems sufficient refutation of Waismann's first objection. As for the constant, gradual changes in usage, such changes do not prevent us from speaking of the United States as the same country from day to day, despite the turnover in its population, nor from calling the Atlantic the same ocean, despite the turnover in its waters. In general, we do not speak as Waismann seems to suppose we do. His objections against Wittgenstein's definition would be valid only if the word "meaning" belonged to a language very different from ours, with standards of precision much more severe—impossibly so.

Samuel Issman's criticism seems to suffer from much the same weakness. "It is evident," he says, "that it would be foolhardy in an interpretative situation to replace 'The use of A is identical with the use of B' by 'A means B.' The first has a descriptive function, the second has an entirely different function."[41] Issman seems to base this distinction on the way definitions are given and on the implicit supposition that synonymity is the relation expressed in definitions. Now in a great many cases those giving a definition do not pretend to know the whole usage of the definiens and definiendum, nor therefore do they mean to assert any equivalence of usage. Rather, adapting themselves to the needs and the cultural level of the one to whom they are giving the definition, they employ words which have only roughly the same use.[42] So Issman's objection is basically the same as Waismann's. It is as though he were to say, "Very often when people say that one thing is as long as another, they have not measured the objects, nor do they mean to say that, if measured, the objects would turn out to be exactly the same length; so it would be foolhardy to identify the 'length' of which they speak with that which might be measured." Of course the correct conclusion in both cases is not that people are talking about something different but that they are applying different standards of exactness.[43]

A difficulty somewhat similar to Waismann's and to Issman's is raised by George Pitcher: ". . . if someone tells me (a non-Latin-speaker) that 'ultus' means revenge in Latin,[44] I thereby know the meaning of that word, but I have no idea how or when to use it."[45] Even here, where the objection is more serious, it seems legitimate to answer that though a non-Latin-speaker could not use the word "*ultus*" in any Latin sentence and therefore his knowledge of the word's use is, to say the least, not exhaustive, nevertheless in being given its rough equivalence with the English word "revenge" he is told quite a lot about its use. The meaning he is told is this much of its use.

A comparison will suggest the reasonableness of such a defense, even when so much of the word's use is left out of the meaning communicated. If, on another occasion, just one meaning out of many were given and if it were asserted that the meaning taught was use, few would object that it could not be, since large areas of the word's use were not mentioned. For instance, if someone told a child, " 'Gravity' means seriousness," he would be leaving out much of the word's use, but this would be no argument against the identification of meaning with use. For no one would claim that the *whole* meaning of the word "gravity" is given in such a definition.

Pitcher's objection implies that if meaning is use and a definition gives the meaning, it must give *all* the use. But this is not so. For it need not give all the meaning. I believe that an attempt to say just what is communicated in such a definition of *"ultus"* would have revealed that even when a definition does not give the whole meaning of a word, what it does give is nevertheless the word's use in the language—this use or that use, or just so much of it, but still use.

In the case he mentions, the noun use is communicated. If Latin did not have parts of speech roughly equivalent in their use to our English nouns, and if *"ultus"* were not such a word, with such a use, and if it were not used in roughly the same way as our noun "revenge," with a similar referent, then the definition Pitcher mentions would not be accurate. It would not give an accurate impression of the word's *use*.

To see more clearly the validity of this defense, consider a slight variant on Pitcher's definition: "The Latin word '*ultus*' means to revenge." Why did Pitcher leave out the word "to"? Isn't it because *"ultus"* is a Latin *noun*? Revenge and the act of revenging amount to the same thing. But noun use and verb use do not. What is given in the definition is a *verbal* equivalence, not a real equivalence. And of course this does not mean that the Latin and English words look or sound alike. The similarity indicated by the definition is similarity of use.

In his criticism of Wittgenstein's definition, Pitcher also makes some of the objections already considered in this section, but in a manner which reveals rather clearly a basic presupposition of considerable importance, one which Pitcher explicitly repudiates but which accounts for objections by him and others which would be unintelligible without it.

> Wittgenstein's identification, he says, is implausible on the face of it. In nonlinguistic areas, at any rate, things which have uses (e.g. tools, instruments) normally cannot sensibly be said to have meanings. Moreover, things which may sometimes have meanings—or (in case nothing non-linguistic can be said to *have* a meaning) things which may sometimes mean something—(e.g., black clouds on the horizon, footprints in the snow, the rising pitch of someone's voice) do not, except rarely, have uses. So one would not expect the meaning of a *word* to be the same thing as its use(s) in the language, and I think it can be shown that it is not.[46]

The facts cited here and later by Pitcher do show how mistaken it would be to assert the universal identity of meaning and use. But of course Wittgenstein did not identify meaning and use. He identified the meaning *of a word* with the use *of a word* in a language. So how do the facts cited make his definition look "implausible on the face of it"? For what reason would they make one "not expect the meaning of a *word* to be the same thing as its use(s) in the language"?

The only connection I can see is one Wittgenstein demolished in his study of general terms. If all meaning is of one sort and all use is of one sort, then the equivalence of meaning and use in any individual case would lead us to expect equivalence in all cases, and lack of equivalence in other cases would lead us to expect non-equivalence in any particular case, for instance the case of words and their meaning. But Wittgenstein has shown to Pitcher's satisfaction that everyday terms like "use" and "meaning" rarely designate invariant "essences." So isn't a situation such as the one Pitcher describes precisely what we should expect? Is it so strange if only *one* member in each of two families bears a close resemblance to the other?

So much, then, for the alleged over-extension of meaning in Wittgenstein's definition. The point is not proved.

III. Too Vague?

The commonest objection against Wittgenstein's definition Professor Findlay expresses thus, in his usual forceful manner: "I wish to make against it the not often raised objection that the use for which it bids us ask, is of all things the most obscure, the most veiled in philosophical mists, the most remote from detailed determination or application, in the wide range of philosophical concepts."[47] By the time Findlay spoke these words, objections like his were by no means uncommon. Nicola Abbagnano, for instance, considered it "one of the most singular deficiencies" in the *Investigations* that "among the many rich, detailed, and exhaustive grammatical analyses which they contain, there is no adequate analysis of the word 'use.'"[48] Complaints of this sort are not generally accompanied by a request that after distinctions are made, the definition of meaning be limited to just part of what has been distinguished, as was the case in some criticisms just considered. Greater precision is demanded for other reasons, not always specified.

Long before Findlay fired his broadside, Jason Xenakis remarked: "Since 'use' sometimes means (i) just use, 'employment,' and some other times (ii) 'correct use,' as well as (iii) 'established use' or 'usage,' and since no use-theorist seems to have noticed this ambiguity (indeed they seem to

vacillate between these uses of 'use'), their theory has rightly been criticized for unclarity and confusion. The word in my view of meaning
occurs in sense (i)."[49] Since Xenakis' "sense (i)" is generic and includes
the last two, more specific senses, as it stands this is not a request for a
narrower definition of meaning, but for missing distinctions.[50]

One "use-theorist," at least, had noticed distinctions such as Xenakis
mentioned, and others besides. Gilbert Ryle devoted a whole article to
making them.[51] He complained in particular that the use-utility[52] and
use-usage[53] distinctions had not been clearly marked. A. R. Louch would
have other distinctions pointed out: "Use and function are fundamentally
ambiguous terms. On some occasions they refer to intentions of the users
of expressions; on others to the reactions of auditors and readers of these
expressions."[54] N. Abbagnano complains that Wittgenstein's reduction of
meaning to use "obscures or overlooks an equally important aspect of
meaning: choice."[55] Both Ryle[56] and J. L. Evans[57] insist on the difference
between the use of words and the use of sentences (if they can be said to
have a use). P. L. Heath would like a neat rule to indicate when words
have meaning and when they don't; neither Wittgenstein's vague definition nor his interminable enumeration of different uses supplies such a
rule.[58] Only confusion can result, he complains, "when syntactical, seman-
tical, social, and other so-called 'rules' are all amalgamated together under
the monistic heading of 'use.'" In particuar, Wittgenstein's "attempt to
reconcile the abstract provisions of use = custom with the concrete diversity of use = employment" results in "a peculiar ambivalence between
'democratic' and 'totalitarian' views of language."[59] J. W. N. Watkins
complains that "loose talk about the meaning of a word being its use
tends to blur the old distinction between connotation and denotation."[60]
Each one has his own way to cut the pie.

Similar requests are made regarding the comparisons with which Wittgenstein illustrated his definition. Katz and Fodor would like to know
"the respects in which talking a language is neither like baking a cake,
nor like playing a game or dancing a dance."[61] L. J. Cohen would like to
see differences pointed out between the use of words and the use of tools,
for instance that in the case of words "we ourselves are both manufac-
turers and users of them at one and the same time."[62] M. J. Charlesworth
adds that "the use of a tool is to some extent dictated by the structure of
the tool itself, but words or expressions in themselves have no use in this
way; it is we who give them a use."[63] Wittgenstein should have made

these distinctions, and didn't. He should have specified more precisely how a *word* is used.

The three writers on Wittgenstein who have made criticisms of Wittgenstein's definition in conversation with me had the same objection to make: Wittgenstein should have supplied some missing distinctions. His definition does not have that "total clarity" which he promised (§ 133). One of the critics agreed to this summary of his objection: In the *Blue Book* Wittgenstein said that "meaning" is an "odd-job" word (BB 43-44), but he never told us then or later precisely what its odd jobs were. He merely told us it was a name for jobs.

If Wittgenstein can be justified against all these criticisms, it is only in the way Strawson suggests:

> The fact that Wittgenstein is content to leave this central notion of use so vague is a manifestation of his reluctance to make distinctions and classifications which are not of direct assistance to the fly in the flybottle (309). Underlying this reluctance is a general, and debatable, doctrine of the nature of philosophy: to which I shall refer later."[64]

What Strawson says is true. However, his remarks might easily suggest that if Wittgenstein's doctrine of the purely negative, thereapeutic role of philosophy is rejected, then his definition will *ipso facto* be found wanting. This would be an illegitimate inference. For even though there is pretty universal agreement that philosophy has some positive work to do, it does not follow that *this* task, the filling out of Wittgenstein's definition, is philosophical work worth doing.

John Austin probably would not have considered it worth his while, nor would his faithful followers at Oxford. For Oxonians too are more interested in the objects of discourse than they are in the words of discourse. And even their strictly conceptual interests are not of the sort to lead them in this direction. The attempt to map a single concept, to determine in detail the boundaries and complex ramifications of a single word's use in the language differs in purpose and nature from the sort of inquiry exemplified in the work of Austin and his followers. Austin, like Wittgenstein, was interested in samples, not definitions. He was interested in differences within an area of inquiry rather than within the confines of a single concept. He did not ask, "What aberrations in actions are called 'defects'? What are the precise contours and contents of this concept?" but rather, "What are the various ways in which an action is defective, as indicated by the various expressions we use in making excuses?"[65] Thus, to make a long story short, if an Oxonian complains of the vagueness of Wittgenstein's definition, analysis of his complaint will probably show it to be directed against defining as an occupation rather than against the way in which Wittgenstein defined this term. The Oxonian prefers greater distinctness, but not in definitions. He would like to know, for instance, how use differs from utility, but not as a first step towards achieving a more precise definition of the word "meaning."

A person who insists on this further step would seem to be confusing philosophy with linguistics. For what philosophical purpose would be served by these further refinements of the definition? By specifying the grammar of "use" or the grammar of "meaning" in all the ways required by Wittgenstein's critics, would we learn something about language (the "world" to which this concept is applied) that we did not know already? I think it is clear we would not. Or if we did, there would have been a much easier way to make the same discoveries.

Let us consider just one proposed distinction, by way of example. If, after considering a wide variety of cases, we arrived at the conclusion that in many cases the "meaning"—"use" identity is an identity with *usage* and in many cases it is not, would this reveal to us the fact that there is such a thing as verbal usage—customary, established, regular, ordinary ways of using words? Or would it bring to light the fact that some word uses are customary and some are not? Obviously neither. Rather the *first step* in our investigation would be to consider cases of both sorts so as to determine whether the word "meaning" is applied to both sorts of use. The grammatical fact, the extension of "meaning," is what requires reflection and investigation, not the linguistic facts, customary and occasional use. As Wittgenstein said, such facts are familiar and open to view, whereas the contours of an individual concept like "meaning" are not nearly so obvious.

However, it is notorious how philosophers can stare past the nose on their face. Might not some absent-minded professor have his memory jogged by an investigation of this sort? But of what sort? By an investigation into the question whether "meaning" refers to both customary and non-customary use of words? No, for this question already contains the distinction he has supposedly overlooked. By an investigation into "meaning"? But how will that proceed, if there is no guiding question? Supposedly by his simply looking at language, at this part of the "world," by looking at lots of examples, considering many and varied cases. But of course he can do this without bothering about any final definitions and distinctions. He will notice the fact of usage long before he maps the grammar of "meaning." And the same is true of the other facts mentioned —utility, denotation, intentions and reactions, differences between words and sentences, choice, and so on.

In at least this case, then, I opt for Wittgenstein's criteria of an adequate formulation. But I still haven't shown that Wittgenstein satisfied his own criteria. Would further distinctions give the definition greater therapeutic value? Is the definition Wittgenstein gave, together with his development of it, an adequate antidote for the problems it was meant to cure? Let us consider some of them.

There is the common and ancient practice of stripping off the leaves of the artichoke in search of the artichoke (BB 125, § 164), as when Socrates went in search of *the* thing which is knowledge (BB 20). The "Fido"-Fido theory is usually responsible for this sort of thing, and to cure that it is quite sufficient to point out that a word's meaning is no one object or essence, but its use.[66]

An elaborate form of the same error brought both Russell and Wittgenstein to an impasse: search as they might, they could find no suitable atomic meanings with which to construct an elementary proposition. This showed that something was wrong with their theory, but what? (M[3]1) The answer, in a nutshell: meanings are not simple objects, but use.

In William James the symptoms were acute and obvious. He was bound to have trouble with ordinary statements after defining the self as a collection of peculiar motions in the head or between the head and throat.[67] This absurdity came from trying to match words with feelings, and this could probably be cured by Wittgenstein's definition, without any further refinements' being required. The meaning of a word is not a feeling, a sensation, but its use.

Other errors and confusions that I have considered as possible evidence for the need of a more precise definition turn out to require no distinction which Wittgenstein's definition does not provide or none which a definition of word meaning might provide. So I cannot support the opposition case with any specific example of a philosophical problem whose cure the definition might have provided and did not.

However, a critic might insist, more generally, that any important distinction regarding the use of words *might* be overlooked and philosophical puzzlement result, and that a more detailed treatment of the concept would forestall such difficulty. Wittgenstein seems to have believed only in cure, not in prevention. If, however, we believe that in philosophy, too, an ounce of prevention is worth a pound of cure, we will not follow his example. A listing of different types of use such as Wittgenstein gave (BB 68, § 23) may suffice for a *Tractatus*-type error, but much present-day puzzlement might no doubt be averted by listing the principal *senses* of the word "use." "Use," like "meaning," is an odd-job word, and so more philosophically dangerous than an ordinary general term like "game." If, as Wittgenstein said, such odd-job words "cause most philosophical troubles" (BB 43-44), a definition of "meaning" is dangerously incomplete which merely substitutes for "meaning" another odd-job word, "use." Wittgenstein's definition is good as far as it goes, but it would have been better had it gone farther.

But how far? The suggestions of various critics indicate what an abundance of distinctions might conceivably be added. There are endless possible distinctions of this sort. So I would reply with Wittgenstein: "an explanation serves to remove or to avert a misunderstanding—one, that is, that would occur but for the explanation; not every one that I can imagine" (§ 87). Wittgenstein did not see any imminent error on the horizon which called for greater precision in his definition, or at least greater clarity in marking the distinctions already made. If his critics do see one, they should name it. They do not do so when they warn about, say, the difference between "usage" and "use."[68] If anybody has overlooked this distinction, the explanation to be given him is not a more precise definition of meaning, but an explanation of "usage" and "use."

Greater precision of another sort has also been called for: not distinctions between the different sorts of use or different senses of "use," but greater precision in specifying the "large class of cases." Arne Naess argues for this sort of descriptive definition:

> A formulation shall . . . be called a formulation expressing a descriptive definition of usage, if and only if it states that a certain expression, the so-called definiendum expression, is used strictly synonymous with a certain other expression, the so-called definiens expression, within a certain class of situations, the so-called field of application of the descriptive definition of usage.[69]

Using previous symbols a descriptive definition may be symbolized by

$$S\ (a\ p_i\ s_j,\ b\ p_m\ s_n)$$

where

a—definiendum expression

b—definiens expression

p_i s_j—intended field of application

p_m—person whose interpretation of "b" shall determine the interpretation of "a"

s_n—"standard" situation in which the person p_m shall be when making the "standard" interpretation of "b."[70]

Definitions seldom live up to such standards.

Thus looking up statements on "democracy" which seem to be intended to be descriptions of usage, the factors symbolized in S $(a\ p_i\ s_j,\ b\ p_m\ s_n)$ are very seldom expressed, and if they are, then only rather vaguely, making it difficult or impossible to test the hypotheses. Thus, for p_i "we" may be found, for s_j "where used correctly" or "hitherto," for "b," the definiens expression, some expressions the preciseness of which seems very questionable. Explicit indications about p_m and s_n are seldom found. More often, only "a" and "b" are indicated, e.g. as in formulas "a means b." The widely held contempt for "definitions" seems well motivated if it were turned against formulations intended to give descriptive definitions which have the defects indicated above and are not based on empirical research.[71]

Leaving the parting shot about empirical method for consideration in the following section, I will limit myself here to the complaint about preciseness. "For a large class of cases" is certainly a very vague indication. Wouldn't a Naessian definition be preferable? A full and, I think, adequate answer to this objection can be found in Wittgenstein's writings.

First there is the pragmatic reply. To demands for ever greater exactness —ideal exactness—Wittgenstein had a standard reply: "Has this exactness still got a function here: isn't the engine idling?" (§ 88). " 'Inexact' is really a reproach, and 'exact' is praise. And that is to say that what is inexact attains its goal less perfectly than what is more exact. Thus the point here is what we call 'the goal' " (§ 88).

Wittgenstein's goal is clear, and it is reached by his definition. If there are some primary uses of "meaning" not included in his "large class of cases," this doesn't matter for his purposes. For of course he not only recognized that in many cases meaning is use, but he knew what cases they were and that they were the ones causing philosophical trouble.[72] Sample contexts of this sort are mentioned in his discussions of language and the meaning of words. Because he saw no point in making a complete

inventory of existing usage, he qualified his definition in a vague manner
to allow not only for the secondary sense of "meaning," but also for
exceptions to the chief primary sense, if there were any; he said, "for a
large class of cases—though not for all."

It is doubtful, furthermore, whether a complete inventory could be
made. Not to mention the practical difficulties, there is also a theoretical
difficulty about undertaking to list all circumstances in which the equivalence holds. Since it is not likely that either the definiens expression or
the definiendum has any clear or stable field of application, neither being
a scientific expression, it is doubly doubtful whether the range of their
equivalence could be accurately defined. Only sample contexts can be
given, and Wittgenstein did that, in accordance with his general method:
"The work of the philosopher consists in assembling reminders for a
particular purpose" (§ 127). Something must now be said about this
method.

IV. UNPROVED?

"Your scruples are misunderstandings," Wittgenstein said. "Your questions refer to words; so I have to talk about words" (§ 120). And that is
what he did. But he did it as an amateur, without undertaking a scientific
study of language. And this might seem to cast doubt on his findings.
For, after all, any quirks of language which have fooled intelligent people
are likely to be fine points of language, about which other intelligent
people may make similar errors if they use the same amateur methods.
For sure results, scientific methods are necessary. So goes the objection.

In its most general form, the indictment takes in a great many contemporary philosophers. "The philosopher's main concern," says W.
Mays, [73] "apparently is the description of certain usages, distinguishing as
many as possible of the contexts, and then sorting the separate senses
under different headings in accordance with the function they fulfill."
"Such semantic studies," he continues,[74]

> are not . . . to be sniffed at. But they can perhaps be better done by the
> philologist who owing to his historical understanding of the language is
> perhaps better equipped for this sort of investigation than is the philosopher,
> and who is also not tempted to indulge in philosophical generalisations.[75]

Doubtless the Oxford brand of analyst is most directly in the line of fire when Mays speaks of making all possible distinctions; but Wittgenstein is sometimes included by name in similar indictments. For instance:

> One of the striking things about many of the recent speculations and theories concerning language by philosophers, more especially by logicians and semanticists, and about Wittgenstein's *Investigations* also, is the fact that they pay too little regard to . . . the findings of experts in the field of linguistics, but instead prefer to go their own empirical way, quite as if this resource were not available to them.
>
> Thus it is that some more or less arbitrary, more or less special, more or less implicit, presuppositions actually determine the results attained by such philosophers, logicians and semanticists from their quasi-empirical gropings into the workings, the modes of functioning of language.[76]

Irwin Lieb makes a similar broad criticism in his review of the *Investigations*:

> Wittgenstein also seems to suppose that differences between uses are simply apparent, that they can be noted by looking. He ends one paragraph, for example, by saying ". . . assimilating the descriptions of the uses of words in this way cannot make the uses themselves any more like one another. For, as we see, they are absolutely unalike" (§10). This is far too offhand to be an acceptable account of the recognition of differences, of important differences, and the possibilities which uses and different uses define.[77]

Arne Naess narrows the attack, picking out synonymity for attention:

> Argumentations in the analytical philosophy seldom lack empirical components, and among the empirical arguments or tacit presuppositions, those of synonymity or, more generally, distance in cognitive meaning between expressions, belong to the most frequent kinds. How is it in this situation possible to continue philosophical inquiry without making empirical investigations a genuine part of one's philosophical activity?[78]

We have already seen Naess's requirements for descriptive definitions,[79] and how signally Wittgenstein's definition of meaning failed to meet them. It is not surprising, then, that the Naessian criticism has been focused precisely on Wittgenstein's treatment of meaning. Hermann Wein objects that if Wittgenstein wished to "bring the question 'What is meaning?' down to earth" (BB 1), this "should mean that in reality the 'Philosophical Investigations' of Wittgenstein penetrate the domain of

empirical linguistic research or at least that some notice should be taken
of such research and of its importance for 'the concepts of meaning, of
understanding, of a proposition.' "[80]

Gilbert Ryle would seem to be both criticizing Wittgenstein's definition
and defending it against such charges when he says:

> The famous saying: "Don't ask for the meaning; ask for the use,"[81] might
> have been and I hope was a piece of advice to philosophers, and not to
> lexicographers or translators. It advised philosophers, I hope, when wrestling
> with some *aporia*, to switch their attention from the trouble-giving words in
> their dormancy as language-pieces or dictionary items to their utilisations in
> the actual sayings of things; from their general promises when on the shelf
> to their particular performances when at work; from their permanent pur-
> chasing-power while in the bank to the concrete marketing done yesterday
> morning with them.[82]

O. K. Bouwsma thinks, similarly, that the only safe way to take the
definition of meaning as use is to interpret it something like this: "If you
will say 'use' and write 'use' instead of 'meaning' in writing and speaking
of words, and can manage to think accordingly, that will help. Help what?
It will help you to rid yourself of the temptation to think of the meaning as
something in the dark which you cannot see very well."[83] It does not
matter much what word you use, provided the cure is worked. We may
understand Wittgenstein's definition "as one which is intended to help
us to a change in perspective. Once that change has come about, the sentence, like the ladder, is of no further use."[84]

A. Naess and S. Issman offer Wittgenstein a similar but slightly different avenue of escape. Besides descriptive definitions, which are empirical
hypotheses and so should be based on research, there are also explicative
definitions, whose whole purpose is practical. They help you to see what
a word refers to, and so long as they do that it does not matter much what
words are used.[85] Here the aim is positive understanding, and not merely
a change of method or viewpoint; but in either case the precise words
used need only be effective. They need not be synonymous with the term
defined.

None of these suggestions is an adequate defense of Wittgenstein's
procedure. For although he had such therapeutic, methodological, and
explicative intentions, he was aware to an unusual degree that "Essence is
expressed by grammar" (§ 371).[86] When he said what meaning *is*, he was

not abstracting from the way the defined and defining terms are *used*. In talking about meaning, he meant to speak the language of everyday (§ 120). In his remarks about meaning, he meant to bring the word "meaning" (and *Bedeutung*) back from its metaphysical use to its everyday use, to its use in the language-game which is its original home (§ 116).[87]

This concern for usage is evident in the phrasing of his definition. He did not say, "The meaning of a word is often its use in the language," but spoke instead of "a large class of cases . . . in which we employ the word 'meaning'" (§ 43). And by "we" he did not mean only himself and a few acquaintances. He meant that this was a prevalent use. So the question remains: How did he know it was prevalent? What was his evidence?

To this we might answer that his evidence was thirty years or so of speaking, hearing, reading, and writing English (and a much longer time for German, in which the *Investigations* were written). "For a native speaker to say, what, in ordinary circumstances, is said when, no . . . special information is needed or claimed. All that is needed is the truth of the proposition that a natural language is what native speakers of that language speak."[88] Someone who knows the language can give a *roughly* accurate definition.

Such a *result* has already been defended. But what of the method? A linguistic philosopher is likely to be far more acutely aware than the ordinary person of how words are used. With his special interests he is likely to be specially observant of various usages. Wittgenstein was. Even so, wouldn't it be better to produce *evidence* to back his assertions? Doesn't such a haphazard method of personal observation replace evidence with trust in the observer? And should we trust a single observer, no matter how observant? Would we do so in establishing any other scientific result?

Naess recognizes the practical impossibility of satisfactory research "in the field."[89] Studying usage only in books, conversations, television programs, and the like would be comparable to studying physical phenomena only as they occur naturally, without ever performing an experiment in a laboratory. If, for instance, we want to find the outer limits of any concept, we shall immediately run into borderline cases, and borderline cases are unusual cases. So it will be difficult enough finding one or two natural reactions to each borderline situation, and probably impossible to find a large sampling for even one borderline situation of a single concept. So if, for instance, we want to know whether people would call a rare chair-like object a "chair," our only recourse is to ask them.

This Naess does by means of carefully prepared questionnaires. This is his scientific method, the only sort that seems feasible. This is the sort of research some critics think Wittgenstein should have undertaken, or should have at least relied on. So what is to be said of it?

First, it seems to me that Naess, or rather those who answered his questionnaires, would inevitably draw some boundaries where none existed.[90] For if only contexts are suggested in which usage is uniform and well established (all English-speakers would call the thing I am sitting on a "chair"), the investigation has no evident interest or utility. If others are included, that means that people will have to *decide*; they will have no established usage to go by, none that they are acquainted with. So the result will not be a report on established usage, but on the reactions of these people to some unusual questions.

There are some special difficulties in using this method to determine synonymity, as Naess does. If we drew an odd-looking object and offered the choice of several names for it, those answering the questionnaire would be making decisions, drawing new boundaries. But at least the expressions would be familiar, and their decision would rest on some analogy with the ordinary use of the expression chosen. In the case of synonymity the situation would often be radically different. It is not merely that the defining combination of words may be quite unusual (e.g., "use in the language"), so that whereas in the example above the expressions were common and the application rare, here the expression is rare and the thing described perhaps quite common (e.g., the use of words). But no explicit equation of the defining and defined expressions occurs in common usage. Whereas we can observe whether people call three-legged seats "chairs" and base our reply on this observation when asked about the meaning of "chair," there is no sort of verbal scale in regular employment wherein we might observe expressions to be neatly balanced. Hebrew parallelism has gone out of style, and even in the Hebrew psalms exact equivalence is not guaranteed. We do not often hear a person say something, then try it over again with the change of just one word; and when we do, it is often a sign that the new word is *not* the equivalent of the first. Nor is our conversation full of definitions or lists of synonyms. Since words are not weighed out for us on scales, on what should our replies to questions about synonymity be based? Guesswork? The relation of Naess's questionnaires to actual usage appears more and more problematical. It seems that all we might conclude from them is that a particular group of people, when asked some rather strange questions, gave these answers.

For let us make a complete disjunction of possibilities:

A. The people interviewed simply *react* to the question, and any correlation between their unthinking reaction and the ordinary use of certain expressions in the question (or any others we care to consider) will have to be determined, if we consider it worth our while to do so, by a statistical examination of common usage. So if it is really common usage that interests us, why bother with the questionnaires? If we offered people colors to name, we might consider their reactions typical; for naming colors is a natural activity, which people acquire from their social milieu. But the same is not true of definitions.

B. The people are expected not merely to react, but to *decide* on synonymity, basing their answers on *knowledge*. Now this knowledge might in other cases be a simple recollection, for instance, that this sort of thing is commonly called a "chair." And if a person's memory was normally good, we would accept his reply as evidence of usage. But, once again, the case is different here; for, when a person is asked whether two expressions would have the same sense in a given context, he is not being asked simply to remember something (e.g., whether these two expressions are ordinarily called synonyms), but to make a rather complex judgment. And for this reason, it is not at all clear what information his answers give about common usage, or whether they give any.

Let us consider this difficulty more in detail, under the following headings:

1) The complexity of "sense," so that amateur answers are practically worthless.

2) The impossibility of reproducing actual speech situations by means of descriptions in a questionnaire.

3) The abstractness of the questionnaire situation, so that the criteria of "sameness" are not clear.

First, relying on the sort of critique made, in Chapter II, of unit meanings, I will suppose that sense, like meaning, is as complex as Wittgenstein said it is. To give useful answers, the people questioned should be aware of this to a degree most people are not. But even if they were

quite conscious of the difficulty of their task, is it likely that *their* answers
—their *impromptu* answers—would be better guides to usage than the
carefully considered conclusions of a Wittgenstein? Here it is quality that
counts, not quantity.

Even if mass, impromptu answers were roughly accurate indicators of
synonymity between words like "pay" and "salary," there would be special
objections against applying Naess's technique to a term like "meaning."
Let us suppose that the definiendum expression is "meaning" and the
definiens expression is "use in the language." We now choose as one
context the sentence "I don't know the . . . of that word" and ask whether,
according to the interpretation of those answering the questionnaire, definiendum and definiens would yield the same sense in this context. The
majority of people would be quite nonplussed by such a question, and
very little could be concluded from their answers. They make frequent
use of "meaning" and of "use" and of "language," but perhaps never in
their lives have they made such a statement as "I don't know the use
of that word in the language," whereas they have said, heard, or read
many times an expression such as, "I don't know the meaning of that
word." Of course this does not show that "meaning" and "use in the
language" would not be cognitively or pragmatically equivalent here.
There are a great many defining expressions which are hardly ever substituted for the definiendum, save by experts. And that is my point; the
opinion of one Wittgenstein is worth that of ten thousand teenagers when
it comes to answering a question such as this one.[91]

So that first ready answer ("Anyone can give a *roughly* accurate definition of common words"), even if it were generally true (which it isn't),
would not be true in this case. Cavell's words, which I quoted when giving
that answer, are quite accurate: expert knowledge is not required to
describe ordinary usage. But it quite often is in giving definitions.[92]

Now a second objection. If questionnaires could reproduce *whole* speech-
situations, they might indicate roughly how words are actually used. But
if only verbal contexts are suggested, the depth grammar of the expressions is at most suggested. And what is suggested is likely to vary con-
siderably from individual to individual; one will imagine one situation
for the sentence, another another. And so the answers about equivalence
may not be answers to the same question at all; one will be denying
equivalence in the circumstances he has imagined, while another will
affirm equivalence in the circumstances he has imagined.

"Full" descriptions are no solution. Suppose the questionnaire starts out: "Imagine that you are on the corner of Fifth and Broadway. . . ." Maybe the person questioned has never been on Fifth and Broadway and so can't imagine what we want him to imagine. So we make the situation more general—and once again leave the rest to his imagination. Even if our subjects were people of very wide experience and great imaginers, the fullest description on paper of what the interviewee is to imagine himself doing, in what circumstances, with what people, would not be full enough to ward off the fundamental objection of Wittgenstein: here language is like an engine idling, it is doing no work (§ 132).[93] An abstract statement of circumstances is not equivalent to a concrete life situation.[94]

Similar difficulties arise from the fact that the questioning situation, like the supposed context, is isolated and abstract. Whether one says that two expressions have the "same" sense in a given context depends on the sort of sameness indicated by the questioning context, the purposes and circumstances, and not solely on the context considered or described in the question.[95] In particular, it needs to be made clear what degree of exactness is desired. For instance, one person might conclude that since the expression "use in the language" is not generally used where the expression "meaning" is, the shorter expression being handier, therefore the two cannot be said to be equivalent. Applying standards like these, Quine has concluded that no two words are synonymous.[96] Another person, applying less rigid criteria of sameness, would give a different answer. In ordinary life, circumstances generally indicate the sort of standards to apply, the aspects to consider, the accuracy required. Thus whereas I might say in a discussion of quite varied compositions, of varied length, that two of them are of the same length, a television official, on the other hand, who had to time a program of music to the second, might expect a quite different answer. Now the mere fact of handing someone a questionnaire would give no such lead; and in trying to be more specific, one would meet difficulties similar to those that arose in regard to the expressions' context.

I do not mean to say that good questionnaires could not give a fairly accurate indication of synonymity. But the reasons mentioned[97] make me doubt that questionnaires would give a more reliable result, especially for a word like "meaning," than did Wittgenstein's personal observation—his careful, intelligent, prolonged reflection on the intricate employment of expressions "in the language-game which is their home." There is, of course, something impressive and reassuring about precise figures and neatly marshalled columns of facts. Beside them a philosopher's mere "seems to me" cuts a very sorry figure indeed. But here appearances may very well be deceiving.[98]

V. UNIMPORTANT?

Panayot Butchvarov believes that Wittgenstein cannot have meant merely to point out how the word "meaning" is used. That is too obvious.[99] But the errors of philosophers are there to show that it isn't so obvious. And the discussion in the preceding section has shown why.

O. K. Bouwsma questions the importance of the definition more pragmatically: "As a definition the sentence is indefensible and if it is defensible, what good comes of it?"[100]

"What good comes of it?" The question is asked in many ways, depending on the questioner and on the kind of good he would like to see come of it. Some are interested in scientific results, others in the consequences for philosophy. The views of Stephen Ullmann,[101] a semanticist, illustrate the former outlook. Ullmann sounds quite sympathetic and open-minded in his comments on Wittgenstein's definition:

> His formula will appeal to the student of language not only because of its neatness and simplicity and because it is very much in line with current trends in linguistics, but also because it offers several advantages. On the negative side, it avoids any recourse to vague, intangible and subjective mental states or processes. On the positive side, it has the merit of defining meaning in contextual, i.e. in purely empirical terms. The crucial question which now arises is this: how does the operational definition compare with the referential (a) as a tool of research, and (b) as a working hypothesis in semantic theory?
>
> (a) What is the value of the operational definition in the study of particular words, for example in lexicography? The answer will depend on how the definition is interpreted. If it is taken to mean that the student must confine himself to collecting and analysing contexts in which the word occurs, then the task would seem to be thankless as well as inconclusive.[102]

Since his subsequent remarks indicate that the "contexts" he here has in mind have nothing to do with what Wittgenstein called "depth grammar" of expressions, it is obvious that this is not the application Wittgenstein would have made of the definition. So let us pass on to Ullmann's second point: "(b) Any definition of meaning should be regarded as no more than a working hypothesis. Its value will depend on how it works: on the help it can give in the description, interpretation and classification of semantic phenomena."[103] From this point of view, he concludes, it would be premature to choose between Wittgenstein's definition and others. The sort of benefit Ullmann has in mind is illustrated by his remarks on another definition, which describes meaning as a "reciprocal and reversible relation between name and sense."[104]

> If this formula is accepted as a working hypothesis, then semantic changes will fall naturally into two categories: those based on an association between the senses and those involving an association between the names. Each of these categories can be further subdivided if we accept the customary distinction between two kinds of association: similarity and contiguity. These two pairs of criteria yield four cardinal types of semantic change, some of which can be broken down into further subdivisions.[105]

One has the impression, in reading Ullmann's book, that Wittgenstein's jejune definition, though courteously received, does not stand a chance in competition with a high-powered definition like this. His definition may be accurate enough as a report of usage, but usage does not interest Ullmann, any more than it interests a physician in search of medical terms and medical definitions.

A comparison with medical terms is instructive. Consider the common expression "heart attack." This vague term covers a number of categories much more precisely named and defined in medical textbooks. To my knowledge, medical terminology does not include any more precise sense of the expression "heart attack." For reasons made clear in Ullmann's book, it would be surprising if it did. Polysemy is not practical and cannot endure when the two senses of a word are not sufficiently distinguished by context. A new, restricted sense of "heart attack," covering perhaps just thromboses, would in many contexts be easily confused with the ordinary, wider sense of the expression. Rather than ruin a perfectly good expression through ambiguous polysemy, or cause needless confusion, the medical profession has left the term alone.

I think Ullmann and his brethren would do well to leave "meaning" alone. It is not a scientific expression. And when it is defined scientifically, as in the definition just quoted, which Ullmann favors, it no longer corresponds with common usage. Consequently, through the sort of chain reaction Ullmann is familiar with, the rest of accepted terminology must be readjusted. Thus his acceptance of the name-sense definition of meaning makes Ullmann dubious about some hundreds or thousands of perfectly good words, those which he calls "form-words." [106] "This," for instance, and "there" are not "full words,"[107] but should probably be called "pseudo-words." For they have no referents.[108] But of course everyone calls them words. So Ullmann would do well to return all such familiar expressions to the language-game which is their natural habitat and find some unambiguous, scientific terms. It seems strange that so many linguists who are intent on making their researches scientific should go on using unscientific terms, and expecting linguistic analysts to give them new meanings for old terms. Their new wine should go in new skins.

Actually the cleavage between Wittgenstein and people like Ullmann (apparently most linguists) is much more profound than Ullmann seems to realize. For the common acceptance accorded the name-sense definition[109] is based on widespread acceptance of views like Ullmann's, that "the theory of signs . . . is concerned with a wide variety of phenomena encountered in everyday life, which have only one thing in common: they are all signs standing for something else, pointing to something other than themselves."[110] Isn't this universal "pointing" which all signs do in quite the same class with the "modifying" which all tools do? (§ 14). There seems to be more than an error here. There is the craving for generality where there is no generality, for simplicity and order where there is no simplicity or order, for rigor where there is no rigor (BB 18).

Wittgenstein knew all about this malady and about this precise form of it; he, too, had made all signs point. In the *Investigations*, though, he had something better, something wiser, to offer. "A scientific hypothesis"—that is precisely what his definition is *not*. Rather, in its willful vagueness, it is a rejection of all such hypotheses as Ullmann craves. "When we say: 'Every word in a language signifies something,' we have so far said *nothing whatever*" (§ 13). Beyond the fact that they are words, that is, sounds or marks with a use in the language, words reveal no common factor which might make a more precise definition of meaning possible.

More precise categories do exist, more precise patterns can be found, which have their own more precise names, or can be given them. But these are not coextensive with meaning nor can their names be introduced into a definition of "meaning." The word "meaning" already has its own allotted use, on a higher level of generality than any such definition would permit.

The attempt to bring it down a notch by means of some precise definition, for instance by making it cover just the more limited area already served by "referring," would seem to be a new variant of the old philosophers' trick of reduction, transposed from the material into the formal mode of speech. The reductionist philosopher said that A is "really" B and B "really" C. In a manner characteristic of his profession, the linguistic scientist speaks instead of words, and gives definitions: he defines A as though it were B, and B as though it were C, thus creating the illusion that he has succeeded where the philosopher failed; he has simplified reality. No doubt he will answer when challenged that he is merely creating a more precise terminology, for scientific purposes. But the same blind tendency would seem to be at work as in the philosophers' attempts. For the linguist is often reluctant to do what has been done in so many other scientific fields; instead of creating an entirely new set of precise, scientific terms, coined perhaps from Latin or Greek, he does violence to the imprecise terms which are still needed for everyday use. To renounce their use would be to renounce the vague aspirations he shares with those philosophers. He wants to be both scientist and philosopher. He would not only make a detailed study of meanings; he would give people a more precise and accurate idea of what meanings "really" are. Thus whereas neither the biologist nor the sociologist nor the anthropologist nor the psychologist, despite vast research and ever new findings, would take it into his head to tell us that many of the things we referred to as "men" are not really men at all, a semanticist like Ullmann is ready to assert that a good many of the things we referred to as "words" are not really words at all, and that they don't really have meanings.

To summarize: (1) Ullmann desires a definition that will both suggest and conform to the structure of the semantic science to be born; (2) this will require the introduction of concepts more specific than "meaning" or "use in the language"; (3) such a definition would not give the ordinary sense of the word "meaning"; (4) it would therefore create needless conflict and confusion; (5) Ullmann should therefore find another term to do the job.

Though Wittgenstein's definition offers no "advantages" of the sort Ullmann looks for, it is beneficial to science. As Friedrich Waismann points out, Wittgenstein's contribution consists precisely in his refusal to be more precise, and particularly in his rejection of a "referential" definition:

> To give just one example of vision in philosophy: Wittgenstein saw through a big mistake of his time. It was then held by most philosophers that the nature of such things as hoping and fearing, or intending, meaning and understanding could be discovered through introspection, while others, in particular psychologists, sought to arrive at an answer by experiment, having only obscure notions as to what their results meant. Wittgenstein changed the whole approach by saying: what these words mean shows itself in the way they are used—the nature of understanding reveals itself in grammar, not in experiment. This was at the time quite a revelation and came to him, so far as I remember, suddenly.[111]

Any science which has not yet made up its own referring or plainly non-referring terms stands to benefit in similar fashion. Only confusion can result from the search for the referents of non-referring terms, from the attempt to pair off items or aggregates in experience with terms that either are not being used to describe or designate anything, or indicate a variable weave in the pattern of our lives rather than any one object, aspect, or experience.

Now, what of the definition's philosophical importance? What effect is it likely to have and should it have on the practice of philosophy? Even a tentative and sketchy treatment of this subject will have to consist in more than answers to objections made by critics. The first question to ask here is whether a definition should have any philosophical consequences whatsoever. If for good reasons a person holds certain values or certain views regarding God, man, the universe, a mere definition, it seems, should make no difference to these. So long as the reasons for the views remain unchanged, won't a new definition demand merely a new terminology in which to express the same old views? This query calls attention to the sort of consequences which should be expected of a definition. They will not be logical consequences of the definition itself, but changes in viewpoint effected by the arguments for the definition, plus various changes in viewpoint and approach attributable to the suggestive power of the definition. It is not the visible part of an iceberg that sinks ships.

Wittgenstein's definition is the visible tip of a whole iceberg of arguments and observations. This has been made clear in previous chapters. Furthermore, to continue the same metaphor, it makes its presence felt in the philosophical seas not merely by the collision of these underlying views with well-defined opposing views, but by a subtle change of temperature in the waters round about it. Where it is accepted and given prominence, it introduces new emphases, new approaches and pre-occupations.

As a definition of words' meaning, it draws attention to language. By equating this meaning with their use in a language, it emphasizes their actual functioning, usage. Therein lies much of its value, and its main limitations.

G. J. Warnock might appear to be making much the same distinction as I have just made when he distinguishes between Wittgenstein's definition and his dictum, "Don't ask for the meaning, ask for the use." Only the dictum, he says, is really important for philosophy. "For, after all, we are only incidentally concerned with the meaning, or with the use, of 'use' or of 'meaning.' "[112]

There is a good deal of truth in this. If we are already disposed to pay attention to word-use, then "meaning" is just one term among many, and the problems connected with it may not have any special or basic importance for us. But very often this is not the case. And if someone rightly believes that the important thing about a word is its meaning, yet has confused or erroneous notions about meaning, he can be brought to follow the advice to look for the use only by being shown that meaning is use. For him, Wittgenstein's definition is dictum and motive rolled into one.[113] Thus the definition not only calls attention to use, but does it most effectively precisely because it is a definition.

Not all philosophers agree. Some find that the definition has merely given rise to new perplexities. "Nothing has been changed," complains Bouwsma. "If before we were puzzled with: What is the meaning of a word? now we are puzzled with: What is the use of a word? (I think I paced up and down in this cage for years.)"[114] "*These* difficulties would not have arisen," says Irwin Lieb, "had Wittgenstein been even bolder, had he refused to provide a formula of the kind he repudiates. Charles Peirce's practice is, I think, instructive by contrast. Instead of giving a single formula, Peirce wrote about different kinds of meanings. . . ."[115]

There is something humorous in a scolding administered to Wittgenstein, the enemy of generalities, for having been too general about meaning. The answer to the complaint is to point out, first, that people who are perplexed by Wittgenstein's definition are just as likely to be perplexed by piecemeal statements, and second, that giving a definition provided a remedy for *any* notion of the sort Wittgenstein wished to extirpate. If someone is looking for an entity which is the meaning of a word, purely negative arguments will merely drive him from one hypothesis to another —from object to essence, from essence to image, from image to composite image, from composite image to feeling, from feeling to idea. He needs to change his whole outlook, and the positive definition does that once for all.

Now, if it be conceded that the definition satisfactorily draws attention to language and the actual use of words in language, its value and importance will depend on the value and importance of this emphasis. How valuable is it? It seems there would be no oversimplification in saying that the definition is important because people tend to ignore the way words are used, that their state is not one of mere ignorance but of positive prejudice, and that both the ignorance and the prejudice with its *a priori* misconceptions show up constantly in the history of philosophy.

To illustrate the first point and make it convincing, I could quote college students. But the words of a professional philosopher who had read his Wittgenstein will illustrate still more strikingly what a blind spot word use can be: "We might say 'I am going to talk about the use of "pitch" in the sense in which it means that black stuff with which you are familiar.' But it would at once be clear that this was a roundabout way of saying 'I am going to talk about that black stuff called "pitch" with which you are all familiar.' "[116] Now, if I said that the word in this sense had a referring use, I would not be talking about pitch. Nor if I contrasted this use as a noun with the word's use as a verb, would I be talking about pitch. We can often take such grammar for granted; but in philosophy serious trouble may easily arise if someone supposes, for instance, that a word has a referring function when as a matter of fact it has no such role in the language. This was the case with "meaning"; philosophers made up imaginary entities or multiplied familiar ones like feelings because they thought the word "meaning" must have a referent.

Of course this division of words into those that refer and those that don't is shorthand for extremely complex differences. In general, the use of words is complex and varied, far more complex and varied than the average pre-Wittgensteinian noticed. How often have I heard it said: "But there *must* be something in common if the same word is used! Otherwise why would it be used?" This preconception has probably been a chief reason for the unabashed, though implicit Humpty-Dumptyism that has plagued philosophy for so long. What resistance there is to the idea that truth, justice, beauty, knowledge, meaning are what people call truth, justice, beauty, knowledge, meaning! Somehow it never occurs to many people that these words do not mean what *I* choose them to mean, that usage—messy, complex, arbitrary useage—has prior rights which should be respected.

True, the philosophers of the past—Plato, Aristotle, St. Augustine, certain medieval scholastics—often surprise us by the amount of attention we find they gave to language and the use of individual words. But rarely has the study of usage been sufficiently thorough. It is Wittgenstein's merit to have met this need by advocating a new manner in the study of language—conceptual, and richly comprehensive—and by providing masterful samples which have served as models for those who have followed.

This is not the place nor do I feel prepared to prescribe the forms linguistic philosophy should take and the goals it should pursue if Wittgenstein's definition is adopted as motto and guide. However, I feel constrained to say at least something on the subject. For to conclude that the definition should result in greater attention to language and the actual use of expressions would be a very meagre indication of the consequences it should have.

First some large distinctions. In its orginal context, the definition is an example of and stimulus to therapeutic linguistic philosophy. As for the more positive, thorough type of linguistic philosophy which also resulted from Wittgenstein's (and others') influence,[117] this is not excluded by the definition itself, or by the reasoning that led to it. However, as was pointed out in the previous chapter, a type of linguistic philosophy which specialized in telling people what they can and cannot say, would be quite at variance with the sort of use Wittgenstein had in mind when he defined the meaning of a word as its use in the language. So it is just the first two sorts of linguistic philosophy that I shall consider, as exemplifying the definition's potentialities.

It is probably evident by now that I believe the therapeutic study of usage is in general both useful and necessary. I would not limit philosophy to such therapy; there are and fortunately will continue to be many mansions in the kingdom of philosophy. But given the extent to which language is both tool and substance of our thought, there will always be need for such therapy.

An area of particular therapeutic concern that I would like to suggest, both because of its vast importance and its close connection with Wittgenstein's definition, is that indicated by the statement: "These concepts: proposition, language, thought, world, stand in line one behind the other, each equivalent to each" (§ 96). This tendency to suppose a parallel, a matching, between thoughts, words, and things, is hardly confined to the pages of the *Tractatus*, which Wittgenstein was here criticizing. And the starting point and direction of inference have very often been those suggested in the *Tractatus*: "To give the essence of a proposition means to give the essence of all description, and thus the essence of the world" (5.4711). Mistaken views on language have led to mistaken representations of thought and thought's objects, peopling the mind with imaginary correlates of words and the world with Platonic and logical objects.

The importance of a tendency that radically affects people's views of language, psychology, and the whole domain of discourse need hardly be stressed. And the therapeutic connection between this tendency and Wittgenstein's definition should be clear from the second chapter of this study. The definition's chief negative implication is: No, meanings are not such correlates, whether in the mind or outside it. The definition is both fruit and expression of Wittgenstein's sustained criticism of the assumption that words are matched with thoughts and thoughts with things.

Let me repeat that Wittgenstein's criticism of this tendency does not make him a behaviorist. And when I say that I agree with it basically, I am not denying that thought, insight, reasoning, and the rest are, at least in part, private, non-sensible. It is the structure, the pattern of internal experience and activity that is falsified by matching theories. When I talk about sounds, scents, skyscrapers, or speeds, I *do not* always "call them to mind." And when I talk about chess or large numbers or values, I *cannot* call them to mind in the sense of internally representing, mirroring them at the moment I speak of them. And the reason for this is that they *are not* the sort of things which can be thus fleetingly represented. These brief, inadequate remarks are not meant to convince anyone; Witt-

genstein's extended treatment would do that better. They are meant
merely to indicate one particular way in which I personally believe that
Wittgenstein's definition should have a beneficial influence in philosophy.

Regarding the positive sort of linguistic philosophy done at Oxford,
J. O. Urmson once affirmed that "if you read the works of the philosophers
in this group, you will discover much more of the common influence of
Wittgenstein than of the rigorous and precise use of the method I have
briefly described to characterize them."[118] From what he has told me, I
gather that Mr. Urmson now regrets having made this statement. Nevertheless, Wittgenstein and his definition did affect the Oxonians too. Consequently, to judge the value and importance of his treatment of meaning,
it is necessary to form some estimate of the Oxonian movement and its
relation to this aspect of Wittgenstein's thought.

The acknowledged master of the Oxford method explains it thus: "Our
common stock of words embodies all the distinctions men have found
worth drawing, and the connexions they have found worth marking, in
the lifetimes of many generations: these surely are likely to be more
numerous, more sound, since they have stood up to the long test of the
survival of the fittest, and more subtle, at least in all ordinary and reason-
ably practical matters, than any that you or I are likely to think up in
our arm-chairs of an afternoon—the most favoured alternative method."[119]
So let the dictionary be our guide to reality.

This approach rests ultimately on the same basic fact by which Wittgenstein justified his method: the obscurity of the obvious, our forgetfulness
of the familiar. Wittgenstein stressed our reflective ignorance of familiar
linguistic facts, whereas Austin stressed our forgetfulness of "the realities
we use the words to talk about."[120]

The identity of their starting point and the early divergence of their
ways can be rather clearly illustrated, I think, by considering the example
of "games." For Wittgenstein the varieties of games are not difficult to
recall; the arm-chair method is quite adequate for his purposes, that is,
for the clarification of the ordinary, familiar ways in which we use the
word "game" (§ 66). Typical of Austin would be an interest in the variety
of games, their major differences and groupings. Wittgenstein's offhand
method and the meagre sampling it yields seem inadequate for such a
purpose. Austin would go through the dictionary in search of names for
games.

A further similarity appears, though, in the next stage of inquiry. Once

Austin has his collection of terms, he does not attempt to give definitions of these terms, that is, to determine the precise boundaries of each concept. For neither he nor Wittgenstein is interested ultimately in words. For their different reasons and in their different ways, both are interested in the things we speak of with words. And neither expects these to include essences.

Thus it is typical of both—and of the British philosophy inspired by them—to study individual *uses* of a word in the language rather than its overall *use* in the language. Wittgenstein gives no definition of "game" or "language," draws no boundaries, maps no concepts. Even in his rare definition of "meaning," he speaks only of "a large class of cases." This approach still characterizes British philosophy, for basically similar reasons. Of course it may be argued that this is more a coincidence than a result. In presenting his case for his favorite form of inquiry, Austin pays no attention to meaning or a doctrine of meaning. So why trace the trend to Wittgenstein and his definition?

Because people read him and were influenced by him. Because without his therapy they might not have espoused Austin's approach so enthusiastically. As Wittgenstein said in a similar context (BB 16-19): "What makes it difficult for us to take this line of investigation is our craving for generality. This craving for generality is the resultant of a number of tendencies connected with particular philosophical confusions. There is— (a) The tendency to look for something in common to all the entities which we commonly subsume under a general term" (BB 17)—that is, the "meaning" of the term. Here is a basic link between Wittgenstein's therapeutic definition of meaning and even an Oxonian interest in the uses of expressions. Wittgenstein's therapy allows us to take the broad look that Austin too urged, and it teaches respect for particulars (BB 19-20).

A good many people regard linguistic philosophy, whether Oxonian or other, as decidedly narrow. It seems to me, though, that a really thorough study of words' uses might turn out to be so comprehensive that there would be little ground for this complaint of narrowness. For example, in studying the "depth grammar" of a term like "pain" we must know how others use the term, and not just how we use it. But to speak with philosophical assurance about others' use of the term, we would have to come to grips with the other-minds problem. Or consider the concept of truth. A full study of this concept would lead well beyond the narrowly empirical limits of Wittgenstein's investigations.[121]

So far I have considered rather general consequences of Wittgenstein's definition—first a general shift of emphasis, then two fruitful sorts of philosophical practice which embody the new emphasis on language and usage. For therapeutic practice there were also more particular consequences to mention, in connection with word-thought-thing parallelism in general, and meaning in particular. In like manner the definition has particular consequences for positive linguistic philosophy of the sort I have just been discussing. Mention of the concept of truth suggests such consequences. The clarification of one important concept, such as meaning, may help to clarify other important concepts which are closely related to it, for instance the concept of truth. The following sketch, in bold and over-simple strokes, may suggest the importance and general direction of this inquiry.

Meaning is more basic than truth; for truth depends partly on the facts and partly on the meaning of the words stating the facts, whereas the meaning of the words or of the sentences does not depend on the truth of the statement. The meaning of individual words, in turn, is more basic than the meaning of sentences, each sentence being, in the circumstances, an original creation, depending for its effectiveness upon the already established meaning of the words used in it. Thus it might be said that by leading us back to the meaning of words and to what is most basic in the meaning of words, Wittgenstein brought us to what is most basic in philosophy, and terminated the centuries-long quest for truth, then for meaning, then for the meaning of meaning.

Perhaps the direction can now be reversed, thanks to his accurate definition. With the general notion of meaning clarified, we can proceed to a more reliable study of individual meanings. Because of the connection of truth with meaning, we can also use the definition to arrive at the definition of statements' truth. And with that concept clarified, we can go on to distinguish more surely between true statements and false statements.

More precisely, my own impression is that Wittgenstein's definition will not help us as much in clarifying the concept of truth, that is, the meaning of the word "true," as it will in more fully and accurately describing the conditions which must obtain if we are correctly to declare a statement true.[122] It suggests a "correspondence theory" of sorts: The statement "It is raining" is true on this double condition: (a) that it is raining when the statement is made, and (b) that it has generally been raining on other occasions when the same statement was made. That is, the particular use corresponds with usage.

Another set of particular consequences deserves at least brief mention. The analytic-synthetic distinction has been much discussed lately; so has the perennial problem of synthetic *a priori* propositions or statements. Mention is still made of the classical statement of these questions, in terms of inclusion or non-inclusion of meanings. Even when other approaches are used, the concept of meaning often is crucial. Wittgenstein's distinction between referent and meaning is especially important, enabling one to recognize statements as synthetic which would otherwise be thought analytic. For instance, if, as seems likely, the ordinary concept "cube" does not specify the number of edges, then a good case can be made for the syntheticity of the statement: "All cubes have twelve edges."[123] But if the meaning of "cube" is identified with some referent—a mental or physical cube—then of course the meaning of the subject term includes the specific number of sides.

The method by which Wittgenstein established the general definition of meaning is also useful here, as a means of determining realistically what is and is not included in the meaning of a term. One can consider what is learned when people learn the meaning of this or that particular term, and conclude that this is the term's meaning. For instance, if after learning the meaning of the term "cube" they need to be informed of the number of edges or to figure it out briefly for themselves, then the meaning they learned does not include the specific number of edges.

So much for the conceptual implications of Wittgenstein's definition.

A final pragmatic lesson taught by Wittgenstein's definition is implicit in what has already been said, but deserves special emphasis and attention. Philosophers sometimes remind me of those men the Bible speaks of, who set out to build a tower to the heavens but got nowhere because they could no longer communicate with one another. Each started to speak a language of his own rather than the common tongue they began with. So too philosophers start out all speaking German or French or Italian and end up speaking a language nobody understands. This is not the worst of it. A Frenchman does not correct an Italian for using Italian, or a German for using German; nor does he argue either into using his own language. But such intolerance is common in philosophical debate. Or rather, such incomprehension. It is not so much that philosophers refuse to accept one another's way of speaking. They often fail to recognize that each one has his own way of speaking. For the words are all French, or English, or Italian. The "surface grammar," to borrow Wittgenstein's expression, is the same, but the "depth grammar" is not.

Now, how did this Babel get started? Why do philosophers come to have their own private languages, at least in part, with the result that their debates so often reflect no difference of opinion but only a difference of language?

Consider, as an example, these words of Austin:

> It is a matter for decision how far we should continue to call such masqueraders [formulae in a calculus, value judgments, performatory utterances, definitions] 'statements' at all, and how widely we should be prepared to extend the uses of 'true' and 'false' in 'different senses.' My own feeling is that it is better, when once a masquerader has been unmasked, *not* to call it a statement and *not* to say it is true or false.[124]

This is the sort of feeling that often gives rise to personal languages. But in Austin it was largely under control—under the control of Wittgenstein's definition, or at least of the truth contained in it. He went on to consider just how the word "statement" is ordinarily used, thus giving implicit recognition to the rights of usage, of a word's "use in the language." It is generally recognized that Wittgenstein's definition has had this effect. Those reached by his influence tend to feel that there is no use arguing with existing usage. It is not for them to decide a word's meaning (though they may of course introduce and employ a personal definition). Usage has already decided its meaning.

Yet Austin speaks of a decision to be made, a decision based not on usage alone, but on investigation of the utterances in question. He is ready to condemn even widespread usage if the utterances turn out to be "masqueraders." Here at last is the crucial question about Wittgenstein's definition, and the crucial danger of its misapplication. Usage alone cannot decide questions of truth. So these must be distinguished from questions of meaning.

Strawson indicates a partial solution to this problem:

> Suppose, in a room with a bird in a cage, I say "That parrot is very talkative." Then my use of the referring expression ("That parrot") with which my sentence begins is correct when the token-object (bird) with which my token-expression (event) is correlated by the conventions of demonstration is

of a kind with which the type-expression is correlated by the conventions of description. Here we do have an event and a thing and a (type-mediated) conventional relation between them. If someone corrects me, saying "That's not a parrot; it's a cockatoo," he may be correcting either a linguistic or a factual error on my part. (The question of which he is doing is the question of whether I would have stuck to my story on a closer examination of the bird.)[125]

If I examined the bird closely and saw everything the other person saw, yet continued to call it by another name, the words we used would have different *meaning* for us.

But suppose that the word in question has no referent and that consequently there is nothing to be examined? Well, at least there will be certain accepted criteria for the use of the word. And may not people be mistaken in certain cases as to the realization of these criteria—perhaps frequently enough to create "usage" of the sort Austin was ready to condemn? Here is the really hard part. How much of the usage is meaning with rights, and how much of it is error with no rights? Where and how shall we draw the line that separates them, when nature no longer draws the line for us, by its neat divisions into species and individual things?

It seems to me that Wittgenstein has given the correct analysis of this sort of difficulty. We feel sure there must be some clear line of demarcation; if we just look long and hard enough we will discern it—not just for this or that word, but for all words: a handy rule to tell where extended sense ends and error begins. But at the present, in the difficult case we happen to be considering, we are so far from detecting any sharp borderline that we feel our task to be extremely difficult. The explanation, Wittgenstein would surely say, is simple enough: there is no such clear boundary, here or in general. That is why it seems so hard to find.

Thus an expression like "statement" has a family of uses, and may easily be extended to others. There are utterances which clearly lie beyond its scope: questions, commands, jokes, and so on. If we called such utterances statements, what we said would be *false*. But as for the cases within the word's range, or borderline cases, there is no question of error here, as there might be were we discussing something unobservable ("ether") or difficult to calculate or observe. To say that people call value judgments or definitions "statements" because they have failed to notice their true logic is very much like saying a person calls a yellowish thing yellow because of a mistake in chemical analysis. As Wittgenstein should have made us expect, a term of ordinary language such as "statement" has no sharply delimited realm of application beyond which use of the term is no longer "extended" but clearly erroneous. If we decide to eliminate certain dubious or infreqent cases, or even quite common ones, if we decide to draw a sharp new line, we should understand that our decision is a personal one for personal reasons, not a decision binding on others. For everyone may have his favorite paradigm, but no one owns the word. If we remember this, that a word's meaning is not your use or mine, but its use *in the language,* the result will be more tolerance and understanding, less babel and more tower.

NOTES—INTRODUCTION

1. Ludwig Wittgenstein, *Philosophical Investigations,* original German facing English translation by G. E. M. Anscombe, 2nd ed. (Oxford, 1958), p. 20, § 43. This second edition contains a number of improvements in the translation. Cf. G. E. M. Anscombe, "Note on the English Version of Wittgenstein's *Philosophische Untersuchungen,*" *Mind,* 62 (1953), pp. 521-22. Sections in the first part of the *Investigations* will be referred to by paragraph number alone (e.g., § 263). "PI" followed by the page number (e.g., PI 217) will be used in references to the Preface, Part Two, or unnumbered notes in Part One.

2. Knowledgeable people have objected to me that Wittgenstein did not give a definition of the term "meaning"; the German word he used is not *definieren* but *erklären*: "Man kann für eine *grosse* Klasse von Fällen der Benutzung des Wortes 'Bedeutung'—wenn auch nicht für alle Fälle seiner Benutzung—dieses Wort so erklären. . . ." In view of my constant references in this work to "Wittgenstein's definition," this is a serious objection, to be dealt with at the very start. It is not enough to point out in reply that Miss Anscombe uses the word "defined" in her translation of § 43. It is apparently necessary to justify her translation. So I would ask how a term can be "explained" without giving its meaning, that is, defining it (at least for some cases, as here). And does not Wittgenstein's "explanation" clearly take the *form* of a definition: "the meaning of a word is its use . . ."? The objections of these critics may result from unclarity regarding the two sorts of statement this form is used to make. If I say "*X* is *y*," I am either giving further information about a subject sufficiently identified by the subject term, or I am identifying the referent of the term "*X*," that is, I am giving the *meaning of the term.* Wittgenstein's statement clearly belongs to the latter category. It does not presuppose agreement regarding the referent of the term "meaning."

However, if someone has a precise and limited notion of what a "definition" is (e.g., designation of an "essence"), and Wittgenstein's statement doesn't seem to fit his notion, let him not be troubled: I am not using the term "definition" in his precise and limited sense. My references to "Wittgenstein's definition" are simply to this statement of Wittgenstein's, in § 43.

3. On the importance of the definition in Wittgenstein's philosophy, cf. Domenico Campanale, *Studi su Wittgenstein* (Bari, 1956), p. 190; J. N. Findlay, "Wittgenstein's Philosophical Investigations," *Rev. Int. Philos.,* 7 (1953), p. 205; P. F. Strawson, critical notice of *Philosophical Investigations,* in *Mind,* 63 (1954), p. 73.

3a. Cf. e.g., Gilbert Ryle, "The Theory of Meaning," in *British Philosophy in Mid-Century* (London, 1957), ed. C. A. Mace, pp. 239-64.

4. P. F. Strawson has called him "the first philosopher of the age" (*op. cit.,* p. 78). Others have gone still further. For a good estimate of Wittgenstein's importance, cf. e.g., Allan B. Wolter, O.F.M., "The Unspeakable Philosophy of the Late Wittgenstein," in *Proc. Amer. Cathol. Philos. Assoc.,* 34 (1960), p. 169.

5. According to Gilbert Ryle (*op. cit.,* p. 239) "Answers to this highly abstract question, What are meanings? have in recent decades, bulked large in philosophical and logical discussions. Preoccupation with the theory of meaning could be described as the occupational disease of twentieth-century Anglo-Saxon and Austrian philosophy. We need not worry whether or not it is a disease. But it might be useful to

172

survey the motives and the major results of this preoccupation." This Ryle then does in an account to which the reader is referred as a complement to my brief remarks. Confer also pages 7-8 of Ryle's introduction to the collection *The Revolution in Philosophy* (London, 1956). For a discussion of the connection between Hume's division of propositions and present-day concern with meaning, cf. Charles B. Daly, "Logical Positivism, Metaphysics and Ethics. I. Ludwig Wittgenstein," *Irish Theol. Quart.*, 23 (1956), pp. 111-23. F. H. Heinemann ("Meta-Analysis," [Summary] *Proc. Xlth Int. Cong.*, Vol. V [Logic; Philosophical Analysis; Philosophy of Mathematics], Amsterdam-Louvain, 1953, p. 125) traces the movement still further back.

6. Cf. G. E. M. Anscombe: *An Introduction to Wittgenstein's* Tractatus (London, 1959), p. 12.

7. Cf. Ludwig Wittgenstein: *Tractatus Logico-Philosophicus*, original German facing English translation by D. F. Pears and B. F. McGuinness (London, 1961), 4.46-4.461. Hereafter references to the *Tractatus* will consist of numbers alone (e.g., 5.52).

8. Cf. G. Ryle, *op. cit.*, pp. 242-54.

9. "Signs are mere proxies for their content" (*Translations from the Philosophical Writings of Gottlob Frege*, ed. Peter Geach and Max Black [Oxford, 1960], p. 10). Cf. Gottlob Frege, *Grundgesetze der Arithmetik*, 2 vols. (Darmstadt, 1962), pp. 45-50; and Frege, *Funktion, Begriff, Bedeutung, Fünf logische Studien*, ed. Gunther Patzig (Göttingen, 1962), p. 42 ("Die Bedeutung eines Eigennamens ist der Gegenstand selbst, den wir damit bezeichnen") and p. 43: "Ein Eigenname (Wort, Zeichen, Zeichenverbindung, Ausdruck) drückt aus seinen Sinn, bedeutet oder bezeichnet seine Bedeutung."

10. Every word, he thought, must have *some* meaning (*The Principles of Mathematics*, 2nd ed. [London, 1937], p. 42). That is, it must refer to or "stand for" something—"a man, a moment, a number, a class, a relation, a chimera" (*ibid.*, p. 47). For a striking illustration of this outlook, cf. *ibid.*, p. 100.

11. Cf. J. O. Urmson, *Philosophical Analysis* (Oxford, 1956), pp. 179, 199.

12. Bertrand Russell and Alfred N. Whitehead, *Principia Mathematica*, 3 vols.; Vol. 1, 2nd ed. (Cambridge, 1925), pp. 71-72. For Russell's own account of his gradual elimination of referents, cf. the introduction to the second edition of *The Principles of Mathematics*, pp. x ff. Cf. also Urmson, *op. cit.*, pp. 188-89.

13. Cf. Georg Henrik von Wright's "Biographical Sketch" in *Ludwig Wittgenstein, A Memoir* by Norman Malcolm (London, 1958), p. 5.

14. Ludwig Wittgenstein, *Notebooks 1914-1916*, ed. G. H. von Wright and G. E. M. Anscombe; with an English translation by G. E. M. Anscombe (Oxford, 1961). In addition to Wittgenstein's notebooks, this volume also includes notes on logic dictated to G. E. Moore in 1914 and excerpts from letters to Russell.

15. This first appeared in 1921 in *Annalen der Naturphilosophie*, then in 1922 with an unsigned English translation by C. K. Ogden and an introduction by Bertrand Russell. Wittgenstein was unhappy about Russell's introduction (cf. NB 131) and nobody liked Ogden's translation. That of Pears and McGuinness, already cited, is considered a great improvement, though its index is not. All quotations will be from this translation.

16. Cf. Urmson, *op. cit.*, pp. 106-07; and G. H. von Wright, *op. cit.*, p. 12.

17. "Some Remarks on Logical Form," *Proc. Ar. Soc.*, Suppl. 9 (1929), pp. 162-71. On the history of this article, cf. von Wright, *op. cit.*, pp. 13-14; G. E. Moore,

"Wittgenstein's Lectures in 1930-33," *Mind*, 63 (1954), p. 2; John Passmore, *A Hundred Years of Philosophy* (London, 1957), p. 358; and Wittgenstein himself, Letter, *Mind*, 42 (1933), pp. 415-16.

18. *Philos. Rev.*, 74 (1965), pp. 3-11.

19. Ed. Rush Rhees (Oxford, 1964). Since this work appeared after I had finished mine, I have not sought to cite all the pertinent evidence in it, but have used it principally as a check on possible errors of interpretation.

20. "Wittgenstein's Lectures in 1930-33," *Mind*, 63 (1954), pp. 1-15, 289-316; 64 (1955), pp. 1-27; later included in G. E. Moore, *Philosophical Papers* (London, 1959), pp. 252-324. In references the first, second, and third parts of this article will be designated as M^1, M^2, and M^3 respectively.

21. Edited by Rush Rhees (Oxford, 1960).

22. Edited by G. H. von Wright, Rush Rhees, and G. E. M. Anscombe; original German facing the parallel English translation by G. E. M. Anscombe (Oxford, 1956). In subsequent references this will appear as FM.

22a. Ed. Cyril Barrett (Oxford, 1964); referred to hereafter as LC.

23. *Zettel*, edited by G. E. M. Anscombe and G. H. von Wright, translated by G. E. M. Anscombe, Oxford, 1966. The *Zettel* are slips which Wittgenstein cut from extensive typescripts which he also left, mostly belonging to 1945-1948. They are accompanied by manuscript material apparently specially written to go with some of the typescript cuttings.

24. Cf. Anscombe's *Introduction*, pp. 11-12, and von Wright, *op. cit.*, p. 5.

25. His familiarity with *Principles of Psychology* will be established later; his reading of Russell's book is shown by, for instance, a comparison of M^3 23-25 with *The Analysis of Mind* (London, 1921), p. 159.

26. Cf. von Wright, *op. cit.*, pp. 20-21.

27. For Wittgenstein's estimate of Russell and Moore and their respective contributions to philosophy, cf. Malcolm, *op. cit.*, pp. 66-67. Pages 33-34 and 87-92 also suggest that Moore's views stimulated Wittgenstein more to criticism than to admiration. Another who knew both Wittgenstein and Moore has said: "Moore's and Wittgenstein's ways of thinking are in fact utterly different. Although their friendship lasted until the latter's death, I do not believe that there is any trace of an influence of Moore's philosophy on Wittgenstein" (von Wright, *op. cit.*, p. 15).

28. Wittgenstein once told Norman Malcolm (*op. cit.*, p. 69) "that in the *Tractatus* he had provided a perfect account of a view that is the *only* alternative to the viewpoint of his later work."

29. Cf. FM 113, 165; §§ 20, 183, 421.

30. Cf. e.g., § 41.

31. The exception which proves the rule occurs on FM 54. In the *Philosophische Bemerkungen*, cf. pp. 144 and 192.

32. This is Ernest Gellner's expression. Cf. *Words and Things* (London, 1959), pp. 40-43.

33. In "Ordinary Language," *Philos. Rev.*, 62 (1953), pp. 178-79, Gilbert Ryle points out "some radical differences between what is meant by 'the meaning of a word or a phrase' and what is meant by 'the meaning of a sentence'" (p. 179). The two questions cannot be identified without more ado. I have limited myself to the former.

34. Cf. Jerrold Katz and Jerry Fodor, "What's Wrong with the Philosophy of Language," *Inquiry*, 5 (1962), p. 201.

35. Cf. M[15-6]; §§ 90, 118-19, 309.

36. On past philosophy as an ailment, cf. FM 57,157. On language as the origin, cf. M[15-6]; BB 6, 35, 58-59, 108; §§ 38, 111, 122-23, 132, 194. For the charge not just against language but specifically against words, cf. BB 1, 6, 17-19, 23, 27, 28, 30, 43-44, 48-49, 55, 72, 108, 150, 173; §§ 11, 120, 182. In BB 17-19 the diagnosis of causes is more diversified than in the *Investigations*.

37. For confirmation that Wittgenstein thought of meaning as the important thing about words, cf. BB 5, § 120, PI 56, common usage, and the amount of attention Wittgenstein gave to the question of words' meanings.

38. For a succinct account of Wittgenstein's later philosophical procedure which makes clear the connection with his definition of meaning, cf. the lecture notes on page 50 of Malcolm, *Ludwig Wittgenstein*.

NOTES—CHAPTER I

1. Second paragraph. Cf. also 3.324.

2. Much that has been written on this subject is misleading. For an accurate account of Wittgenstein's early views, cf. P. F. Strawson, "Analyse, science et metaphysique," with discussion, in *La philosophie analytique*, ed. L. Beck (Cahiers de Royaumont, Philosophie No. 4 [Paris, 1962]), pp. 105-06. Pages 111-13 reflect Wittgenstein's later views on the same subject.

3. Cf. NB 48, 70, 95, 96.

4. Compare 6.122 with this in Heinrich Hertz's *Principles of Mechanics* (translated by D. E. Jones and J. T. Walley [London-New York, 1899]), p. 420: "*Corollary 2*. The property which one system possesses of being a model of another, is independent of the choice of the coordinates of one or the other system, although it is only clearly exhibited by a particular choice of coordinates." Cf. also *Corollary 2* on page 426, and compare both passages with e.g., 3.143, 4.002, 4.001-4.0141. I will cite Hertz rather frequently in this chapter, partly to make up for commentators' neglect of him in their explanations of the *Tractatus*. Wittgenstein's frequent references to him (NB 36; 4.04. 6.361; M[1]13; BB 26, 169) and his invitation to consult Hertz (4.04) have till recently (cf. James Griffin, *Wittgenstein's Logical Atomism* [Oxford, 1964], pp. 99-102) gone unheeded. Yet reading Hertz's *Principles* quickly reveals what these references already suggest, the great likelihood that Hertz had no small share in shaping the thought of the *Tractatus* and that therefore it can be better understood by consulting him. The present citation is a typical example of numerous passages which might have kept commentators from what seem to me mistaken interpretations of the *Tractatus*, in the present case the interpretation that Wittgenstein considered an unperspicuous language to be logically defective or senseless. As an antidote to this particular error, cf. also Hertz, *op. cit.*, p. 2.

5. Cf. 4.0031.

6. If there is no meaning outside use, then obviously meaning can be discovered only by examining use, which is the second principle. The reverse is not true; if meaning can be discovered only by examining use, this does not necessarily mean that there is no meaning except in use. Just as weight is best discovered by weighing yet is had off the scales as well as on, so meaning might be best discerned by examination of use even if it were not limited to use.

7. As will be shown later, the word "meaning" here has a quite limited sense and the names referred to are not the ordinary names of everyday language. But, since the names and expressions in question occur only in analytic translations from everyday propositions, the principles here stated apply to everyday language as well.

8. Gottlob Frege, *The Foundations of Arithmetic*, transl. J. L. Austin, with the original German text facing the English (Oxford, 1953), p. 71.

9. Frege, *ibid.*, p. 78; cf. also p. 79.

10. P. x. Cf. also pp. 71, 116.

11. Frege, *Grundgesetze der Arithmetik*, pp. 45-50.

12. Cf. e.g., Frege, *Translations from the Philosophical Writings of Gottlob Frege*, p. 105.

13. Frege, *The Foundations of Arithmetic*, p. 69.

14. Frege, *Funktion, Begriff, Bedeutung*, p. 89; *Foundations*, p. 22.

15. These were especially *Principia Mathematica*, which was in process of publication when Wittgenstein arrived at Cambridge, and *The Principles of Mathematics*, first published in 1903, of which G. H. von Wright says: "It seems clear that this book profoundly affected Wittgenstein's development" ("A Biographical Sketch," in Malcolm, *Ludwig Wittgenstein*, p. 4). When I speak of their influence, of course I also have in mind the direct influence of Wittgenstein's friend and teacher, whose thought they reveal.

16. I.e., assumed.

17. PM, I, 67.

18. PM, I, 66. For similar remarks, applied to ordinary names, cf. Russell's "The Philosophy of Logical Atomism," in *Logic and Knowledge, Essays 1901-1950*, ed. Robert Charles Marsh (1956), pp. 243-44.

19. Cf. 3.31.

20. An explanation which might seem tempting but is not correct is the following, in terms of the picture theory. A dab of blue is nothing outside a painting. Inside a painting it may be a patch of sky or a patch of sea, but it cannot be a patch of tree or a patch of brick. In the conventional realistic style, its color determines this much; its place in the picture determines the rest. Likewise a sign might be the sign for an atomic object through convention, but the sign for *this* atomic object through its context. However, though the dab may be a patch of sea in a picture, the picture does not determine what sea it represents a part of. For it may be an incorrect picture or there may be many similar seascapes. In Wittgenstein's word-pictures this problem is solved by the names. "Names are necessary for an assertion that *this* thing possesses *that* property and so on. They link the propositional form with quite definite objects. And if the general description of the world is like a stencil of the world, the names pin it to the world so that the world is wholly covered by it" (NB 53; cf. e.g., 5.526). The picture does not determine what objects are named, but rather the names determine what objects are pictured.

21. Commenting on this point in the *Tractatus*, Gilbert Ryle says: "Un concept est, pour ainsi dire, déja façonné en vue des affirmations, questions, ordres, etc., auxquels il conviendra; et non façonné, par conséquent, pour combler d'autres places vacantes grammaticalement permises" ["La phénomènologie contre *The Concept of Mind*," with discussion, in Beck, ed., *La philosophie analytique*, p. 73].

22. Cp. BB 9-10.

23. Cf. e.g., *The Foundations of Arithmetic*, p. 71.

24. Cf. § 49: "Naming and description do not stand on the same level: naming

is a preparation for description. Naming is so far not a move in the language-game—any more than putting a piece in its place on the board is a move in chess. We may say: *nothing* has so far been done, when a thing has been named. It has not even *got* a name except in the language-game. This was what Frege meant too, when he said that a word had meaning only as part of a sentence." This quotation, showing how Wittgenstein had understood Frege (and approved), supports both the explanations I give for the *Tractatus* restriction of meaning to use.

25. Max Black has finally pointed out the surprising mistranslation of 3.328, even in the second, improved English translation. Cf. *A Companion to Wittgenstein's Tractatus* (Ithaca, 1964), p. 134.

26. Anscombe, *Introduction to Wittgenstein's Tractatus*, pp. 65-67, 75; D. S. Shwayder, "Uses of Language and Uses of Words," *Theoria*, 26 (1960), p. 34; H. R. G. Schwyzer, "Wittgenstein's Picture-Theory of Language," *Inquiry*, 5 (1962), p. 58.

27. Cp. 6.233-6.2331.

28. In the light of NB 7 and the following pages, it seems that Wittgenstein cannot have been in the trenches yet when he made his discovery.

29. "A Biographical Sketch" in Malcolm, *Ludwig Wittgenstein*, pp. 7-8. Cf. Malcolm's briefer account on pages 68-69.

30. A statement like this might suggest that Wittgenstein had a very simplified notion of the relation between objects and words and that he would attempt to find this sort of one-one correlation between words and things even in ordinary sentences. More than one commentator has made this mistake and so had an easy time pointing out Wittgenstein's error. Cf. E. Daitz, "The Picture Theory of Meaning," *Mind*, 62 (1953), p. 184; and Charles B. Daly, "New Light on Wittgenstein," *Philos. Stud.*, 10 (1960), p. 19. A sufficient indication of Wittgenstein's more sophisticated notion of picturing is 4.0141, which indicates the possibility of widely varying projective relationships between pictures and things pictured. The commentators mentioned should perhaps have distinguished more carefully between the elements of a propositional sign (e.g., "*p*") and the elements of a proposition, whose multiplicity would necessarily match that of any situation which might verify the proposition. Wittgenstein's use of the German word *Satz* for both sentence and proposition makes this distinction easy to overlook.

Statements like this one (4.0311) and 4.221 help to show the error of Wilfrid Sellars' interpretation: "I have attempted to explain how a propositional sign can consist of *one logically articulated name*" ("Naming and Saying," *Philosophy of Science*, 29 [1962], p. 20; italics are his).

31. Cf. e.g., § 23.

32. *Wittgenstein's Logical Atomism*, pp. 129-31. A full refutation of Griffin's position does not seem appropriate here.

33. I prefer "statement" to both "sentence" and "proposition" as the usual translation of *Satz* in the *Tractatus*. As Griffin points out (*ibid.*), if by *Satz* one means sentence plus its sense in use, "proposition" is not the best term to use. For the same proposition may be stated in different sentences in different languages. But we do not usually employ the term "statement" in this way. So it seems to me just the right term. However, to link my brief treatment with both of the existing translations of the *Tractatus* and with the translation of the *Notebooks*, I have for the most part used "proposition."

34. In discussions I have had with her on the subject and in her introduction to

the *Tractatus*, pp. 64-65. Rush Rhees's chief criticism in his review of her book is aimed at this part of Miss Anscombe's interpretation. Cf. "Miss Anscombe on the *Tractatus*," *Philos. Quart.*, 10 (1960), pp. 29-30. For an interpretation similar to Miss Anscombe's, cf. Anfinn Stigen, "Interpretations of Wittgenstein," *Inquiry*, 5 (1962), p. 173.

35. Cf. 2.15; 3.1432; 4.022; 4.21; 4.431; 4.442; 4.5; also NB 25, 33.

36. For a good presentation of the case against Miss Anscombe's interpretation, cf. H. R. G. Schwyzer, "Wittgenstein's Picture-Theory of Language," *Inquiry*, 5 (1962), pp. 46-64. To Schwyzer's reasons I would add, for instance, that neither in the *Notebooks* nor in the *Tractatus* does Wittgenstein suggest any such analysis of non-assertive sentences as that proposed by Miss Anscombe, that such expressions are left totally out of consideration. This is not only evidence for my own view that Wittgenstein simply disregarded non-assertive sentences, but it suggests how risky it is to attribute to Wittgenstein *any* particular analysis of such sentences.

37. His attitude is summed up, I think, by Russell's remark in his introduction to the *Tractatus*: "The essential business of language is to assert or deny facts" (p. x), and by an almost identical remark of Moritz Schlick (*Gesammelte Aufsätze 1926-1936* [Vienna, 1938], p. 155). For a description of this viewpoint in Russell and Carnap, cf. Albert Levi, *Philosophy and the Modern World* (Bloomington, 1959), pp. 442-43.

38. Cf. W. M. Thorburn, "The Myth of Occam's Razor," *Mind*, 27 (1918), pp. 345-53. For the formula quoted, cf. p. 345. On Mill, whom I quote merely as evidence of a tradition that was likely to have reached Wittgenstein, cf. p. 352.

39. In the following pages I might just as easily center my remarks about disparity of form as the reason for eliminating various signs (e.g., a sign, being an object, would not have the same logical form as an external relation, or an internal relation, or a mere possibility, and so could not be their representative in the logical mirror, the proposition). But the pragmatic view of language expressed in Occam's razor grew still stronger in Wittgenstein's later philosophy, in which I am chiefly interested, whereas the idea of the logical mirror would disappear from his thought.

40. G. H. von Wright, "A Biographical Sketch," in Malcolm, *Ludwig Wittgenstein*, p. 11.

41. Ved Mehta, "A Battle Against the Bewitchment of Our Intelligence," *The New Yorker*, 37 (December 9, 1961), pp. 110-11.

42. Wright, *op. cit.*, pp. 24-25.

43. *Principles of Mechanics*, p. 2. Compare this also with the discussion of mechanics, in 6.231-6.342. Such passages in Hertz show how well prepared Wittgenstein was to receive the illumination of 1914 regarding the picturing function of language.

44. *Principles of Mathematics*, p. 466. Cf. also "The Monistic Theory of Truth," in Bertrand Russell, *Philosophical Essays* (London, 1910), p. 169: "In this world, whatever is complex is composed of related simple things."

45. Cf. e.g., 3.1431; 3.21. Karl Britton disagrees. Cf. *Communication: A Philosophical Study of Language* (London, 1939), p. 117.

46. Cf. e.g., 2.201-2.21; 2.223; 2.225.

47. Failure to do so leads to errors such as those already alluded to. 2.03 may be partly responsible for the impression that propositions express internal relations, for do not the links of a chain fit one *inside* the other? However, the chain simile is meant merely to emphasize that the relation is not another object in addi-

tion to the terms of the relation—not another link between the links. Cf. I. Copi, "Objects, Properties, and Relations in the *Tractatus*," *Mind*, 67 (1958), p. 159, for a correct explanation.

48. NB 115; 2.14; 3.1431-3.1432; 4.022; 4.031; 4.0311; 4.221. Partly, perhaps, because they pay no attention to the way Wittgenstein invoked and employed Occam's razor (a general failure of commentators), a good many writers on the *Tractatus* give such a broad interpretation of the *Tractatus* objects and names as to eliminate Wittgenstein's clearly marked distinction between objects, which are named, and their configurations or external relations, which are not. This tendency might be roughly indicated as the tendency to consider *"aRb"* (3.1432) a sample atomic proposition and *"R"* a sign in it. In "Wittgenstein's Three Languages," *Rev. Meta.*, 15 (1961), p. 280, Richard Bernstein points out that this is a basic mistake which permeates the whole of Stenius' treatment of the picture theory. Cf. Erik Stenius, *Wittgenstein's Tractatus* (Ithaca-Oxford, 1960), e.g., p. 63. Irving Copi has a full criticism of such views in "Objects, Properties, and Relations in the *Tractatus*," *Mind*, 67 (1958), 145-65. Cf. especially pp. 155-56. Cf. also Judith Jarvis's criticism in "Professor Stenius on the *Tractatus*," *J. Philos.*, 58 (1961), pp. 586-89.

49. 4.123; 4.124; M²315.

50. 5.53. Cf. 3.203; NB 130. Cp. 4.041.

51. Cp. Russell: "If it were really a name, the question of existence could not arise, because a name has got to name something or it is not a name" (*Logic and Knowledge*, p. 243).

52. On the necessity of common form in sign and signified, cf. e.g., 2.171; 2.18; 2.2; 2.151; 4.12. The above discussion might be transposed onto the level of complex signs thus: complex signs could have the same form as structure only if they were not facts but pure structures. But all our complex signs are facts (3.14-3.143).

53. "In order to be able to represent logical form, we should have to be able to station ourselves with propositions somewhere outside logic, that is to say outside the world" (4.12). Much of the discussion to which this statement (and the whole say-show distinction) has given rise seems somewhat irrelevant. Commentators seldom pay close attention to the principles on which the distinction is based. Cf. e.g., Russell's discussion of metalanguages on the last page of his introduction, and a similar discussion by Gustav Bergmann in terms of mirrors, in "Intentionality," *Arch. Filos.*, 1955 (*Semantica*), p. 194.

54. It has, that is, if we suppose a debated point which I think is nevertheless clear, namely that in the *Tractatus* Wittgenstein envisaged only relational propositions, composed entirely of names. F. McGuinness ("Pictures and Form in Wittgenstein's *Tractatus*," *Arch. Filos.*, 1956 [*Filosofia e Simbolismo*], pp. 207-28) holds (on page 226) that Wittgenstein rejected the "all propositions are relational" thesis not only in the notebooks (NB 103), but also in the *Tractatus*, where he "seems still to do so at 5.553. 2.01 etc., when taken in conjunction with 4.24 imply the doctrine, however odd it may sound, that a proposition such as '*fa*' asserts a 'sich verhalten' or 'Verbindung' of the object *a*." I do not see how 5.553 is evidence against exclusively relational propositions or for some other sort; whereas numbers like 2.14, 3.1431, 3.2-3.201, 3.202, 4.031-4.0311, 4.221 are evidence that Wittgenstein admitted only relational atomic propositions, composed of names alone. What 5.553 does help to prove is that we should not take 4.24 as introducing analytic forms. This would make *fa* a non-relational atomic proposition, and Wittgenstein would be saying that some of the atomic propositions we came across would certainly turn out

to have the analytic form *fa*. Analytic forms cannot be decided *a priori*. What can be decided *a priori* is that any atomic proposition one found could be re-presented in the non-analytic form *fa;* even if the elementary proposition named twenty-seven objects, one of the terms, *a*, could be selected as the argument of a function in which the other twenty-six terms of the relation would be included under *f* in *fa*. Thus in the notebooks Wittgenstein had said: "The proposition *fa* speaks of particular *objects*" (NB 75; italics mine). In 4.24 he was merely introducing the notation with which he intended to work in the ensuing passages of the *Tractatus*, since he was not yet prepared to offer any completely analytic forms (5.55).

His elimination from elementary propositions of signs for predicates is suggested already by the view quoted from page 466 of Russell's *Principles of Mathematics*, and still more strongly by Wittgenstein's innovation, the comparison of propositions with pictures, as in 4.0311.

55. This is an important anticipation of Wittgenstein's later attack on essences. The essences he later attacked were actual properties or sets of features; but the "forms" of the *Tractatus*, common to all the members of a class, were not, as will be seen, such essences. They were possibilities. In the later period such essences as these got treated as linguistic conventions; what things logically could or could not do depended on what situations grammar permitted to be described in these or those terms and which it excluded (§ 371).

56. Cf. e.g., NB 119.

57. Thus in the *Tractatus* logical constants are not limited to logical operations, quantifiers, or the like, as some commentators seem to believe. In fact, these barely qualify as logical constants, in the (rather vague) manner suggested by 5.47: even elementary propositions, and therefore all propositions, have all the logical operations in common. Not that they are all negations (a negative proposition is not elementary; cf. NB 130) or disjunctions or conjunctions; but they can all be written as such, are all truth-functional equivalents of such expressions (p is equivalent to $\sim \sim p$); all show at least the possibility of actual negation, disjunction, and so on. Wittgenstein's full idea of logical constants as the constants of logic, taking in signs for relation, proposition, object, and so on, is suggested in Russell, *Principles of Mathematics*, pp. xvii, 8-9.

58. 5.47. Cp. NB 29.

59. 2.201-2.203; 2.221; 4.12-4.1212.

60. These examples of the way Wittgenstein used the term "content" suggest why he used it; expressions with "content" are contrasted with "empty" variables which are "filled" when specific arguments are substituted for them. For instance, x might be the sign for a form, the form of objects; a would fill the form with "content"—a particular object designated by a.

61. This is just one of several reasons for questioning the connection which F. Barone makes between Wittgenstein's insistence that logical constants are not representative and another fundamental thesis of the *Tractatus*, that atomic states of affairs are independent of one another (2.061-2.062). Did fact q follow from fact p, Barone suggests, then there would be an "and" in reality; did fact q exclude p, then there would be a "not" in reality. And therefore there would be such logical realities to be represented by signs, namely by our logical constants. However, Barone has overlooked Occam's razor, which would eliminate the constants as superfluous signs if the propositional signs already did their job, as they do in the case of internal relations. Not all aspects of reality can be named in the *Tractatus*.

Cf. F. Barone, "Il solipsismo linguistico di Ludwig Wittgenstein," *Filosofia*, 2 (1951), p. 553, for his suggestion.

62. 4.1271; 4.127; 4.53.

63. 5; 6-6.002.

64. Cf. William and Martha Kneale, *The Development of Logic* (Oxford, 1962), p. 423.

65. This (direction) is a second sense of *Sinn* in the *Tractatus*, quite distinct from the principal one, soon to be considered (possible state of affairs). For its origin, consult common German usage and the writings of Bertrand Russell which preceded the *Tractatus*, e.g., PM, I, 26; *The Principles of Mathematics*, p. 95; "On the Nature of Truth," in *Philosophical Essays*, pp. 182-84. Cf. also the remark quoted by H. T. Costello in "Logic in 1914 and Now," *J. Philos.*, 54 (1957), p. 257. There is no third sense of *Sinn* in the *Tractatus*.

66. 4.0621; 4.2; 5.2341. Cp. B. Russell, "On Propositions: What They Are and How They Mean," *Proc. Ar. Soc.*, Suppl. Vol. 2 (1919).

67. There are various other indications that the signs for logical operations are not representative, especially this general argument: whatever is expressed by operational signs can be expressed by a truth table marked with T's and F's (4.44). And "It is clear that a complex of the signs 'F' and 'T' has no object (or complex of objects) corresponding to it, just as there is none corresponding to the horizontal and vertical lines or to the brackets" (4.441). These signs merely state correspondence or lack of correspondence with reality; they do not add reference to any further reality.

68. 4.466; 5.461; 6.124; and especially 6.126. Russell would have called it "the proper strict logical sense of the word" ("The Philosophy of Logical Atomism," in *Logic and Knowledge*, p. 201; cf. *ibid.*, p. 196). On the necessity of logical constants and their difference from names, cf. *ibid.*, p. 197: "In a logically perfect language the words in a proposition would correspond one by one with the components of the corresponding fact, with the exception of such words as 'or,' 'not,' 'if,' 'then,' which have a different function."

69. A. Maslow claims that "It is an abuse of his own terminology on Wittgenstein's part to say that a sign has meaning" (*A Study in Wittgenstein's Tractatus* [Berkeley-London, 1961], p. 62). Maslow seems to have overlooked the fact that in ordinary usage there is both intrinsic "having" and extrinsic "having" (a man "has" a liver and he also "has" a wife). Neglect of this distinction is often noticeable in discussions of Wittgenstein's "objects" and the properties which they do or do not have.

70. Notice that neither here nor elsewhere in this chapter do I mention the famous verification principle, according to which a sentence has meaning (Wittgenstein would say *Sinn*) only if there is some way of verifying it empirically. With no stronger support than texts like 2.223, 3.02, and 4.031, a number of commentators have claimed to find the verification principle in the *Tractatus*. It is extraordinary that Colombo (p. 65) supposes the verification principle to be almost explicitly contained in 4.063, pointing to words which few philosophers would hesitate to accept. For Wittgenstein's own statement on the matter, cf. D. A. T. G(asking) and A. C. J(ackson), "Ludwig Wittgenstein," *Aust. J. Phil.*, 29 (1951), p. 79. Compare *Philosophische Bemerkungen*, pp. 62, 282, 289 and especially 174.

71. To say that the sense is a possibility is not to say that the sense is potential. Thus this is an inaccurate account of Wittgenstein's view: "The sense of a proposi-

tion is its ability to represent a reality by means of its form of representation" (Benjamin R. Tilghman, "For the Best Account Showing That There Is or Is Not a Significant Difference Between the Views of the Earlier and the Later Wittgenstein," *Rev. Meta.*, 16 [1962-1963], pp. 380-381). Tilghman has put the potentiality in the wrong place; the sense is always determinate, but the situation may not be realized.

72. Already in 1914 Russell was insisting on the same point. Cf. Harry T. Costello, "Logic in 1914 and Now," *J. Philos.*, 54 (1957), p. 248.

73. 2.012-2.0121; 6.124.

74. 2.024; 2.026-2.0271.

75. Cf. B. Russell, *Logic and Knowledge*, pp. 187-88.

76. 2.21-2.22; 2.223-2.224; 4.022.

77. A. J. Ayer apparently overlooked this distinction when he said: "To refute the logical atomist theory, in its extreme form, it need only be remarked that a sentence which consisted entirely of logically proper names could not be used to say anything false. Either it would express a truth, or it would be meaningless" ("Meaning and Intentionality," *Proc. XIIth Int. Cong.*, I [Florence, 1960], pp. 143-44). For a criticism of these remarks, cf. Y. Bar-Hillel, "Critical Comments on the Introductory Papers on Logic, Language and Communication," *Proc. XIIth Int. Cong.*, IV (Florence, 1960), p. 14.

78. NB 59-60, 64-65.

79. The *Investigations* have almost as much to say on this matter as the *Tractatus*; for before criticizing his former views in the *Investigations*, Wittgenstein presented them anew, often more fully than in the cryptic *Tractatus* itself.

80. Even were it not already clear from the *Tractatus* itself (e.g., 2.025) that the *Tractatus* objects are not mere forms, that is, mere possibilities which are realized only in facts, this passage from the *Investigations* would demonstrate the error of those who thus explain them.

81. Cf. the passage already quoted from *Principia Mathematica*: "Whenever the grammatical subject of a proposition can be supposed not to exist without rendering the proposition meaningless, it is plain that the grammatical subject is not a proper name, i.e., not a name directly representing some object. Thus in all such cases, the proposition must be capable of being so analyzed that what was the grammatical subject shall have disappeared" (p. 66). Cf. Russell, *Logic and Knowledge*, pp. 242-43.

82. There is no doubt that this line of thought was one of the reasons for Wittgenstein's own atomism in the *Tractatus*, even though he does not expressly say so in the *Investigations*. For one thing, his own former views are under fire in the section of the *Investigations* from which I have quoted. In particular, the passage cited forms part of the criticism of a viewpoint Wittgenstein had expressed already in 1915: "What seems to be given us *a priori* is the concept: *This*.—Identical with the concept of the object" (NB 61; cp. §§ 38-39).

83. Cp. Russell, "Particular colours and sounds and so on are events" (*An Outline of Philosophy* [London, 1927], p. 288).

84. This interpretation is contested. The disagreement is part of a controversy about three related questions: Can any *Tractatus* simples be empirical? Are all *Tractatus* simples empirical? Are all propositions empirical? The three questions are distinct, but an affirmative answer to the second entails an affirmative answer to the third, and, of course, to the first. There is no direct evidence in the *Tractatus* in favor of an affirmative answer to any of these questions. In view of Wittgenstein's

general principles I favor a negative answer to all three questions. A quite cogent case for empirical objects has been made by A. B. Wolter, O.F.M., in "The Unspeakable Philosophy of the Late Wittgenstein," *Proc. Amer. Cathol. Philos. Assoc.*, 34 (1960), p. 176. Others agree. On the other hand it is frequently (and rightly) argued that in the *Tractatus* Wittgenstein abstracted from such questions and that the matter is not decided there, one way or the other.

85. The existence of atomic simples (as distinct from atomic meanings, the arguments for which are being discussed here) seemed evident especially for this reason: "It seems that the idea of the SIMPLE is already to be found contained in that of the complex and in the idea of analysis" (NB 60; cf. NB 50, 62, 65). Analysis implies complexity and complexity implies simplicity. For this reason Wittgenstein felt sure that even were the world infinitely complex, it would still consist of absolutely simple objects—infinitely many of them (4.2211).

86. On the background of Wittgenstein's insistence on precision, confer Keynes's observations on the contemporary climate at Cambridge: "It was all under the influence of Moore's method, according to which you could hope to make essentially vague notions clear by using precise language about them and asking exact questions. It was a method of discovery by the instrument of impeccable grammar and an unambiguous dictionary. 'What *exactly* do you mean?' was the phrase most frequently on our lips. If it appeared under cross-examination that you did not mean *exactly* anything, you lay under a strong suspicion of meaning nothing whatever" (quoted by Levi, *Philosophy and the Modern World*, p. 449).

87. My translation.

88. In his introduction to the *Tractatus*, p. x.

89. This statement suggests the precise way in which to elucidate a text which might seem to contradict what I said earlier about Wittgenstein's attitude toward ordinary expressions and about his aim in constructing an analytical notation. When he says that "Without philosophy thoughts are, as it were, cloudy and indistinct: its task is to make them clear and to give them sharp boundaries," his meaning is, I think, that the meaning of our ordinary assertions is precise and clear, but that we do not know precisely and clearly what it is (4.112).

90. My translations. Cf. also NB 64.

91. If we think of this "application" as mental application, as the mental connecting up of thing and sign (cf. e.g., NB 64, where "syntactical application" is conceived of as having preceded all explication), Wittgenstein's explanation remains homogeneous; "applied" and "thought out" have roughly the same meaning. But 3.262 (cp. 6.2331) suggests that the use of both expressions is a sign of incipient schism, of a tension in Wittgenstein's thought which would be resolved only when he dropped the occult act of "thinking out" and gave full prominence to the "application" of signs as the reason for their significance. (In NB 59 and 65-68, the only other places I have found which are of interest for the interpretation of the term "application" in 3.5, Wittgenstein's use is noncommittal, indicating neither mental nor non-mental application, neither instantaneous nor non-instantaneous.)

92. J. M. B. Moss calls this a "serious error of interpretation, perhaps comparatively uncontroversial," and a "doctrine for which I can see no support in the writings of Wittgenstein or his commentators" (Review of George Pitcher, *The Philosophy of Wittgenstein*, in *Philosophical Books*, 6 [1965], p. 23). I hope the preceding paragraphs have shown that my interpretation (and Pitcher's) is at least controver-

sial and that there is support for it in Wittgenstein's writings. A much fuller proof could be given.

93. Cf. Russell's introduction, p. xix.

94. NB 64; 5.1311; 6.12-6.1201; 6.2331.

NOTES—CHAPTER II

1. Maslow, *A Study in Wittgenstein's* Tractatus, p. x.

2. "The motto here is: Take a *wider* look around" (FM 54).

3. Cf. BB 68.

4. Cf. e.g., BB 6-7, 34-35, 38-39, 43, 65; §§ 358, 454.

5. Cf. BB 25.

6. This same argument is cited by Moore (M^19), together with a couple Wittgenstein did well to forget about (M^18-9).

7. Charlesworth (*Philosophy and Linguistic Analysis*, p. 115) gives Wittgenstein's remarks a strange twist: "It seems from what he says that all such 'transcendental' words as 'composite,' 'simple,' 'one,' etc. which pretend to have a use in all language games, are *ipso facto* meaningless. So he says: 'to the philosophical questions: "Is the visual image of this tree composite and what are its component parts?" The correct answer is "That depends on what you understand by composite." (And that is of course not an answer but a rejection of the question.)' " It is strange to say that words "pretend" anything. And it is strange to read a general theory into Wittgenstein's remarks, one which would rule out *a priori* a certain sort of word use. The long paragraph 47 from which Charlesworth quotes is rich in examples of the various meanings "composite" and "simple" do actually have. Wittgenstein argues from this diversity of meanings to the complete ambiguity of the atomic theory, not from a universal lack of meaning to lack of meaning in this particular case.

8. E.g., BB 27, 81; §§ 88, 91, 99.

9. Nor, for that matter, can they be the meanings of definite descriptions; though Wittgenstein does not explicitly extend the argument, what he says about proper names applies equally well to definite descriptions.

10. Cf. also BB 73 and § 36, which suggest how the transition occurs from object meanings to mental meanings.

11. This is a reference to the first language-game in the *Brown Book* (BB 77), which corresponds to the first language-game in the *Investigations* (§ 2). The present paragraph corresponds (less closely) to § 6.

12. It is necessary to distinguish, in this connection, between Wittgenstein's discussion of "mental states" as states of a hypothetical mechanism (BB 117), supposedly enabling us to speak, count, and so on, and "mental states" as conscious states (e.g., BB 78).

13. "On the Nature of Truth," in *Philosophical Essays*, p. 109. Alan White attributes somewhat similar notions to Wittgenstein's friend, G. E. Moore: "I shall call Moore's view the concept theory of meaning, for it is the view that the meaning of an expression is the concept—or the proposition, as it is called when the expression is a complete sentence—which the expression stands for, signifies, names or expresses. One often comes to this view on discovering certain mistakes in a somewhat

similar and perhaps more natural view called the *object theory*. This is the view that the meaning of an expression is the object which the expression stands for, signifies, names or refers to. Since both of these views are based on the common assumption that the function of words is to *name* something, and differ primarily on what is the something which is named, they may be both called the *naming theory* of meaning" (*G. E. Moore*, p. 40; cf. also p. 57).

14. p. 202.

15. *Ibid.*, p. 191. This passage suggests the close connection there is likely to be between an object theory of meaning and an image theory of meaning, a blow against images generally being a blow against object meanings as well, since the images supposedly make the connection between word and object. So the present section may be considered a continuation of the last. Furthermore, though Russell did not call images the meanings of words, his explanation does suggest what Wittgenstein had in mind when he spoke of "the view that the meaning of a word is some image which it calls up by association" and his reason for calling it a "causal" theory of meaning (M[1]8).

16. *Confessions*, Bk. X, ch. xv, no. 23. Cf. also Russell's "On Propositions: What They Are and How They Mean," *Proc. Ar. Soc.*, Suppl. Vol. 2 (1919), p. 21: ". . . it is nevertheless the possibility of the memory-image in the child and an imagination-image in the hearer that makes the essence of the 'meaning' of the words."

17. I have presented a very truncated version of Russell's views, citing only statements which Wittgenstein would consider misleading, since my aim here is to suggest the sort of thing he objected to. Though he considered them "essential," Russell recognized that images are not *always* present to give words meaning.

18. The general importance Wittgenstein attached to this approach appears when, in the midst of a discussion regarding the image theory of meaning, he remarks: "Now I don't say that this is not possible. Only, putting it in this way immediately shows you that it need not happen. This, by the way, illustrates the method of philosophy" (BB 12).

19. Cf. M[1]13-14.

20. Cp. M[1]14.

21. "It is no more essential to the understanding of a proposition that one should imagine anything in connexion with it, than that one should make a sketch from it" (§ 396).

22. Cf. Russell, *The Analysis of Mind*, pp. 219-21.

23. Symptomatic of Wittgenstein's later outlook is the fact that on BB 28, where he contrasts the complicated use of some words with the comparatively simple use of others, these latter, though mentioned for contrast, are not words with a single meaning, but words "with *several* clearly defined meanings" (italics mine). For five good pages on Wittgenstein's anti-Socratic treatment of universals, cf. Hermann Lübbe, " 'Sprachspiele' und 'Geschichten,' Neopositivismus und Phänomenologie im Spätstadium, zu Ludwig Wittgenstein, *Philosophische Untersuchungen*, und Wilhelm Schapp, *Philosophie der Geschichten*," *Kant-Studien*, 52 (1960-1961), pp. 220-24.

24. Cf. also § 251: "Now can I imagine 'every rod having a length'? Well, I simply imagine a rod. Only this picture, in connexion with this proposition, has a quite different role from one used in connexion with the proposition 'This table has the same length as the one over there.' "

25. Cf. BB 131.

26. Cf. BB 12.

27. Cf. §§ 169-170.

28. *The Principles of Psychology*, 2 vols. (London, 1905), I, 222.

29. *Ibid.*, p. 269.

30. *The Analysis of Mind*, p. 187.

31. This familiarity is indicated by the relative frequency with which Wittgenstein mentions James by name (BB 78, 103; §§ 413, 342, 620; PI 219); by numerous passages in which the views discussed by Wittgenstein resemble closely those expressed by James in the *Principles* (cf. e.g., BB 42-43, 45, 118, 143ff.; §§ 337, 584, 607, 609, 637, 640; PI 181-183, 188); and finally by phrases or passages in the *Principles* cited by Wittgenstein (compare § 342 with Vol. I., pp. 266-69; § 413 with p. 301; BB 78 with p. 245; BB 181 with p. 459). There is external evidence as well. Passmore says (*A Hundred Years of Philosophy*, p. 428): "If I were asked to mention the two books, apart from the *Tractatus* (and the Frege-Russell tradition it incorporates), most suitable as background reading to the *Philosophical Investigations*, they would be Schlick's *Gesammelte Aufsätze* (especially his lectures on 'Form and Content') and William James's *Principles of Psychology*, supplemented by his *Pragmatism*. Wittgenstein several times refers to James—a rare distinction—but not, I think, quite so as to bring out the nature of his relationship to James. . . (I had written of James's influence on purely internal evidence. One of his former pupils, Mr. A. C. Jackson, tells me that Wittgenstein very frequently referred to James in his lectures, even making on one occasion—to everyone's astonishment—a precise reference to a page-number! At one time, furthermore, James's *Principles* was the only philosophical work visible on his bookshelves)."

32. *Op. cit.*, I, 253.

33. *Ibid.*, p. 236.

34. *Ibid.*, p. 253.

35. *Ibid.*, p. 255.

36. *Ibid.*, p. 266.

37. *Ibid.*, pp. 265-66.

38. *Ibid.*, p. 269.

39. *Ibid.*, p. 477.

40. *Ibid.*, p. 278. For evidence that this pulse is meaning, cf. e.g., pp. 252-53, 281.

41. *Ibid.*, pp. 277-81.

42. *Ibid.*, p. 279.

43. *Ibid.*, p. 281.

44. *Ibid.*, p. 245.

45. *Ibid.*, pp. 279-80.

46. Cf. e.g., §§ 39, 40, 44.

47. Cf. e.g., BB 35.

48. BB 144; §§ 510, 557, 592.

49. BB 35, 103, 145, 148. Cp. BB 113; § 151.

50. PI 33; §§ 20, 595, 607. Cp. § 35.

51. For a development of this point by means of the same comparison with friendly facial expressions, cf. BB 156-157.

52. It was in the present context that Wittgenstein said: "A main cause of philosophical disease—a one-sided diet: one nourishes one's thinking with only one kind of example" (§ 593).

53. For an expression of this attitude, cf. the passages already quoted from James, *op. cit.*, I, 255, 269.

54. That is, the same positive point. The adversary immediately in view in §§ 522-523 was the *Tractatus* view of propositions. This same point is most fully developed already in M³18-19. Cf. also LC 29-30, 34.

55. §§ 522, 526-527. Cp. PI 218.

56. Cp. M³19.

57. The two points are, of course, intimately connected, yet obviously distinct. To illustrate: a bank teller may accompany all his counting operations by a clicking noise. This is a mere fact. It does not show that his counting would go wrong without the clicks.

58. Cf. BB 65, 78-79; PI 215, 219.

59. James, *op. cit.*, I, 222.

60. Cf. *ibid.*, p. 245.

61. *Op. cit.*, I, 459.

62. *Ibid.*, p. 265.

63. This tendency is especially noticeable not only in James, but also in Russell's *The Analysis of Mind*.

64. BB 166; §§ 527, 534; PI 182, 206.

65. The close similarity between these sorts of experience has been hinted at already in Wittgenstein's insistence that pictures and images can be signs much as words can. A close parallel is also suggested when Wittgenstein speaks of sights or sounds that seem to "say something" to us (Cf. e.g., BB 179). Then too he often contrasted drawings with mere "scribbles," on the one hand (BB 163, 165, 170), and words with mere "scribbles," on the other (BB 167, 172-173), and on page 174 of the *Brown Book* left no doubt about the intended parallel: "When I say 'I don't see mere dashes (a mere scribble) but a face (or word) with this particular physiognomy' . . . ." Sometimes his intention is clear from the way he passes from one to the other (BB 168; PI 145, 198, 212), as in the *Investigations*, Part II, section xi, as a whole, where pages of non-verbal examples lead up to pages of verbal examples. The parallel is clear in other ways as well, including some that will now be mentioned. Finally, Wittgenstein sometimes expressly points out the parallelism (PI 210) and indicates that his purpose in giving the non-verbal examples is to throw light on our verbal experiences (BB 165). Near the end of his longest discussion in this vein he says, "Aspect-blindness will be *akin* to the lack of a 'musical ear.' The importance of this concept lies in the connexion between the concepts of 'seeing an aspect' and 'experiencing the meaning of a word' " (PI 214).

Gustav Bergmann ("Intentionality," *Arch. Filos.*, 1955 [*Semantica*], p. 192) gives a description of the same sort of experiences as Wittgenstein discussed at such length—then claims that Wittgenstein denied their existence! This is supposed to demonstrate how he was "overly impressed by the behaviorists."

66. Cf. PI 196, 197, 198, 201, 203, 204, 205, 206, 209.

67. Cf. also BB 165-166, 174-177, 180; PI 202.

68. Cf. BB 178; PI 182.

69. Cf. PI 182, 216.

70. Cp. § 646.

71. By means of italics, Peter Geach brings out Wittgenstein's intention on PI 217 to refer us to a larger field of observation: "If God had looked into our minds,

he would not have been able to see *there* whom we were speaking of" (*Mental Acts, Their Content and Their Objects* [London, 1957], p. 72).

72. BB 20-21, 40, 145, 183-185; §§ 572-595, 638-659; PI 174, 219, 231.

73. The punctuation of this passage is obviously faulty in the English translation. I have repunctuated it in keeping with the punctuation in the German text.

74. Cp. §§ 179-180.

75. "It is useful to observe Frege's distinction of sense (*Sinn*) and reference (*Bedeutung*) in stating Wittgenstein's position; what Wittgenstein wanted to deny was not the private *reference* of psychological expressions—e.g., that 'pain' stands for a kind of experience that may be quite 'private'—but the possibility of giving them a private *sense* . . ." (Geach, *Mental Acts*, pp. 3-4).

76. BB 24; §§ 210, 362, 381-82, 384.

77. This is more difficult to do than might be imagined. For in describing the "private" language, we must use public words like "sensation," and so introduce a public grammar into the private language. The thing we call a sensation will on that account have to satisfy the ordinary criteria for sensations—not in virtue of the game, but in virtue of its description (§§ 256, 261, 270).

78. For brevity's sake, I pass over the difficulties and the fuller pragmatic development suggested by §§ 26, 260, 268-270, 389, and PI 228, and simplify by supposing that the private-language user is acquainted with the activities of naming and identifying and that he knows how these games are to be transposed into the strange new circumstances Wittgenstein has suggested (Cp. §§ 350-351).

For a good exposition of this part of the argument, cf. P. F. Strawson's critical notice on the *Investigations* in *Mind*, 63 (1954), p. 81.

79. Cf. §§ 293, 376.

80. Cp. §§ 250, 650; PI 174, 229.

81. The Ariadne's thread which leads most surely through this labyrinth is the question: "How do these remarks tend to solve, or rather dissolve, the 'other minds' problem?" One sure way to run into dead-ends is to follow the lead suggested by Norman Malcolm, in his review of the *Investigations* (*Philos. Rev.*, 63 [1954], p. 537): "The argument that I have been outlining has the form of *reductio ad absurdum*: postulate a 'private' language; then deduce that it is not a *language*." One then wonders, for instance, why there should be criteria in every language, and why checking should be possible. Wittgenstein was not out to establish general theses, but he was interested in clearing up important philosophical puzzles like the "other minds" problem, which was agitating Anglo-Saxon philosophers.

82. M³312; BB 7, 13, 19, 59, 65, 67, 72, 77, 84, 96, 147, 183, 185; §§ 31, 33, 108, 136, 197, 199, 200, 205, 316, 357, 365, 563; PI 59, 174, 181.

NOTES—CHAPTER III

1. Cf. also FM 136, #5; §§ 30, 43, 120, 138, 197, 454, 508, 532, 556, 557, 561, and PI 147 (note), 175, 176, 220.

2. Already in the *Blue Book* the definition of meaning as use can be found explicitly and implicitly expressed, for instance, implicitly on pages 65 and 73, and explicitly on page 69: "The use of the word *in practice* is its meaning"; "The word 'mind' has meaning, i.e., it has a use. . . ."

2ª. Compare with PB 178: "Das System von Regeln, welche einen Kalkül bestimmen, bestimmt damit auch die 'Bedeutung' seiner Zeichen. Richtiger ausgedrückt: Die Form und die synthetischen Regeln sind äquivalent. Ändere ich alsi die Regeln —ergänze ich sie etwa scheinbar—so ändere ich die Form, die Bedeutung."

3. "The essential difference between grammar and lexicon," says Ullmann (*Semantics*, p. 35), "is that the former deals with the 'general facts of language' and the latter with 'special facts.'" Wittgenstein used the term "grammar" to cover the special facts as well.

4. This broad use of the word "grammar" (which I have adopted in this book) is now very common, largely as a result of Wittgenstein's influence. But Wittgenstein did not originate it. Russell used the term in the same wide sense as for instance on page 42 of his *Principles of Mathematics* (in a passage quoted by F. Barone in "Il solipsismo linguistico di Ludwig Wittgenstein," *Filosofia*, 2 [1951], pp. 549-50).

Wittgenstein's transition views on meaning, as well as his use of "grammar," are reflected by what Moritz Schlick wrote in 1936, several years after his discussions with Wittgenstein: "Thus, whenever we ask about a sentence, 'What does it mean?,' what we expect is instruction as to the circumstances in which the sentence is to be used; we want a description of the conditions under which the sentence will form a *true* proposition, and of those which will make it *false*. The meaning of a word or a combination of words is, in this way, determined by a set of rules which regulate their use and which, following Wittgenstein, we may call the rules of their *grammar*, taking this word in its widest sense" ("Meaning and Verification," *Philos. Rev.*, 45 [1936], p. 341).

5. Cf. BB 25, 97-98; §§ 82-83, 190ff., 205-206, FM 184-85.

6. Cf. BB 97-99; §§ 31, 54, 68, 206-208. Contrast what Wittgenstein says in these passages with the following words of Moritz Schlick. Speaking of the rules which determine the meaning of words, he said in 1936: "These rules are not facts of nature which could be 'discovered,' but they are prescriptions stipulated by acts of definition. And these definitions have to be known to those who pronounce the sentence in question and to those who hear or read it. Otherwise they are not confronted with any proposition at all, and there is nothing they could try to verify. . ." (*Op. cit.*, p. 349). This contrast is the same as that between Wittgenstein's later treatment of "rules" and his views expressed in Moore's notes, between a descriptive view and a prescriptive view.

Reporting on the general trend in the early thirties, C. W. Morris said: "The general direction of the change is clear. . . the meaning of a word is considered to be constituted by the syntactical rules within a given speech which determine its usage." Cf. "The Concept of Meaning in Pragmatism and Logical Positivism," *Actes du huitième congrès international de philosophie* (Prague, 1936), p. 135. Cf. also Alan White, "A Note on Meaning and Verification," *Mind*, 63 (1954), p. 68.

7. Cf. §§ 79-80, 82-83, 190-206. Wittgenstein further undermined the rigid view of language by pointing out, as J. N. Findlay sums it up, that "a rule can be neither so expressed nor so exemplified as to exclude all variety of interpretation," so that even if speech were perfectly law-abiding, it would not thereby be reduced to predictable, regular patterns. Cf. Findlay's review of the *Investigations*, in *Philosophy*, 30 (1955), p. 176. He cites §§ 85, 86, 189, 222-226, 229, 239. Cf. also e.g., FM 3, ⫟#3; 6-7; 33-35; 37-40;116, #8; 171, #12.

8. The possibility that emphasis on rules might stand in the way of a definition

of meaning as use is shown to be real enough by the number of those who define meaning as rules of use (cf. n. 6, *supra*), and especially by those who reject Wittgenstein's definition precisely because it does not indicate as clearly as they would wish that meaning is *rules* of use. Cf. e.g., Jason Xenakis, "Meaning," *Methodos*, 6 (1954), pp. 310-11. Wittgenstein's opposition to such a definition will be explained more fully in Chapter IV.

9. These two developments are to some extent independent. For a person might recognize that there is far more to language than mere signs and their combination, and still suppose that it is a calculus in which all signs are defined in terms of their use with other signs. Even if the calculus provided for the possibility of occasionally using a sign by itself, still, if the sign might also be used with other signs, its "grammar" would include this use as well and so integrate the sign with the rest of the system. The "meaning of the word," as opposed to its meaning on a particular occasion, would depend on other words. However, once it is recognized that the rules of combination are only one aspect of words' grammar, that is, once attention is paid to "depth grammar" as well as to "surface grammar," either meaning will not be defined as a word's "place in the system" or the word "system" will be given a much wider meaning than Wittgenstein first gave it.

10. "Wittgenstein and P. Sraffa, a lecturer in economics at Cambridge, argued together a great deal over the ideas of the *Tractatus*. One day (they were riding, I think, on a train) when Wittgenstein was insisting that a proposition and that which it describes must have the same 'logical form,' the same 'logical multiplicity,' Sraffa made a gesture, familiar to Neapolitans as meaning something like disgust or contempt, of brushing the underneath of his chin with an outward sweep of the finger-tips of one hand. And he asked: 'What is the logical form of that?' Sraffa's example produced in Wittgenstein the feeling that there was an absurdity in the insistence that a proposition and what it describes must have the same 'form.' This broke the hold on him of the conception that a proposition must literally be a 'picture' of the reality it describes" (Malcolm, *Ludwig Wittgenstein*, p. 69). Malcolm remarks in a footnote: "Professor G. H. von Wright informs me that Wittgenstein related this incident to him somewhat differently." However, according to the explanation Professor von Wright has given me, if there was a difference in the two accounts, it was mainly verbal.

11. Cf. PB 59, #14: "Ein Wort hat nur im Satzverband Bedeutung: das ist, wie wenn man sagen würde, ein Stab ist erst im Gebrauch ein Hebel. Erst die Anwendung macht ihn zum Hebel."

12. In his preface to the *Blue and Brown Books* (pp. vi-vii), Rush Rhees draws a contrast between Wittgenstein's conception of language games in the *Blue Book* and his conception in the *Brown Book* and later. This contrast seems to me illusory. For instance, saying that "we can build up the complicated forms from the primitive ones" (BB 17) does not imply that the latter are incomplete or that they are parts abstracted from actual language; nor, on the other hand, when Wittgenstein denies in the *Brown Book* that his language games are incomplete does this imply that similar games are not incorporated or could not be incorporated in our more complex languages.

13. Cf. also BB 19; § 18.

14. According to K. Baier ("The Ordinary Use of Words," *Proc. Ar. Soc.*, 52 [1951-1952], p. 54), "We hardly ever use a word by itself." However, not only do we very frequently use words by themselves (think of all the one-word answers to

questions and all the one-word questions, of the orders of waiters shouted back to the kitchen), but independent use is typical of quite a few words, like "yes," "no," "goodbye," "hello," "thanks," "fore," "hooray." Cf. BB 103: "As an exercise ask yourself: in which cases would you say that a certain word uttered by the people of the tribe was a greeting? In which cases should we say it corresponded to our 'Goodbye,' in which to our 'Hello'?"

15. Cf., for instance, PB 118-19, which is merely an expansion of, say, 4.002 in the *Tractatus*.

16. M. Schlick, "Meaning and Verification," *Philos. Rev.*, 45 (1936), p. 342.

17. BB 17-19; §§ 109, 124, 126, 129, 340. "This general identification of 'meaning' with 'use,'" says Harry A. Nielsen ("Wittgenstein on Language," *Philos. Stud.*, 8 [1958], p. 119), "is not an observation but an upshot of his whole way of looking at language." The following paragraphs will show that it was also the result of observation.

18. Norman Malcolm has an apt comparison to illustrate this point: "It is one thing to know the common use of a word in the sense of being able to *use* it, and it is another thing to know it in the sense of being able to *describe* that use, just as one may be able to tie a necktie without being able to tell another how one does it" ("Philosophy and Ordinary Language," *Philos. Rev.*, 60 [1951], p. 338).

19. §§ 116, 124, 132-133; PI 200.

20. §§ 11, 122, 182, 664.

21. For copious references, refer back to the Introduction, p. 6, and p. 175, note 36.

22. Some commentators not only interpret the *Tractatus* as forbidding all talk about language, meaning, and the like, but even attribute the same attitude to the later Wittgenstein. Cf. e.g., Campanale: *Studi su Wittgenstein*, preface and pp. 6-8. My remarks about a say-show distinction even in the later period should not be mistaken for agreement with such views.

23. FM 54; BB 19-20; §§ 182, 593.

24. Cf. John Wisdom, "A Feature of Wittgenstein's Technique," *Proc. Ar. Soc.*, Suppl. Vol. 35 (1961), pp. 1-14.

It may still seem that the parallel is forced; for whereas the later objection to general descriptions of grammar was based on the diversity of use, the former objection was based on the picture theory, not on diversity. But this objection is only half valid; for, after all, the picture theory was a theory of one-to-one correspondence, of pairing off signs, or at least symbols, with simple objects; and Wittgenstein's objection in the *Tractatus* to picturing grammar itself was based on the realization that the use of a sign is not this sort of thing, not some simple, supplementary element in the world which might be represented by its own sign— much as later he recognized that a single general term cannot adequately suggest or represent the use of an expression, precisely because its use is not simple enough to be helpfully described in this way. There is indeed a basic affinity between the *Tractatus* method of laying out in minute detail the grammar, the structure, of an expression and thereby *revealing* (not stating) its structure, and the later technique of citing a list of concrete examples and thereby *revealing* (not stating) the grammar of an expression.

25. The present elucidation of meaning is an example of an explanation which is neither a mere exchange of expression for expression nor a demonstrative definition. Many words are not used as names of things; consequently in their case a non-

verbal explanation, one which does more than provide a synonymous expression, cannot consist in pointing to anything.

26. And that is how Schlick did put it. The following remarks, in which he brings the whole edifice of logical positivism to rest its full weight on this narrow point, explain amply why Wittgenstein considered it worth so much attention, and throw a great deal of light on his treatment of it: "It is clear that in order to understand a verbal definition we must know the signification of the explaining words beforehand, and that the only explanation which can work without any previous knowledge is the ostensive definition. We conclude that there is no way of understanding any meaning without ultimate reference to ostensive definitions, and this means, in an obvious sense, reference to 'experience' or 'possibility of verification.'

"This is the situation, and nothing seems to me simpler or less questionable. It is this situation and nothing else that we describe when we affirm that the meaning of a proposition can be given only by giving the rules of its verification in experience" ("Meaning and Verification," *Philos. Rev.*, 45 [1936], p. 342). My next paragraph shows Wittgenstein attacking Schlick's view head-on.

27. The present paragraph shows how misleading is H. R. Smart's comment ("Language-Games," *Philos. Quart.*, 7 [1957], p. 224): "As a special kind of case, the 'meaning of a name' may be explained simply 'by pointing to its bearer' (sec. 43)." The word "simply" throws the whole thing off and turns Smart's statement into an error Wittgenstein was specially interested in refuting.

28. For a fuller development of these points, cf. the commentary in Albert Shalom, "Wittgenstein, le langage et la philosophie," *Études Philosophiques*, 13 (1958), pp. 487-88.

29. Alan White states Wittgenstein's argument in this way, using a comparison of Wittgenstein's (§ 120): "This is quite correct; what is not correct is to suppose that the object signified by the expression is the meaning of the expression. We are led to suppose so by not distinguishing the correct point that it belongs to the meanings of those [words] which do signify or refer to objects and which, consequently, are taught and learnt ostensively, *that they are used to* refer to or signify these objects, from the incorrect point that the *objects* referred to or signified *are* the meanings of those words. The object theory takes the relation of expression and meaning as analogous to that of money and what it buys, e.g., a cow, instead of as analogous to money and its use, e.g., to buy a cow" (*G. E. Moore*, p. 40). Cf. Strawson's critical notice of *Philosophical Investigations* in *Mind*, 63 (1954), p. 71.

30. This would seem to be a misprint. The sense requires "what," not "that."

31. M[17]; BB 5, 18; § 1.

32. It is true that generally a name or noun does not by itself "refer to" an object. Rather, a sentence does, by means of it. It is also true that such a sentence may contain words of the most disparate types, including ones I would not describe as referring words. The sentence refers "by means of" them too. So why do I call one group referring words and the others not? Since only the existence of a difference is relevant here, and since it seems evident that there is a difference, I shall not attempt to explain exactly where it lies.

33. Cp. § 578.

34. Cp. § 403.

35. Stanley Cavell, in his excellent article, "The Availability of Wittgenstein's Later Philosophy," *Philos. Rev.*, 71 (1962), pp. 67-93, sums up Wittgenstein's view-

point well in this criticism of David Pole's interpretation (in *The Later Philosophy of Wittgenstein* [London-Fair Lawn, N.J.], 1958): "He finds Wittgenstein supposing that 'experiential elements play no part' in determining the way language is used (p. 88; cf. p. 86), whereas what Wittgenstein says is, in these terms, that what is experiential in the use of a word is not an element, not one identifiable recurrence whose presence insures the meaning of a word and whose absence deprives it of meaning" (p. 90).

NOTES—CHAPTER IV

1. That is, sometime in 1932 or 1933. Cf. M¹4.

2. This remark, since it must be reconciled with § 43, where Wittgenstein purports to be reporting usage, is not incompatible with another explanation for Wittgenstein's extended use of the term. The Würzburg school of experimental psychology extended it in a practically identical way, and made quite similar observations about the sort of experience to which they extended it. Cf. Gustav Bergmann, "Intentionality," *Arch. Filos.*, 1955, pp. 188-90.

3. Another similar case, in fact almost identical, is the concept "understanding": "We speak of understanding a sentence in the sense in which it can be replaced by another which says the same; but also in the sense in which it cannot be replaced by any other. (Any more than one musical theme can be replaced by another.) In the one case the thought in the sentence is something common to different sentences; in the other, something that is expressed only by these words in these positions (Understanding a poem).

"Then has 'understanding' two different meanings here?—I would rather say that these kinds of use of 'understanding' make up its meaning, make up my *concept* of understanding. For I want to apply the word 'understanding' to all this" (§§ 531-532).

4. Hartnack, *Wittgenstein und die moderne Philosophie*, p. 57; P. Butchvarov, "Meaning-as-use and Meaning-as-correspondence," *Philosophy*, 35 (1960), p. 316; Charlesworth, *Philosophy and Linguistic Analysis*, p. 108; Campanale, *Studi su Wittgenstein*, pp. 187, 189. The same error may account for Harry A. Nielsen's remark: "in the *Investigations* . . . for many though not all common words, if we know how they are used we need ask no further questions about their meanings" ("Wittgenstein on Language," *Philos. Stud.*, 8 [1958], p. 119).

5. Cf. *The Later Philosophy of Wittgenstein*, pp. 18-19, where he argues well for the view I am defending.

6. P. F. Strawson, critical notice of *Philosophical Investigations* in *Mind*, 63 (1954), p. 70.

7. That is, *Verwendung* and *Gebrauch* in German—both, with about equal frequency.

8. For examples, cf. BB 15; §§ 458, 492; PI 222. Another, important example of the verbal part of "grammar": "what a proposition is is in one sense determined by the rules of sentence formation (in English for example), and in another sense by the use of the sign in the language-game. And the use of the words 'true' and 'false' may be among the constituent parts of this game; and if so it *belongs* to our concept 'proposition' but does not 'fit' it" (§ 136).

9. Cf. § 45.

10. This expression in § 664 may have led Tsu-Lin Mei to this misinterpretation of the whole paragraph, and in fact of Wittgenstein's whole philosophy: "Moreover, depth grammar is a logical—that is, a nonempirical—enterprise. For the aspect of language that misleads is exactly coextensive with the aspect that can be studied empirically. Thus, if we follow the observable patterns of language, we will find ourselves in conceptual confusion" ("The Logic of Depth Grammar," *Philos. Phenom. Res.*, 24 [1963], p. 98). Much more is empirically observable than the surface grammar—the marks on paper, the sound of the words.

11. Cf. BB 35, 142; PI 18; PB 118-119. In 1931, in unpublished notes (Cf. Rush Rhees, "The *Tractatus*: Seeds of Some Misunderstandings," *Philos. Rev.*, 72 [1963], pp. 214-215), Wittgenstein illustrated the contrast between the "surface" of words, in a more limited sense, and their grammar by means of a comparison with a transparent glass figure, only one surface of which is painted and made visible, but whose movements obey the geometry of a cube or whatever form the figure has. Thus regarding the word "is" in "2 × 2 is 4" and "The rose is red," he said: "I want to make this comparison: that the word 'is' has a different verbal body (*Wortkörper*) behind it in the one case and in the other. That in each case it is the same surface, but belonging to a different body; as when I see a triangle in the foreground which is now the end surface of a prism and now of a tetrahedron." Rhees comments: "This idea of a 'word body' (more often he used the term 'meaning body') was analogous to an earlier idea of a *Beweiskörper* or body of a proof. A year or more earlier he had written, 'We might also say: a completely analyzed proposition is just the immediately visible surface of the whole body of proof (*des ganzen Beweiskörpers*), the boundary or side facing us. . . .'" According to Rhees, "Wittgenstein came to distrust speaking or writing of *Bedeutungskörper*, for he thought it opened the way to 'mythology.'" The expression occurs only once, parenthetically and without explanation, in the *Investigations* (§ 559).

12. Cf. § 559.

13. Cp. § 584.

14. Cf. § 420. This is a way in which Wittgenstein treated many concepts closely related to the concept "meaning." His description of them suggests ways in which he might have filled out what he said about meaning. For instance: "To intend a picture to be the portrait of so-and-so (on the part of the painter, e.g.) is neither a particular state of mind nor a particular mental process. But there are a great many combinations of actions and states of mind which we should call 'intending . . .'" (BB 32). Or:

There may be cases where the presence of a sensation other than those bound up with gestures, tone of voice, etc. distinguishes meaning what you say from not meaning it. But sometimes what distinguishes these two is nothing that happens while we speak, but a variety of actions and experiences of different kinds before and after (BB 145).

"'But is there no difference between saying something and meaning it, and saying it without meaning it?'—There needn't be a difference while he says it, and if there is, this difference may be of all sorts of different kinds according to the surrounding circumstances" (BB 145).

In these instances and a number like them (e.g., BB 20, 152; § 164), Wittgenstein spoke of a "family" of cases designated by the concept word (BB 33, 145). He never applied this figure in a general way to *Bedeutung*, but every instance of a word designating a family of cases or used in a family of cases (BB 133) is *ipso facto* an instance of a word having a family of uses, as the present discussion aims to point out. Cf. e.g., BB 125: "And the explanation of the use of this word, as that of the use of the word 'reading,' or 'being guided by symbols,' essentially consists in describing a selection of examples exhibiting characteristic features, some examples showing these features in exaggeration, others showing transitions, certain series of examples showing the trailing off of such features." That is, to describe family features is to give a partial description of the use of the word.

15. Malcolm, *Ludwig Wittgenstein*, p. 93; italics mine.

16. Cf. BB 5.

17. BB 82, 83, 108; §§ 11, 17, 22, 260, 340, 559.

18. *Passim.*

19. BB 93, 94, 108; §§ 30, 50, 182, 557.

20. BB 77-80, 82-85, 92-95; § 2.

21. BB 172; § 1. Cf. also BB 69.

22. E.g., BB 72; FM 165; §§ 30, 43, 47, 120, 138-139, 247, 560.

23. E.g., BB 69, 82, 83, 84; §§ 11, 274, 280, 559.

24. BB 67, 80, 84; §§ 11, 14, 23, 360, 569.

25. Cp. § 385.

26. Cf. pp. 79-80.

27. Cf. PI 179; §§ 88, 545. Cf. also PB 51: "Wenn man quasi die Klasse der Sprachen beschreibt, die ihren Zweck erfüllen, dann hat man damit ihr Wesentliches gezeigt. . . ."

28. Compare this discussion with remarks in the *Tractatus* (5.4733; 3.31); there whatever he judged to be accidental he did not include in the meaning, in the symbol. Cp. also FM 133.

29. Compare FM 153, #41 ("Concepts which occur in 'necessary' propositions must also occur and have meaning in non-necessary ones") and FM 178, #21 (the tautologies of logic are not significant propositions).

30. Cf. FM 165.

31. Cp. § 83.

32. This is David Pole's chief criticism of Wittgenstein's later philosophy. C. B. Daly, "New Light on Wittgenstein," *Philos. Stud.*, 10 (1960), p. 36, cites both Pole (*The Later Philosophy of Wittgenstein*, pp. 56-62, 81-84, 91-92) and Gellner (*Words and Things*, pp. 44, 99 ff., 120 ff., 180) as accusing Wittgenstein "of prohibiting linguistic advance, excluding the creation of new languages, e.g., new scientific or mathematical languages," then cites BB 17, 81 and §§ 18, 23, and 79 against their interpretation. P. F. Strawson, in his review of the *Blue and Brown Books* (*Philos. Quart.*, 10 [1960], p. 371) also criticizes Pole's interpretation. J. O. Urmson makes the same point in "L'Histoire de l'analyse," in Beck, ed., *La philosophie analytique*, p. 18. Philip P. Hallie, in "Wittgenstein's Grammatical-Empirical Distinction," *J. Philos.*, 40 (1963), p. 566, points out that "His is not a philosophy whose main purpose is to slap the wrists of people who talk extraordinarily." The impression that it is is no doubt connected with the common but mistaken notion (cf. Pole, *op. cit.*, p. 6) that Wittgenstein traced philosophical problems to the misuse of language; this would suggest that his whole aim was to prevent misuse, whereas his aim was to remove misunderstandings and misrepresentations of ordinary usage and all the statements and problems which result from such misunderstanding. Philosophers' misuse of language (§ 116) arises from their basic misconceptions

about language (§ 117), not vice versa. This connection between the two errors of interpretation appears in E. Riverso, "L'analisi del linguaggio come metodo d'indagine filosofica," *Rass. Sc. filos.*, 16 (1963), p. 52. N. Abbagnano, who dwells long on the unreasonable rigidity of Wittgenstein's supposed view ("L'ultimo Wittgenstein," *Riv. Filos.*, 44 [1953], pp. 451-53) takes these words in the *Investigations* as representing Wittgenstein's own position at that time: "There must be perfect order even in the vaguest sentence"! So does Campanale (*Studi su Wittgenstein*, p. 208). They are, of course, an echo of the *Tractatus* view which he was criticizing.

33. Cp. BB 139-140.

34. I quote the German because in English the word "milk" can be a verb, and therefore the surface grammar is not so obviously awry in "Milk me sugar" as in *Milch mir Zucker*.

35. See the first section of this chapter.

36. PB 175, #150; FM 30, #105; 52, # #15-17; 61, #12; 63, #18; 113; 140, #11; 141; 150-151.

37. §§ 116-117; PI 178; LC 69; BB 8-9, 65-66.

38. Or activities proper to other institutions, as rhyming in verse, or winning a game of anagrams. The distinction being made here corresponds to Saussure's distinction between *la langue* and *la parole*. Cf. Stephen Ullmann, *Semantics, An Introduction to the Science of Meaning* (Oxford, 1961), pp. 19-21.

39. Cf. BB 58.

40. Cp. Malcolm, *Ludwig Wittgenstein*, p. 92.

41. This distinction between the total use of a sign and a particular application suggests one reason for saying, as Wittgenstein so often did, that meaning is determined by use. Concrete particular applications of a word establish the general manner of its employment, and it is the general use of words and not concrete cases which Wittgenstein generally had in mind when he said that meaning is determined by use (cf. e.g., BB 65, 69, 73, 94, 170; § 10). Often such expressions can be understood in the sense of an equivalence, that is, as implying a definition, as pointing toward the definition of meaning as use. After the very explicit definition in § 43, such expressions practically disappear from the *Investigations*. There is still mention, however, of the reverse process, the determination of meaning in particular cases by the general way in which the word has previously been used (§§ 139, 270).

42. Much as language cannot be completely irregular and still be called language (§ 207).

43. This distinction is quite similar to one Moore made, though he had a different sort of analysis in mind: ". . . philosophy only analyses words of which we already *know* the meaning, in the sense that we can use the word right, although we could not perhaps *say* what it means" (from "The Justification of Analysis [a Lecture Note]," *Analysis*, 1 [1933], pp. 28-30). Cf. White, *G. E. Moore*, pp. 53-65.

44. Cf. PI 224; cp. the end of § 89.

45. This remark, together with Wittgenstein's development of the simile, is given by D. A. T. Gasking and A. C. Jackson, two of his pupils, in "Ludwig Wittgenstein," *Aust. J. Phil.* 29 (1951), p. 76. Cf. PI ix and § 203 for something similar.

46. F. C. S. Schiller ("The Meaning of 'Meaning'" [Symposium], *Mind*, 29 [1920], p. 388, footnote) gives interesting quotes from William James (*Principles of Psychology*, I, 472), who represents meaning as "evanescent and transitive," and from McDougall (*Body and Mind*, p. 303), who though he calls meaning "the

essential part of consciousness," describes it as "eluding introspection." Wittgenstein often had such statements as these in mind when he criticized the "hidden," and not stomach-aches or silent words, which, compared with these questionable entities, are wide open to view.

47. Cf. PI 181.

48. Cp. § 271. Endless examples of this sort might be given. Probably none of those that I have cited here caused P. F. Strawson any difficulty; yet in his critical notice on the *Investigations* (*Mind*, 63 [1954], pp. 70-99) he accused Wittgenstein of "prejudice against the inner" (p. 91), especially in his treatment of sensation words (pp. 83-89), thinking (90-92), and mental states (93). Norman Malcolm countered Strawson's charges in the closing pages of his own article on the *Investigations* (*Philos. Rev.*, 63 [1954], pp. 530-59), finding fault both with many of Strawson's interpretations and with his criticisms of some points which Strawson understood correctly. On pages 2-4 of *Mental Acts*, Peter Geach comments briefly on some of the same debated points of interpretation. For similar remarks, cf. Stanley Cavell, "The Availability of Wittgenstein's Later Philosophy," *Philos. Rev.*, 71 (1962), p. 90. Some go much farther than Strawson in their accusations of behaviorism. Cf. e.g., Charlesworth, *Philosophy and Linguistic Analysis*, p. 118; Gustav Bergmann, "Intentionality," *Arch. Filos.*, 1955, p. 192; and John W. Yolton, "Philosophical and Scientific Explanation," *J. Philos.*, 55 (1958), pp. 135-36.

49. The italics are mine. The manner in which Wittgenstein here leaves place for the inner, without mentioning it (though he does a few lines earlier), is typical. Cf. e.g., PI 187, 189.

50. If we adopt an "all or nothing" attitude, or start thinking in terms of objects and their parts, this may seem confusing. We will then ask, "Is the image the meaning or isn't it? Is it part of the meaning or isn't it?" Yet it is obvious that in endless cases categories like these—"identity" or "non-identity," "part," "include," "belong to"—simply do not fit. For instance, is a bank the same thing as a bank account? Is a bank "part" of a bank account? Is it "included in" a bank account? Does it "belong to" a bank account? No, yet any definition of a bank account, by whatever name you call it, will have to bring in the bank. So it is with meaning and the various aspects of word use. A very close comparison, suggested by Wittgenstein himself (§ 120), would be with a coin and its value. (As the important thing about a coin is its value, so the important thing about a word is its meaning.) The things a coin can buy are obviously not its value, nor "part" of its value. For instance, a chocolate bar is not the value of a dime in my pocket, nor is it part of the dime's value. We do not use the expression "value" that way. Yet (slipping into the formal mode of speech) we may rightly say that any full account of the coin's value would have to mention our ability to buy things like chocolate bars with it. Now just as chocolate bars, shoe-shines, tips and subways would enter into a full account of this coin's value, so images or feelings might enter into the account of some word's use.

51. The idea of inner criteria would seem to be implicit in doubts about the truth of others' accounts or my accounts of their pains, fears, thoughts, feelings, desires, and so on. Wittgenstein explained such problems about truth as misunderstandings about meaning; neither others nor I do or could make use of inner criteria in using psychological terms. Such is not their use, their meaning. Cf. e.g., §§ 202, 239-317.

52. §§ 68, 71, 76-77, 79.

53. In *Communication*, pp. 187-88, Karl Britton develops this theme, using an example gotten from Wittgenstein but not found in his published writings.

54. *Words and Things*, London, 1959, p. 30.

55. *Ibid.*, p. 40. Cp. M³9.

56. *Ibid.*, p. 29.

57. *Ibid.*, p. 43.

58. Cf. M³17-19 and Cyril Barrett, "Les leçons de Wittgenstein sur l'esthetique," *Archives de Philosophie*, 28 (1965), pp. 13-15; and, most recently, LC 1-4, 11.

59. A view summarized by A. C. Ewing in *Second Thoughts in Moral Philosophy*, (New York, 1959), p. 30, which in the light of all the evidence seems a plausible interpretation of Wittgenstein's position in § 77, assimilates the analysis of ethical and aesthetic terms to the *Brown Book* analysis of terms used "intransitively."

60. For a fuller view of Wittgenstein's thought on this question, treated here only briefly and negatively, see also the following pages: PB 85-86, 90, 139-140, 150, 266, 269-271, 285, 290; FM 121, #29; 140, #12; 142, #17; 153, #41; 183, #31; LC 69; BB 54, 71; PI 221.

61. "What I give is the morphology of the use of an expression. I show that it has kinds of uses of which you had not dreamed. In philosophy one feels *forced* to look at a concept in a certain way. What I do is to suggest, or even invent, other ways of looking at it. I suggest possibilities of which you had not previously thought. You thought that there was one possibility, or only two at most. But I made you think of others. Furthermore, I made you see that it was absurd to expect the concept to conform to those narrow possibilities. Thus your mental cramp is relieved, and you are free to look around the field of use of the expression and to describe the different kinds of uses of it" (lecture notes of Norman Malcolm, *Ludwig Wittgenstein*, p. 50).

62. Hawkins, *Crucial Problems of Modern Philosophy*, p. 66.

63. I am aware that someone might argue in the following vein: "Even in the paradigm case of families, there are certain things common to all the members. For instance, they are all white, or all colored." However, the present point is not important enough for me to elaborate the answer that might be given to this objection. The important thing is to recognize the structure of the concept "meaning."

NOTES—CHAPTER V

1. London, 1962.

2. *Ibid.*, p. 1.

3. *Ibid.*, p. 29.

4. *Ibid.*, p. 123.

5. *Ibid.*, p. 5.

6. *Ibid.*

7. *Ibid.*, p. 15.

8. *Ibid.*, p. 16.

9. *Ibid.*, p. 21.

10. *Ibid.*, p. 16.

11. Of course it might be truly argued that no exception, however important, would be an objection against Wittgenstein's definition, since he did not pretend to be giving a definition that holds in all cases. However, if I show that the definition

can be defended in all contested cases, this is not only to confirm Wittgenstein's claim that the definition holds in "a *large* class of cases," but also to demonstrate its value and importance.

12. *Ibid.*, pp. 123-4.

13. *Ibid.*, p. 131.

14. "It seems to me," says William P. Alston ("Meaning and Use," *Philos. Quart.*, 13 [1963], p. 114), "that when one tells someone what an expression means, he is in effect telling him that two expressions have the same use." This is just *one* way, though probably the commonest. So it is quite incorrect to say, " 'And' has a meaning, but (again) we can't say what it is" (*Ibid.*, p. 123).

15. *Philosophy and Linguistic Analysis*, p. 218.

16. On the "egregious confusion between the behavior of 'What do you mean by the sentence?' and 'What does the sentence mean?' " cf. J. Fodor, "What Do You Mean?," *J. Philos.*, 57 (1960), pp. 499-506. Cf. also Colin Strang, "Meaning and Intention," *Proc. XIIth Int. Cong.*, IV (Florence, 1960), pp. 323-24. Alan White answers a similar confusion in slightly different fashion. Commenting on pages 139-44 of R. M. Chisholm's article, "Sentences About Believing," in *Proc. Ar. Soc.*, 56 (1955-1956), he says that when "Chisholm objects that we cannot talk about the meaning or use of a word without referring to what people who use that word in that way *believe* or perceive or know," he "confuses the question *what* is the use (i.e., meaning) of a given expression and the question *why* someone uses a given expression on a given occasion" ("Meaning, Intentionality, and Use," *Proc. XIIth Int. Cong.* IV [Florence, 1960], p. 382). The confusion between meaning words and the meaning of words pervades A. M. MacIver's article, "Do Words Mean Anything?", *Proc. XIth Int. Cong.*, V (Amsterdam-Louvain, 1953), 172-75.

17. "Function and Meaning of Names," *Theoria*, 22 (Copenhagen, 1956), pp. 49-60.

18. *Ibid.*, p. 55.

19. *Ibid.*, p. 53.

20. This is the answer to Jon Wheatley's similar objection: "This theory suffers from two serious difficulties: (a) certain words that have no meaning have a use, e.g. names, 'slithy,' 'a' . . ." ("Some aspects of Meaning and Use" [abstract], *J. Philos.*, 60 [1963], p. 643). The fact that proper names are not said to have meaning would seem to confirm Wittgenstein's definition rather than disprove it. For the "meaning" of proper names would seem to be ruled out by the qualifying phrase in his definition which so many critics overlook: "in the language." The majority of individual proper names do not have a use "in the language," but only among a limited number of people, within a narrow circle. "Jerome Kern," for instance, is not a word of the English language, even though, *per accidens,* in this case the expression's use to designate a certain person is known to many users of the English language. A mother might give her child the name "Jerome Kern" tomorrow, without consulting anyone or promulgating her decision to any appreciable number of English speakers, which is a procedure quite at variance with the way words acquire meaning "in the language," and with quite different results; the name she chose would lack the general acceptance and use which are characteristic of "meaning." The paradigmatic force of the commonest types of names may explain why even names like "Germany" or "the Rockies" are not said to have meaning. P. F. Strawson briefly suggests the same explanation ("On Referring," *Mind*, 59 [1950], p. 338). For a fuller comparison of names and nouns, cf. Ullmann, *Semantics*, pp. 72-77.

21. J. Xenakis, *op. cit.*, pp. 53-55, 57, 60; A. White, *G. E. Moore*, p. 41; G. Ryle, "Meaning and Necessity," *Philosophy*, 24 (1949), p. 70; P. H. Nowell-Smith, *Ethics* (Oxford, 1957), p. 60; P. F. Strawson, critical notice of *Philosophical Investigations*, *Mind*, 63 (1954), pp. 74-75; *Idem*, "On Referring," *Mind*, 59 (1950), p. 338. In "Meaning, Intentionality, and Use," *Proc. XIIth Int. Cong.*, IV (Florence, 1960), pp. 377-79, Alan White not only mentions that proper names don't have meaning, but suggests and refutes an argument to the contrary.

22. "Use and Meaning," *The Cambridge Journal*, 4 (1950-1951), p. 755. J. W. N. Watkins mentions these remarks with approval in "Farewell to the Paradigm-Case Argument," *Analysis*, 18 (1957-1958), p. 28.

23. *Op. cit.*, p. 756.

24. For a full development of this distinction, cf. Charles E. Caton, " 'What-for' Questions and the Use of Sentences," *Analysis*, 17 (1956-1957), pp. 87-92, especially p. 91. An objection similar to Gellner's would be more difficult to answer. So as not to appear to be letting Wittgenstein off too easily, I will mention it here, though it is not among those I have seen raised against his definition. It would go something like this. Though there can be no question of mass misuse of a term like "fifth," the debate regarding the paradigm-case argument seems to have shown that terms with a more complicated logic might actually be misused by the majority of men. Thus at one time the majority of men may have used the term "ether" in a referring way when there was nothing for the term to refer to. A better-informed person might recognize that they were misusing the term—misusing it even though theirs was the majority use. The correct use of the term would then resemble that isolated use of the term "fifth"—yet be correct. Had Gellner used his examples merely to suggest this sort of difficulty, his objections would have been more difficult to dismiss.

One answer to the difficulty would be to distinguish between meaning and truth: In such a case as the one imagined, people would be making perfectly correct use of the word "ether" to convey incorrect beliefs. The debate would not end here, but I think it could be terminated in Wittgenstein's favor.

25. *Op. cit.*, p. 114.

26. *The Diversity of Meaning*, p. 124.

27. "A propósito del último Wittgenstein: observaciones sobre el convencionalismo" (trad. por J. J. Casalduero), *Crisis*, 3 (1956), p. 478.

28. Critical notice of *Philosophical Investigations*, *Mind*, 63 (1954), p. 72. These authors mention uses of words which are not uses "in the language." William P. Alston dwells on much the same distinction when he contrasts "the sort of rules and the sort of correctness which is involved in use in this [Wittgenstein's] sense, from the sort which are not. . . . For example, many speakers recognize rules forbidding them to use certain racy or obscene words in certain circumstances, or rules forbidding them to use crude or vernacular locutions in certain social circles. . ." ("Meaning and Use," *Philos. Quart.*, 13 [1963], p. 108. Cf. also pp. 109-115). Such rules would most naturally be termed rules of society or rules of etiquette rather than rules of language. Later in the same article, which at the start looks like a criticism of Wittgenstein's definition, Alston makes much the same distinction as that which Wittgenstein made by adding the words "in the language"; after developing Austin's distinction between illocutionary and perlocutionary functions, he restricts meaning-use to the former (*Ibid.*, pp. 115-117).

29. "Meaning," *Methodos*, 6 (1954), p. 310.

30. *Ibid.*, p. 315.

31. "Esotericism," *Philosophy*, 34 (1959), p. 343.

32. Xenakis,' Wisdom's, and Findlay's fuller remarks suggest how J. Wheatley probably filled out the second of his two "serious difficulties" already mentioned: "(b) the use of a word is often dependent on what it means" ("Some Aspects of Meaning and Use" [abstract], *J. Philos.*, 60 [1963], p. 643).

33. J. N. Findlay, "Use, Usage, and Meaning," a symposium, *Proc. Ar. Soc.*, Suppl. Vol. 35 (1961), p. 233.

34. *Idem*, "Meaning, Fulfillment and Validation," *Proc. XIIth Int. Cong.*, IV (Florence, 1960), pp. 105-11.

35. *Ibid.*, p. 105.

36. *Ibid.*, p. 106.

37. For a similar view, cf. Gustav Bergmann, "Intentionality," *Arch. Filos.*, 1955 (*Semantica*), p. 191.

38. "Explanation of Meaning," *Proc. XIIth Int. Cong.*, IV (Florence, 1960), pp. 29-35.

39. *Ibid.*, p. 34. To Black's arguments I would add this evidence, that in giving definitions we readily drop the indefinite article (in defining a noun) or the word "to" before a defining verb. This would be inexplicable were we using the definiens to mention an object, even a possible, indefinite object. For such objects we use the indefinite article "a." To this difficulty Findlay would probably reply that it was his reason for saying that most meanings are mere aspects, not whole objects. But of course there is a standard way of mentioning aspects; one uses abstract terms. So even if we take mere surface grammar as our guide, as Findlay does, we should conclude that there is something very fishy about his explanation.

40. "Analytic-Synthetic," II, *Analysis*, II (1950-1951), p. 29.

41. "Signification et usage," *Theoria* (Copenhagen), 22 (1956); p. 151.

42. *Ibid.*, pp. 150-52.

43. On the roughness of usual talk about meaning, cf. William P. Alston, "Meaning and Use," *Philos. Quart.*, 13 (1963), p. 123.

44. Though both the wording and the punctuation of this definition are open to objection, for the sake of simplicity I shall proceed without quibble to use Pitcher's form in the present discussion.

45. *The Philosophy of Wittgenstein* (Englewood Cliffs, 1964), p. 252.

46. *Ibid.*, pp. 251-52.

47. J. N. Findlay, "Use, Usage, and Meaning," a symposium, *Proc. Ar. Soc.*, Suppl. Vol. 35 (1961), pp. 232-33.

48. "L'ultimo Wittgenstein," *Riv. Filos.*, 44 (1953), p. 451. D. Campanale quotes Abbagnano and agrees. Cf. *Studi su Wittgenstein*, p. 204.

49. "Meaning," *Methodos*, 6 (1954), p. 312.

50. For a similar broad criticism, cf. William P. Alston, *op. cit.*, p. 107. K. W. Rankin, too, criticizing Wittgenstein's definition, speaks of "the need to introduce a distinction between different modes of significance" ("Wittgenstein on Meaning, Understanding, and Intending," *American Philosophical Quarterly*, 3 [1966], p. 4).

51. "Ordinary Language," *Philos. Rev.*, 62 (1953), pp. 167-86.

52. *Ibid.*, pp. 173-74.

53. *Ibid.*, pp. 174-80.

54. " 'The Use' of Moral Language," *Theoria*, 27 (1961), p. 78.

55. *Op. cit.*, pp. 453-54.

56. *Op. cit.*, pp. 178-79.

57. "On Meaning and Verification," *Mind*, 62 (1953), p. 8.

58. "Wittgenstein Investigated," *Philos. Quart.*, 6 (1956), p. 71.

59. *Ibid.*, p. 69.

60. "Farewell to the Paradigm-Case Argument," *Analysis*, 18 (1957-1958), p. 28.

61. Jerry Fodor and Jerrold Katz, "What's Wrong with the Philosophy of Language," *Inquiry*, 5 (1962), p. 214.

62. "On the Use of 'the Use of,' " *Philosophy*, 30 (1955), p. 8.

63. *Philosophy and Linguistic Analysis*, p. 181.

64. Critical notice of *Philosophical Investigations, Mind*, 63 (1954), p. 73.

65. Cf. J. L. Austin, "A Plea for Excuses," in *Philosophical Papers* (Oxford, 1961), pp. 123-52.

66. See Gilbert Ryle, "The Theory of Meaning," in C. A. Mace (ed.), *British Philosophy in the Mid-Century*, p. 242.

67. *Principles of Psychology*, Vol. I, p. 301; referred to by Wittgenstein in § 413.

68. A. Flew, "Philosophy and Language," *Philos. Quart.*, 5 (1955), pp. 27-29.

69. "Toward a Theory of Interpretation and Preciseness," in L. Linsky, ed., *Semantics and the Philosophy of Language* (Urbana, 1952), p. 266.

70. *Ibid.*

71. *Ibid.*

72. Objections like those of Xenakis, Wisdom, and Findlay make me think that Wittgenstein was probably right in judging that the misunderstandings of language which cause most trouble in philosophy are misunderstandings of common usage. However, I think he paid too little attention to philosophers' familiarity with philosophical terminology. Such terminology is sometimes mentioned as a difficulty for his analyses, for instance, of the word "meaning." It is sometimes objected that philosophers use the word in other senses than the one Wittgenstein mentioned and that their uses cannot be overlooked in an account of usage. But I think their terminology raises more serious difficulties for Wittgenstein's therapeutic technique than it does for the accuracy of his definition. After all, only some philosophers use the word "meaning" in any one technical sense, and in comparison with all those who speak the language they form a negligible group. That is, we may generally ignore their idiosyncrasies in giving an account of some common word's use "in the language." However, can their terminology be ignored in a therapeutic account of usage? Philosophical problems arise and are discussed principally among philosophers familiar with philosophical uses.

73. "Linguistic Rules and Language Habits," a symposium, *Proc. Ar. Soc.*, Suppl. Vol. 29 (1955), p. 171.

74. *Ibid.*, p. 172.

75. Cf. also Benson Mates, "On the Verification of Statements About Ordinary Language," *Inquiry*, 1 (1958), p. 166; and David Braybrooke, "Personal Beliefs Without Private Languages," *Rev. Meta.*, 16 (1962-1963), pp. 680 ff.

76. H. R. Smart, "Language-Games," *Philos. Quart.*, 7 (1957), p. 230.

77. "Wittgenstein's Investigations," *Rev. Meta.*, 8 (1954), p. 141, footnote. Cf. also David Gruender, "Wittgenstein on Explanation and Description," *J. Philos.*, 59 (1962), pp. 523-30.

78. "Synonymity and Empirical Research," *Methodos*, 8 (1956), p. 22.

79. Cf. also S. Issman, "Problèmes de la définition," *Methodos*, 4 (1952), pp.

102-03; and *idem*, "Signification et usage," *Theoria* (Copenhagen), 22 (1956), pp. 151-52.

80. "Le monde du pensable et le langage. Quelques réflexions sur la critique linguistique wittgensteinienne et sur ses conséquences," *Rev. Mét. Mor.*, 66 (1961), p. 112.

81. This famous saying of Wittgenstein's, frequently mentioned as his (cf. e.g., W. P. Alston, "The Quest for Meanings," *Mind* 72 [1963], p. 84), is not to be found in his published writings.

82. "Use, Usage, and Meaning," a symposium, *Proc. Ar. Soc.*, Suppl. Vol. 35 (1961), p. 229. Elsewhere Ryle observes that "appeal to prevalence is philosophically pointless, besides being philologically risky" ("Ordinary Language," *Philos. Rev.*, 62 [1953], p. 177). This is too sweeping. Had Wittgenstein spoken of a way in which the word "meaning" *might* be used, or if when he spoke of a large class of cases in which "we" employ the word "meaning," he had been speaking of just himself and a few friends, what philosophical importance would his remark have had? In "Philosophical Analysis and Structural Linguistics," *J. Philos.*, 59 (1962), pp. 715-17, W. Alston shows that Ryle himself is interested in usage, and not just use.

83. "The Blue Book," *J. Philos.*, 58 (1961), p. 159.

84. *Ibid.*

85. S. Issman, "Problèmes de la définition," *Methodos*, 4 (1952), p. 104.

86. Cp. § 574. Thus, for instance, meaning is what we call meaning. If someone were to say, "No, just *this* is meaning, not all that," he would simply indicate his intention to use the word in a more restricted way than is generally the case. But he would be expressing his determination in a misleading manner; for by saying, "This *is* meaning," he suggests rather that whenever somone talks about meaning, he talks about this. Having performed this sleight of hand, the philosopher sees no need to explain or justify his introduction of the new terminology. From such confused and murky beginnings little clarity is likely to result.

87. So Wittgenstein was even farther from F. Waismann's view: "A definition behaves in many respects like a rule, e.g., a rule of chess: it is *pre*scriptive rather than *de*scriptive—it tells us how a word, or a symbol, *is* to be used, not what its actual, or predominate, usage is. If I wish to assert that a definition given is in accord with the actual, or the prevailing, use of language, then I am, truly or falsely, making a *statement*, and no longer laying down a mere definition" ("Analytic-Synthetic," I, *Analysis*, 10 [1949-1950], p. 29). Wittgenstein had no intention to legislate when he gave his definition, nor do I think that Waismann's remarks about definitions are generally true.

For a perfect parallel with the present case ("meaning"), see § 100, where Wittgenstein equates the question of what a game is with the question of how we actually use the word "game."

On the empirical nature of linguistic philosophy such as Wittgenstein's, see a good article by Jerry A. Fodor and Jerrold J. Katz: "The Availability of What We Say," *Philos. Rev.*, 72 (1963), e.g., p. 71.

88. Stanley Cavell, "Must We Mean What We Say?", *Inquiry*, 1 (1958), p. 176. Cf. also p. 175; and O. K. Bouwsma, *op. cit.*, p. 148.

89. "Synonymity and Empirical Research," *Methodos*, 8 (1956), pp. 17, 20.

90. Cf. § 68.

91. The teenagers would have one advantage, though, in not having been ex-

posed to philosophical jargon. In this respect Wittgenstein was better off than most philosophers, since his philosophical reading was very limited and confined more and more to philosophers who made use of ordinary terms in more or less ordinary fashion. But even he did not avoid contamination, as is shown perhaps by his reference to experienced "meanings" and certainly by his talk about the "meanings" of proper names. These examples do not cast grave doubts on his definition of meaning as use, for he did not take this over uncritically from any predecessor, as he did his talk about names' meanings.

92. For a similar distinction between what native speakers say about surface grammar and what they say about depth grammar, cf. Jerry A. Fodor and Jerrold J. Katz, "The Availability of What We Say," *Philos. Rev.*, 72 (1963), pp. 64-65.

93. Cf. § 38.

94. S. Issman makes a similar criticism of Naess's method, briefly, in *op. cit.*, p. 99.

95. Cp. § 556.

96. W. V. Quine, "Le mythe de la signification," in Beck, ed., *La philosophie analytique*, pp. 170-87.

97. I might have included *ad hominem* arguments as well, pointing out that enthusiasm for questionnaires sometimes derives from a confusion between meaning words and the meaning of words, and from the mistaken idea that meaning words is an isolated act in the mind, something therefore which can be supposed to occur in the questioning situation much as it does in the natural use of words. For an example of this attitude, cf. e.g., Benson Mates, "On the Verification of Statements About Ordinary Language," *Inquiry*, 1 (1958), p. 167. Similar misconceptions have motivated statistical studies by means of questionnaires conducted by C. E. Osgood, G. J. Suci, and P. H. Tannenbaum (cf. *The Measurement of Meaning* [Urbana, 1957], p. 9, quoted by Ullmann, *Semantics*, p. 70).

98. Campbell Crockett remarks: "Naess is thoroughly aware of the wide chasm that often separates an occurrence and a meta-occurrence of an expression, and does everything that one can to allow for these separations. In this area, however, perhaps doing all that one can is not enough" ("An Attack upon Revelation in Semantics," *J. Philos.*, 56 [1959], p. 109).

99. "Meaning-as-use and Meaning-as-correspondence," *Philosophy*, 35 (1960), p. 317.

100. "The Blue Book," *J. Philos.*, 58 (1961), p. 159.

101. *Semantics: An Introduction to the Science of Meaning* (Oxford, 1962).

102. *Ibid.*, p. 66.

103. *Ibid.*

104. *Ibid.*, p. 57.

105. *Ibid.*, p. 211.

106. *Ibid.*, p. 44.

107. *Ibid.*, p. 45.

108. *Ibid.*, p. 47.

109. *Ibid.*, p. 58.

110. *Ibid.*, p. 15.

111. "How I See Philosophy," in H. D. Lewis, ed., *Contemporary British Philosophy*, third series (London, 1956), p. 489.

112. "Verification and the Use of Language," *Rev. Int. Philos.*, 5 (1951), p. 320. Ullmann, too, recognizes only this value in Wittgenstein's definition, that it reminds us to look for a word's meaning by studying its use (*Op. cit.*, p. 67).

113. Therefore I would apply to the definition too Warnock's excellent remarks on the dictum: "To say that we must look for the use of a sentence solves no problems; but it turns the philosopher's gaze in the right direction, it points out the road down which solutions lie. Many people can follow a path when it is marked out for them; some can go far along it; but to discover the path is perhaps the most difficult, and certainly the most useful, task of all." *Op. cit.*, pp. 319-20. In like vein, W. B. Gallie considers Wittgenstein's definition "one of the greatest achievements of modern philosophy" (*Aesthetics and Language* [Oxford, 1957], p. 22).

114. O. K. Bouwsma, "The Blue Book," *J. Philos.*, 58 (1961), p. 159.

115. "Wittgenstein's Investigations," *Rev. Meta.*, 8 (1954), p. 130.

116. John A. Passmore, "Professor Ryle's Use of 'Use' and 'Usage,'" *Philos. Rev.*, 63 (1954), p. 62.

117. Cf. J. O. Urmson, "L'Histoire de l'analyse," in Beck, ed., *La philosophie analytique*, pp. 19-21.

118. *Op. cit.*, p. 28.

119. "A Plea for Excuses," in *Philosophical Papers*, p. 130.

120. *Ibid.*

121. It is not clear to me to what extent an empiricist tendency was responsible for this narrowness and to what extent it might be explained instead by, for instance, the fact that in the *Investigations* he was concerned so largely with more empirical concepts (for instance, psychological ones), or the fact that, his aim being therapeutic, he wanted to avoid controversial matters and to rely on easily accepted fact, especially since he felt that neglect of the obvious accounted for the ills he sought to cure (Cf. § 109).

122. Cf. P. F. Strawson, "Truth," (a symposium) *Proc. Ar. Soc.*, Suppl. Vol. 24 (1950), p. 156.

123. Cf. D. H. Langford, "A Proof that Synthetic *A Priori* Propositions Exist," *J. Philos.*, 46 (1949), pp. 21-22.

124. J. L. Austin, "Truth," (a symposium) *Proc. Ar. Soc.*, Suppl. Vol. 24 (1950), p. 125.

125. *Op. cit.*, p. 144n.

INDEX NOMINUM

207

INDEX RERUM